Organizational Health

Organizational Health

An integrated approach to building optimum performance

Naomi Stanford

LONDON PHILADELPHIA NEW DELHI

First published in Great Britain and the United States in 2013 by Kogan Page Limited

120 Pentonville Road	1518 Walnut Street, Suite 1100	4737/23 Ansari Road
London N1 9JN	Philadelphia PA 19102	Daryaganj
United Kingdom	USA	New Delhi 110002
www.koganpage.com		India

© Naomi Stanford, 2013

The right of Naomi Stanford to be identified as the author of this work has been asserted by her in accordance with the Copyright, Designs and Patents Act 1988.

ISBN   978 0 7494 6602 2
E-ISBN   978 0 7494 6603 9

British Library Cataloguing-in-Publication Data

A CIP record for this book is available from the British Library.

Library of Congress Cataloging-in-Publication Data

Stanford, Naomi.
   Organizational health : an integrated approach to building optimum performance / Naomi Stanford.
      p. cm.
   Includes bibliographical references.
   ISBN 978-0-7494-6602-2 – ISBN 978-0-7494-6603-9   1. Organizational effectiveness.
2. Organizational change.   3. Organizational behavior.   4. Corporate culture.   I. Title.
   HD58.9.S7383 2012
   658–dc23

                                                                                    2012020105

Typeset by Graphicraft Limited, Hong Kong
Printed and bound in India by Replika Press Pvt Ltd

CONTENTS

LIST OF FIGURES

LIST OF TABLES

ACKNOWLEDGEMENTS

In writing this book I've had the help, support, involvement, and encouragement from a wide array of people. Some have reviewed, some have provided examples, some have edited, some have brought me food and drink as I worked. All these roles have helped me along the way. I'm particularly grateful to my family members, Roger Woolford, Hannah Barugh, Rosa Barugh, Michael Stanford and Rosie Stanford for bearing with this project at the expense of time with them.

Martha Johnson and Cynthia Metzler have been my admirable managers and good companions as I strove to combine full-time work with the writing process. A special thank you to them.

Along the way Matt Nixon, Barry Horgan, Craig Yeatman, Kate Lister, Bridget Hardy, Michael Bloom, and Gillian Fogg reviewed chapters and made improving suggestions. Martina O'Sullivan has been a delightful commissioning editor to work with keeping me grounded and to schedule.

Behind all these are the legions of people I work with daily at all levels of an organization hierarchy, in all walks of life, and at all skills and capability levels. Without them there would be no organizations. Organizational health depends on their health, and I am continuously humbled by the vast majority of them who work cheerfully, often in a difficult setting and against the odds to do good work.

Additionally I would like to acknowledge the good work done by Freedom from Torture, **http://www.freedomfromtorture.org/**, a UK-based organization dedicated solely to the treatment of survivors of torture. The royalties from this book are donated to that organization.

FOREWORD

This book started out as an idea that came to me while I was running. As I conceived it then, it would be an organizational consultant's or manager's look-up guide that took an informed look at the critical and interdependent elements of an organization that must be maintained in a healthy state for managers to meet their business goals. These are many and varied. It is not enough to concentrate on, for example, financial performance, if it is at the expense of employee well-being. A healthy organization is just that in all its aspects: people, process, structures, systems, behaviours and governance. It is one where appropriate adaptive, maintenance and development activities are integral to maintaining performance and alignment in the operating environment.

Most managers understand the concepts of a 'systems or holistic' approach to organization and are all too aware that treating organizational symptoms of dysfunction – perhaps deciding to do 'team building' because a team's members are not performing well together – does not necessarily address the underlying causes of below par performance. They understand that low performance might have as much to do with inadequate resources, faulty business processes or demotivating reward and recognition systems as with the team member's interpersonal skills.

Managers are less skilled in knowing how to recognize and interpret early indicators that suggest things might be going awry, and in accurately diagnosing overall health and well-being. This book offers them the opportunity to develop both these skill sets and then apply them in their organizations.

It is aimed at helping managers nurture and monitor the health of their organizations and giving them practical guidance as to when and what type of action may be needed to maintain the organizational equivalents of mental, emotional and physical equilibrium and with this successful functioning in order to meet the business goals.

As a look-up guide it is not intended to be comprehensive and there are some obvious omissions – for example financial health is not specifically covered; rather the line taken on this is that if the organization is healthy then financial (or other success measures) will be the outcome. But it is intended to point the way towards preventive organizational health in order to mitigate the risk and expense of having to take after-the-fact action.

Following an introductory chapter the book covers seven topics. Each chapter is organized in a similar way:

- a description of the aspect the chapter covers and how essential good health in this aspect is to an organization's overall functioning;
- examples of what can happen in practice – using cases to illustrate healthy and unhealthy organizational manifestations of this aspect;
- the indicators of health (positive and negative) related to this aspect;
- tips, actions, strategies for developing and maintaining good health (eg preventive health actions);
- an exercise to work with;
- key messages.

At the end of the book there is a glossary of terms, and a list of resources organized by chapter topic.

There are numerous short examples and quotes from various organizations, used to illustrate points at a specific moment in time. As with human health, organizational health is a moving target – sometimes organizations are healthy, sometimes they are unhealthy and the degree of health or ill health affects performance. Things move on, so take the examples as they appear and use them as a jump-off point to do some research on what has happened to the organizations since they were mentioned here. Readers may learn something from the ongoing experiences of the organizations mentioned to apply in their own work of contributing to their organization's health.

Where there are unattributed quotes or general references to 'an organization' this is because the people or organization quoted have requested anonymity.

My own work as an organizational member – both as an employee and as a hired consultant – continues to fascinate me. I find there's nothing more interesting (and usually fun and enjoyable) than participating in efforts to improve organizational performance, however difficult, frustrating, or challenging this is in the day to day. I hope that with this book in hand readers will be able to apply, reflect on, or just read about some ways to develop and maintain organizational health.

Organizational health

Complex problems have simple, easy to understand,
wrong answers. (H L MENCKEN)

Objectives

At the end of this chapter you will be able to:

- present the idea that most organizational problems have presenting symptoms and there are underlying causes for these;
- compare organizational health with human health;
- describe the importance of developing and maintaining organizational health;
- outline how to recognize and assess the state of organizational health.

Most problems, big or small, that organizations face are complex ones. Some big ones that come to mind are how to enter a new market, how to respond effectively to a 20 per cent budget cut without loss of customer service, how to introduce a new technology and maximize the investment in it, how to divest a product/service line, or how to become more innovative. In everyday working life people are constantly coming up against smaller things that they would like an easy answer for – how to agree protocols for working in open-plan space, for example, or how to make meetings effective.

When asked what was the most important leadership lesson he had learned, Joseph Jimenez, CEO of pharmaceutical company Novartis, said that before he starts to address a problem he always asks himself and others whether they are fixing the root cause of the problem or simply fixing the symptoms (Bryant, 2011). He told the story of how he learned that lesson. Earlier in his career he had joined a company and was heading up a division which constantly missed its sales forecast. The simple fix was to assume poor sales and operations planning processes. So they streamlined these and introduced better analytics. This fix had no impact on achieving the sales forecasts – they still were not met. Jimenez and his team took a deeper look at the situation and came to the conclusion that people made forecasts that they knew they would not be able to meet. They did this because they felt that their leaders, Jimenez included, only wanted to hear good news, not unpalatable truths. This turned out to be a complex problem and the missed sales forecasts were only a symptom of this.

This realization that symptoms, more likely than not, have underlying causes that need to be investigated and treated is one that many management thinkers have observed. Art Kleiner, a management author, makes the point that organizations are systems like living beings and are 'as unpredictable, unruly, self-organizing, and even sentient as any living beings'. He notes that 'although organizations may not literally be alive, when it comes to running and changing them, they might as well be' (Kleiner, 2011).

Taking the view that an organization is similar to a human being makes it easier to grasp that symptoms – for example, not meeting sales forecasts, or the need to agree protocols in open-plan space – are rarely cured by a quick fix. It makes for a healthier organization if some investigation is done of the symptoms. It makes for an even healthier organization if preventive measures are taken that minimize the likelihood of things going wrong.

The human being analogy

Why is it helpful to think about an organization's health in similar ways to that of the health of a human being? Although this is not an examination question, it is a question worth reflecting on, discussing and answering.

The analogy is apt for a number of reasons. Organizations and humans:

- *Are often described in the same language.* Managers use such words and phrases as organizational 'sensing abilities' and 'intelligence', while being concerned with their organizations' 'systems' and 'processes'. They worry about organizational 'dysfunction' as they look for 'indicators' of organizational health and talk about aspects

FIGURE 1.1   Organization systems model

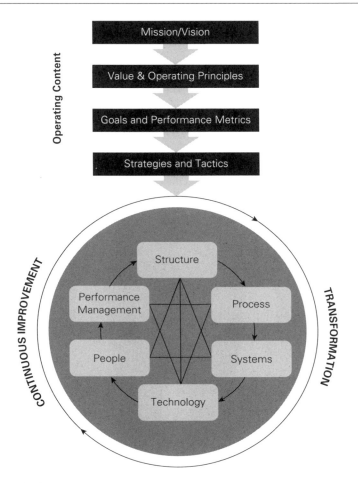

SOURCE: Stanford, 2010.

of their organization as 'being in the DNA'. This commonality of language makes the human/organization analogy easy to grasp for several reasons.

They are both complex, adaptive open systems. Look at Figure 1.1, which is a systems model of an organization, to see a representation of the relationships between the parts in the organizational system. Similarly there are representational models for the human body. Figure 1.2 shows the circulatory system and its various connections.

FIGURE 1.2   Human circulatory system

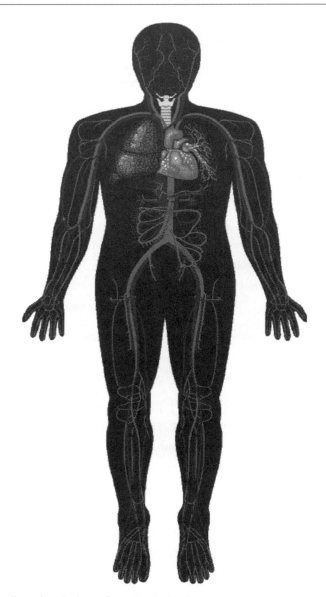

SOURCE: http://www.innerbody.com/image/cardov.html

- *They are both frequently 'diagnosed' and 'treated' following similar methodologies.* Managers are glad when a consultant's 'diagnosis' of an issue comes up with some possible solutions ('treatments'), and consultants deploy a variety of 'diagnostic tools' even though these may come up with a simple response to a complex situation. (See Chapter 8 for more on quack remedies.)

- *They both have life cycles that follow similar paths*: some live into maturity and old age, some get 'sick' and either fail to flourish from birth or die young. Larry Greiner (Greiner, 1998) wrote an article in 1972, 'Evolution and revolution as organizations grow', that is as fresh today as it was when first written. In the article he notes that he has drawn from 'the legacies of European psychologists' to extend their observations on human development to that of organizational development and growth. Unlike Shakespeare, who describes seven ages of man, Greiner describes five phases of organization life cycle, omitting Shakespeare's last two stages which are decline and finally 'mere oblivion', though both of these are discussed in relation to organizations in James Collins' book *How the Mighty Fall* (2009).

- *They both tend to thrive if they are consciously nurtured and developed*. Going into any bookshop will reveal the stacks of information on parenting, managing illnesses, child and adult learning, self-help, diet, nutrition, stress management and so on, all aimed at developing people's mental and physical health. Similarly information on organizational health, traditionally the realm of human resource (HR) departments, is addressed in the professional development of HR practitioners. The UK's Chartered Institute for Personnel and Development's HR Profession Map, for example, lists the ten competences required in HR practitioners. Seven of these are related to the health of the organization.

  - organizational design;
  - organization development;
  - resourcing and talent planning;
  - learning and talent development;
  - performance and reward;
  - employee engagement;
  - employee relations.

But it is not just an HR responsibility to look to the well-being of the organization. It is the responsibility of every organizational leader, line manager and individual employee. Terri Kelly, CEO of Gore, has an interesting perspective on this. Focusing on emotional health, her view is that organizations do well where there are few external rules, and little in the way of trading on power and status. For her a healthy organization is one where people are trusted to do a good job and make local decisions in small 'communities' where they feel a sense of identity and ownership (Caulkin, 2008).

- *They are both responsive to cultural and environmental conditions.* Look at the business newspapers or websites on any day of the week and there are reports of companies responding to changes in their operating contexts. As an example, on 31 October 2011 the *Wall Street Journal*, Europe edition (Cimilluca *et al*, 2011) on the front and first inside page were reports that:

  - Truck maker Scania plans to pare production by as much as 15 per cent, beginning in November.
  - Volvo intends to scale back truck manufacturing next year.
  - PSA Peugeot Citroën plans to suspend production at a plant in Slovakia. The company also said it would lay off 6,000 workers, mostly in France.
  - Liquor maker Diageo restructured its European operation by centralizing certain functions and shifting investment away from Western European markets.
  - Saab Automobile agreed to sell Saab to Chinese companies Pang Da and Zhejiang Youngman for $141.9 million, following a two-year struggle to turn the company around after decades of losses.
  - BT Group said it will complete the roll-out of its fibre broadband network to two-thirds of UK premises by the end of 2014, one year earlier than originally planned.
  - Yahoo has been exploring a potentially tax-free way to dispose of its roughly 40 per cent stake in the Chinese e-commerce company Alibaba.
  - Google announced the creation of about 100 online video 'channels' on its YouTube website, which will have new original programming involving celebrities such as the singer Madonna.
  - Meg Whitman is moving to stabilize H-P after 14 months in which the company removed two CEOs. Some seem to think her efforts are working, so far.

All of these major shifts in company strategy were attributed, for the most part, to the financial turmoil and the aftermath of the recession going on in Europe at the time. People too respond to cultural and environmental conditions: they adjust their behaviours to suit the context – office formality is different from home informality. They cut their spending if they have been laid off, and so on. Failure to adapt rapidly to change is a symptom of lack of adaptation capability and will take both humans and organizations the way of the dinosaur.

- *They both require intense and continuous communication and co-ordination between the elements* to stay functioning efficiently and effectively. In the human body this 'communication' is conducted through neural pathways, via the bloodstream and via the signalling molecules (Kleiner, 2011). In organizations it is conducted through various formal and informal channels (see Chapter 3).

With this comparison in mind, the purpose of this book is to demonstrate that the analogy of an organization to a human being is useful to organizational employees, leaders and managers. Using the analogy they see why leaders in more successful enterprises monitor their organizations' health in the same way that people have regular physicals/check-ups. They take actions to keep the organization healthy as in preventive health, and when symptoms of ill health appear they diagnose and treat the causes and not just the symptoms.

Analogy limitations

Generally speaking then, patterns and insights from anatomy and physiology are useful in thinking about organization design, development, management and growth. The human body, its anatomy and physiology – how it is structured, functions and then what it takes for it to work optimally – provide a striking analogy to that of a successful organization. Considering a definition of physiology illustrates this:

> Physiology is the study of the functions of living matter. It is concerned with how an organism performs its varied activities: how it feeds, how it moves, how it adapts to changing circumstances, how it spawns new generations.
>
> (Pocock and Richards, 2006)

It is easy to change a few words and get an organizationally apt parallel definition:

> Organizational physiology (to coin a term) is the study of the function of organizations. It is concerned with how the organization performs its varied activities; how it learns, how it competes in its environment, how it adapts to changing circumstances, how it sustains growth.

However, this pure physiology focus illustrates the limitations to the analogy, and these should be borne in mind. First, it ignores the spirit, culture and emotion of both human and organizational health.

Second, it misses the point of what is changeable and what is not. Take the notion of DNA, which in remarks like 'It's in the DNA' is a frequently referenced human and organizational term. Here's how one writer explains organizational DNA (Govindarajan, 2005):

> There are fundamental rules that determine how organizations behave – policies and practices that have a tremendous impact on motivations, capabilities, and behaviour. These rules are so powerful, and so often taken for granted, that it is entirely apt to refer to them as organizational DNA.

For humans their DNA, even given modern gene therapies, is pretty much fixed, whereas for organizations the elements that are the proxies for DNA, which include policies, rules, values, principles, control methods and power structures, can be changed to a greater or lesser extent. This illustrates one of the limitations of the analogy – it is not perfect.

Third, taking a single perspective of an organization – that it is like a human body – blinds us to other ways and perspectives of thinking about and interpreting organizations. An advert for raising awareness about cyclists – how many passes does the white team make – put out by TfL (Transport for London) illustrates this tendency to focus on one thing at the expense of other important information. In this advert, asking people to concentrate on the white team means they do not notice what is happening in the black team (Dothetest, 2008). Gareth Morgan, in his book *Images of Organization* (1997), presents eight metaphors for organizations each compelling in its own way. He discusses organizations as:

- machines;
- organisms;
- brains;
- cultures;
- political systems;
- psychic prisons;

- flux and transformation;
- instruments of domination.

But although he talks of them as independent 'lenses', Morgan also makes the point that the insights gained from one metaphor are helpful in interpreting another. In this book it is not the aim to labour the analogy of organizational health as akin to human health, if only because organizations are complex and multi-faceted, and contain inherent contradictions that defy being interpreted in one way. However the analogy will pop up as the discussion proceeds in order to highlight, show connections and contribute to understanding of effective organizational functioning.

Pause for thought

What is the value of analogy and metaphor in thinking about organizations?

Why do so many management books rely on metaphor and analogy to make their points?

Describing organizational health

Beyond the use of the analogy, organizational health is an important and fairly extensively written about topic in its own right, and writers and researchers have come up with various definitions and characteristics. Here are four definitions:

- Organization health is an organization's ability to function effectively, to cope adequately, to change appropriately, and to grow from within. Organizational health, like personal health, may vary from a minimal to a maximal level (Organizational Health Development and Diagnostic Corporation, 2011).
- A healthy organization is one where people like to come to work and are proud to be part of the organization (Lyden and Klingele, 2000).
- A healthy organization is the combination and co-ordination of people and practices that produce exceptional performance (Bruhn, 2001).
- Health is a state of physical, mental, and social well-being and not merely the absence of disease. As applied to an organization, the health of an organization is its body, mind, and spirit:

- Body refers to the structure, organizational design, uses of power, communication processes, and distribution of work.
- Mind refers to how underlying beliefs, goals, policies, and procedures are implemented, 'how conflict is handled, how change is managed, how members are treated, and how the organization learns'.
- Spirit is the core or heart of an organization... what makes it vibrant, and gives it vigor. It is measurable by observation (Bruhn, 2001).

Turning to those who prefer to describe organizational health in terms of attributes or characteristics makes it somewhat easier to gain some clarity on what it is. Below are four descriptions.

- Healthy organizations are characterized by four features:
  - a unity of purpose (strong culture);
  - responsive components;
  - reaction to environment;
  - interrelationships on individual, team, and organizational levels (Bruhn, 2001).
- Healthy organizations have three core capacities: (Hamel, 2010)
  - the ability to renew;
  - the ability to get deep alignment around purpose;
  - the ability to execute.
- Beckhard (Beckhard and Rueben, 1977) suggests 15 characteristics of a healthy organization, which include:
  - a strong sense of purpose;
  - keeping communication open;
  - congruent reward systems;
  - high tolerance for innovation and creativity;
  - identification and management of change;
  - making decisions closest to the customer;
  - respecting customer service;
  - using team management;
  - driving management through information (taken from Bruhn, 2001).

- Bruhn (2001) provided a categorized list of attributes of organizational health (column 1 in Table 1.1) and a comparison of this with a description of healthy individuals (column 2 in the table).

In these lists of characteristics and attributes, the more expressive side of the enterprise is revealed. With both the definitions and the characteristics in hand, it becomes easier to understand the scope of organizational health: it covers the continued and effective functioning of mind, body, spirit, in a context of changing circumstances.

But it is not easy to go from a scope description to a singular definition or set of universally applicable characteristics of health. Given the number of competing definitions, and the rather wide range of characteristics of organizational health, there are a number of 'maybes':

- It may be wishful thinking to believe that it is possible to reach agreement on the meaning of the phrase 'organizational health'.
- It may be a concept that is resistant to single definition and comparable measurement.
- It may be difficult to operationalize a uniform construct of 'organizational health'.
- It may be that it is more useful for organizations to define and characterize health in their own situations, related to their own missions and goals.

It is with these 'maybes' in mind that this book takes the view that 'organizational health' is not amenable to a single definition or a single prescription for attaining it. Nevertheless it is useful to have the differing definitions and characteristics as framing devices – that is, collectively they give an impression of what a healthy organization is. With these it is possible to explore what the outcomes are of organizational health. Four outcomes that are implied in the definitions and characteristics mentioned are:

- effective performance or functioning (body);
- well-managed adaptation, change and growth (body and mind);
- a strong sense of alignment interdependency and community (mind);
- a spirit of energy, vibrancy and vigour, perhaps what the online shoe retailer Zappos defines as WOW.

As Zappos' CEO Tony Hsieh says: 'We're a service company that just happens to sell shoes. We are not an average company, our service is not

TABLE 1.1   Attributes of health

Attributes of organizational health	Attributes of healthy individuals
Leading a life of purpose • Clear mission and goals • Gives back to the community • Integrity • Quality focus • Principled • Provides opportunities for growth • Rewards or recognizes achievement	**Leading a life of purpose** • Clear mission and goals • Balanced – living within one's value system • Integrity • Productive • Purposeful work • Spiritual or higher purpose basis • Passion or motivation to achieve for the better good
Quality connections to others • Open, honest communication norms • Fairness or justice in practices • Opportunity • Trust and safety norms • Mutual purpose and sense of belonging to the bigger whole • Embraces and encourages diversity of people, skills and ideas • Cohesiveness and positive affiliation • Pride in group accomplishments • Facilitates interdependent workers (high autonomy with strong social supports)	**Quality connections to others** • Interdependent: strong, positive social support system • Emotional competence • Mature, intimate connection to family and significant others • Communication competence
Positive self-regard and mastery • Encourage balance • Growth opportunities • Support systems for problems • Fitness support systems • Positive physical work environment • High safety focus	**Positive self-regard and mastery** • Humour • Hope and optimism • Self-efficacy or confidence • Self-awareness – strength focus – a component of emotional competence • Subjective well-being/happiness • Hardiness, self-reliance, and adaptability • Vigour, physical and mental energy • Personal challenge and growth goals

average, and we don't want our people to be average. We expect every employee to deliver wow' (Butler, 2011).

Pause for thought

What makes striving for an agreed definition or list of characteristics of organizational health unrealizable and/or unnecessary?

How far is a base list of organization health characteristics useful to help develop organization effectiveness?

The importance of organizational health

In a discussion with Gary Hamel (a business school professor) on organizational health, Colin Price of McKinsey (a management consultancy) notes that:

> The long-term performance of organizations is enhanced if in addition to a focus on performance, they have a long-term, sustained, deep, and authentic focus on building what we call the underlying health of the organization. It's not a 'nice to have', it's not an optional extra; it turns into the money. Without a focus on health, performance doesn't occur (Hamel, 2010).

Note that these remarks could equally apply to the field of personal health. It is not a 'nice to have' but an essential if one is to live a fully functional life.

Price goes on to propose that although a focus on health is 'merely lip service in most organizations... there is a set of principles and approaches which the best organizations have managed to use which will bring the same degree of rigor and robustness to the development of health as to the development of performance.'

Take the example below of the 2009 oil spill, known as the Macondo Blowout, in the Gulf of Mexico. The *Financial Times*, discussing the report into the spill, comments on four things that contributed to the disaster:

- Various procedures were not followed.
- A key safety test was ignored.
- The cement that was injected to seal the well had not been tested for suitability.
- The crew had not had sufficient disaster training.

It concludes, 'Not only does the report criticize BP's lax processes but also its poor communications – both internally and with contractors' (*Financial Times*, 6 January 2011). What is interesting about this is the fact that four months earlier the owners of Deepwater Horizon, Transocean, had suffered a similar but less catastrophic accident on their oil rig Sedco 711. Following this accident:

> [A] PowerPoint presentation from Transocean, produced in response to the Sedco 711 event, looked at shortcomings in the company's manuals for dealing with such events, and at the need for heightened vigilance in such circumstances. 'Are we ready?' it asked, and 'WHAT IF?' Yet Transocean told the commission [investigating Deepwater Horizon] that neither that sobering presentation, nor a subsequent advisory notice, ever made it to the Deepwater Horizon.
>
> (*Economist online*, 2011)

Map the elements of the story to the elements of the systems model (Figure 1.1) and it becomes clear that there were failures through the whole Transocean organizational system. There is no evidence of what Price calls a set of principles and approaches that develop health. These failures are all outcomes of system-wide ill health. Table 1.2 takes each of the elements in the systems model (Figure 1.1) and maps the failures to this, illustrating the interdependencies between system elements.

The costs to Transocean of the Sedco 711 accident were significant. The internal report generated to investigate it stated that it had resulted in 11.1 days of lost time at a cost of approximately £5.2m (approximately $8.1m) and 'significant loss of reputation to Transocean' (Maritime Law Staff, 2010). Costs of the Macondo incident to Tansocean are currently (November 2011) being apportioned.

Using these two examples it is likely that had Transocean been a healthy organization it would have maintained a good reputation, averted serious accidents, avoided disaster recovery costs and so on.

Thus, in the same way human ill health has damaging consequences, so does organizational ill health. As Price says, organizational health is not a 'nice to have'. It is critically important to value, maintain and develop it and, rather than treat a problem when it appears, introduce the principles and approaches that develop long-term health. One way of doing this is through preventive healthcare.

TABLE 1.2   Failure by systems element

Systems element	Transocean failure
Mission/vision	Deciding to trade off safety for time/money. 'Whether purposeful or not, many of the decisions that BP, Halliburton, and Transocean made that increased the risk of the Macondo blowout clearly saved those companies significant time (and money).' (National Oil Spill Commission, 2011)
Values/operating principles	Playing play fast and loose with procedures.
Goals and performance metrics	Ignoring a key safety test when it delivered the wrong result.
Strategies and tactics	Not circulating the sobering [what if] presentation, nor a subsequent advisory notice to the Deepwater Horizon teams.
Structure	Having weak structures of control and oversight: '... the Macondo blowout was the product of several individual missteps and oversights by BP, Halliburton, and Transocean, which government regulators lacked the authority, the necessary resources, and the technical expertise to prevent.' (National Oil Spill Commission, 2011)
Processes	Maintaining lax processes.
Systems	Allowing failing management systems. As the Commission reports 'most of the mistakes and oversights at Macondo can be traced back to a single overarching failure – a failure of management.' (National Oil Spill Commission, 2011)
Technology	Using inadequate technologies – or failing to maintain them effectively. In the Deepwater Horizon accident a cement seal at the bottom of the well – had given way. In the Sedco 711 it was a valve blow out that triggered the accident.
People	Giving the crew insufficient training to deal with the calamity.
Performance measures	Going ahead with insufficient information. Cement that was used to seal the well was injected before studies had been completed to assure its suitability for the task.

Preventive health care

In human health terms, preventive care means taking steps to prevent disease and ill health – physical and psychological – from occurring in the first place. It includes taking steps, decisions and specific positive actions to avert and avoid disease, in order to stay functioning optimally. The steps involved are not sequential but rather cover a wide spectrum of ongoing activity ranging from one-time vaccinations to sustaining an existing state of good health to making complex behavioural changes in relation to things such as weight control and stress management. In most cases preventive health activity requires sustained effort in many dimensions over time.

Organizations whose stock in trade is individual preventive health position themselves to 'encourage consumer behaviours most likely to optimize health potential (physical and psychosocial) through health information, preventive programmes, and access to medical care' (Reference MD, 2007). A preventive approach makes sense because prevention costs less than expensive medical interventions when things go wrong, and in the long run prevention brings more benefits.

A very similar approach can be taken by organizations, and those organizations that choose not to take a preventive healthcare approach run high risks of incurring unnecessary costs and reputational damage, as Transocean did.

The value of organizational preventive health becomes clear if we take another look at the Transocean example and do a 'what if exercise'. What if Transocean had been a healthy company, what would it look like? Table 1.3 illustrates this by going down the organizational elements again but this time substituting against each item some examples of what healthy functioning might have looked like.

This Transocean example of poor health and preventive health shows that taking a systems approach to both assessing ill health and taking preventive care action is a useful one. This becomes clearer when considering the Macondo case. Strong arguments were put forward that a bad cement job was the cause of the accident, essentially painting the problem (bad cement job) as a single and simple one to address, in much the same way that a single and simple approach to treating a headache is to take an aspirin. However, the Investigation Commission's findings about the incident rebut this single 'cause/effect' argument by providing evidence that the failure was the outcome of a system-wide complex problem.

TABLE 1.3   Health by systems element

Systems element	Transocean – what the outcome of preventive health care might look like
Mission/vision	There is clear evidence executing on the vision of being 'universally recognized for innovation and excellence in unlocking the world's offshore resources. • We will be our customers' trusted partner and their preferred solution provider. • We will conduct our operations in an incident-free workplace, all the time, everywhere. • Our people's passion and commitment to overcoming challenges will be our trademark. • We will deliver outstanding value to our customers, our employees, and our shareholders.' (Transocean, 2011)
Values/operating principles	There is clear evidence of living up to the organizational values: 'We want to create an environment in which different cultures can interact in a positive way to create a competitive advantage, and we will be united by our commitment to our core values of Transocean FIRST, which stands for: • Financial Discipline: Our decisions will be made to ensure long-term growth for the benefit of employees, customers and shareholders. • Integrity and Honesty: Our actions will be conducted following the highest standard of ethics, honesty and personal integrity. This will foster and maintain trust and confidence of our employees, customers and suppliers. • Respect for Employees, Customers and Suppliers: Our employees will be developed and motivated to meet the challenges ahead. Individuality and diversity will be valued and performance recognized. We will provide our customers with unsurpassed value-added service. Our relationship with suppliers will reflect respect, understanding and sound business practice. • Safety: Personal safety and employee health is our greatest responsibility, followed by the protection of our environment and company property. • Technical Leadership: Our competitive advantage is based on continually improving our processes and finding innovative solutions to the technical challenges in meeting the needs of our customers.'

TABLE 1.3 *continued*

Systems element	Transocean – what the outcome of preventive health care might look like
Goals and performance metrics	People are taking care to use the objective data to guide decision making.
Strategies and tactics	Problems are seen as a company-wide responsibility and not a local one. The April 14th Transocean report on the December 23 2010 Sedco 711 incident report was limited to the North Sea Division. A healthy response would be distributing the information to all three major Divisions and deciding to correct the problems company-wide rather than trying to treat the one incident in the North Sea as an isolated incident. Commentators suggest that if this had happened the Deepwater Horizon accident would have been averted. (Maritime Law Staff, 2010)
Structure	The internal and regulatory controls are in place for assessing and mitigating the risks of this type of event occurring. (Feilden, 2010)
Processes	Safety and other processes are being followed appropriately.
Systems	Managers are using consistent and well understood systems to execute on their responsibility to coordinate the organizational activities across the enterprise.
Technology	Technology is selected with reference to a range of factors, not just speed and cost.
People	High quality training is available, required, and monitored for efficacy for people who work in the offshore drilling industry.
Performance measures	Financial and time measures are balanced with other measures. The balanced scorecard is one approach to this.

As stated at the start of this chapter most organizational problems are more complex than first sight suggests. In most cases, rather than assuming a cause/effect from a single symptom, a better approach is to start by judging that a presenting symptom may signify a more deep-rooted problem, assessing whether this is the case or not, and if it is then addressing the issue as a complex whole-systems organizational one (and usually also an inter-organizational one), and treating it accordingly.

The key thing to note in the previous sentence is 'treating it accordingly'; not all systems are directed at the same vision, values or goals, so what is deemed healthy in one system may not be so for another. 'Treatments' for organizational ill health, and principles and approaches for organizational preventive health, need to be tailored to the specific organization. As is the case in human health, what works for one person may not work for another.

Pause for thought

What is the value of considering whole-system health rather than treating the presenting symptom or issue?

Why assess the risks of not taking preventive health care action against the benefits of taking it?

Different systems, different health approaches

If we think about human health, it is clear that what is considered 'health' or 'healthy' falls on a spectrum and is dependent on a number of factors, including people's visions, values and goals in wanting to maintain health, the cultural norms they are familiar with, and their genetic inheritance.

Thus a competitive athlete will have very different health goals, and ways of realizing them, from a pregnant woman or cancer survivor. Additionally, although there are common indicators of human health – blood pressure, heart rate, cholesterol levels and so on; these are always expressed within a range of 'normality' which itself depends on various factors. So, for example, blood pressure ranges are different for children and adults. Paula Radcliffe, world record holding marathon runner, has had asthma all her life. Here she talks about how she manages that inheritance using a preventive health care approach (NHS Choices, 2010):

I take my peak flow readings regularly to make sure I'm always getting the right level of treatment. When training, I take my preventer inhaler first thing in the morning, and I always take my reliever inhaler before I start exercising.

It's very important for me to warm up gently and gradually before I compete. This ensures that my asthma doesn't interfere with my training.

Look back at the range of definitions and characteristics of organizational health presented on page 9 and notice that for organizations too what is deemed health in one organization may not hold true for another.

What does hold true for both humans and organizations is to relate the profile of health to the specific vision/mission/purpose, as this has a direct bearing on the type of preventive health measures that a person or organization chooses to take. Remember, as in human health, there are some common indicators of organizational health and ill health – financial performance is one in the for-profit world – but again these indicators are not fixed points but ranges that depend on the unique circumstances of each organization.

Indicators of health and ill health

Walking into the offices of an organization, or interacting with employees via chat, phone, e-mail or website gives some indicators of the health of that organization. Below is one customer's experience of a retail outlet:

Four times this week I went to a UK shoe repairer and key cutting retailer. Each time was about a mailbox key. The first outlet I went to, the assistant initially said the key would be a special order and it would take a week to come in. When I told him I was leaving within a week he spent several minutes looking for an appropriate blank and found one that he thought would do the job.

I watched him cutting it. Splinters of metal were showering off the equipment and, out of interest, I asked him if he had eye protecting goggles. 'Oh yes,' he said. 'They're in my apron pocket.' He pulled them out to show me. 'Why aren't you wearing them? Aren't you worried about your eyes?' I asked. 'No,' he said, 'I just look away.'

I looked around the shop. It had a number of cheerful posters proclaiming the high calibre of the employees, the benefits they get, the selection processes and so on. I noticed that the clock was showing the wrong time and asked what had happened.

'Oh,' said the same assistant who cut my key, 'the hour hand doesn't work. We just go by the minute hand and guess the hour.' The other assistant was busy serving another customer, and I listened to the exchange. The customer wanted a tag engraved for his dog's collar. It was 5:20 pm. The store shut at 5:30 pm. The assistant said 'It'll take more than 10 minutes to engrave the tag. We're shutting now. You'll have to come back tomorrow.' Hmm – not what I'd expect from a high-calibre employee.

I tried out the key when I got home. It was stiff but finally worked after a fashion – it opened the mailbox. Then I realized that I needed a second key. The following day I went back to the same outlet. I hadn't brought the key I'd had cut the day before but just the original. I explained to the assistant that he'd cut a key from that same original the day before, it worked well enough and I needed another. He glanced at the original key. 'Oh, I don't know which blank I used. Bring back the one I cut and then I'll know.' So I went back later in the day with the one he'd cut the previous day plus the original.

This turned into a big production. He found the right blank. I suggested that he cut from my original but he said no he would cut it from the reproduction, and then 'if it doesn't work you can bring it back.' Still no goggles on, and then he couldn't get the clamp to work. The second guy suggested that he take the clamp off a different machine and put it on the one he was working on. This took a bit of time but finally he produced a second key. Guess what? It didn't work.

I went back for the third time. Since I needed the key I asked for it to be re-cut. It turned out that there were no more blanks. 'You can try the other shop,' the second guy said. I asked for my money back on the second key. He was reluctant to give it to me since he said I could produce my receipt in the other shop and they would cut it for free. As I had no idea whether the other shop had the blank and this shop didn't offer to call through and find out, I pressed for my money (and got it).

Fourth go. I walked over to the other shop and produced the duplicate, more-or-less working key and the second duplicate, non-working key. I said I wanted a re-cut of the second duplicate key. The assistant looked at it and said: 'It's been very badly cut.' He compared it with the first duplicate key and said: 'This key hasn't been finished properly either. Give me the original and I'll cut a new one and then finish the other one properly.' He wasn't wearing goggles at the time. I watched what happened next. He approached the machine, pulled out the goggles from his apron pocket and put them on. He cut the key from the original and then took it to a different machine to finish it (this hadn't happened in the first shop). He then compared his duplicate with the other duplicate and took that to finish. 'OK – that should do it,' he said. 'There's no charge. Sorry for your difficulties.' I got home to find that both keys worked perfectly. (Oh, and the clock in the shop showed the right time.)

Taking the situations described as examples of a healthy and unhealthy organization – a systems table, like Table 1.2, could be compiled illustrating failures (ill health) and outcomes of preventive health, as the Transocean example illustrates (Table 1.3).

But, in brief, in the first shop some of the indicators were:

• reputation of the organization ignored by employees;
• low level of motivation;

- reduced productivity;
- increased costs (having to rework).

In the second shop the opposite indicators were evident.

The interesting thing is that both these stores were part of the same chain. So how is it that two stores, part of the same organization, in the same city, have such opposite approaches to their work and to their customer service? Various immediate and simple answers present – it might be due to employee selection, local management, some tie-up to performance measures, a link to customer feedback and satisfaction, and/or the right tools to do the job.

The customer telling the story above also e-mailed it to the CEO of the company and by return got the following response:

> Dear
> Thanks for the feedback, which proves we don't always get it right. But your e-mail gives us the chance to learn from the mistake.
> I will check it out
> CEO

She got a second response from a customer care advisor:

> Please be assured that a copy of your e-mail has been sent to the Area Manager for follow-up with the branch concerned.
> As a company we place great emphasis on our standards of customer care and workmanship and it is only through our customers keeping us informed that we are able to monitor and indeed improve standards. I am therefore grateful to you for bringing this matter to my attention.

This story illustrates three points:

- First, that an organization is not totally healthy or totally unhealthy. Like a human being an organization can function well enough in a range of circumstances. Recognize however, that even with the most assiduous preventive health care humans will get headaches, colds and other malaises, but these are likely to be temporary and recognizable as simply treatable (or just lived with for a short time).

- Second, that in this case (and in any case) the challenge for the CEO is to know what the indicators are of good health and how to optimize these, where poor health is developing, and the extent of any presenting health issues. The skill is assessing what is simply treated, and what is a symptom of a deeper-rooted and pervasive problem.

- Third, it is striking that both the CEO and the customer care advisor said that reading the story gave them an opportunity to learn and improve. Going back to the characteristics of organizational health one of the key, and repeated, ones is the capacity to learn and adapt.

Learning and adaptation can take place as a reaction to an event (and should if an event occurs) – but as has been stated at several points a better approach is to introduce a rigorous process for regularly assessing health in order to take any actions to prevent untoward events occurring. Rather like an individual's physical/check-up, a regular organizational health assessment leads to actionable information.

Assessing organizational health

There are many methods of assessing organizational health, and there are many more consultancies and consultants willing to assess it. As with individual health, choosing the assessment method and assessment team is not straightforward, but rather 'horses for courses'.

People vary in the way they address their own health care. Some take a do-it-yourself approach, reading self-help books on wellness, nutrition, stress management and fitness, for example. Others go to traditional or conventional providers of services, while others opt for 'alternative' approaches; in all cases the choice of provider of health assessment tools is wide.

Harry Levinson (an academic and consultant) offers some sage advice on determining the scope of an organizational health assessment. He makes the point that traditional assessments tend to concentrate on things like structure, roles, status, attitudes, which he describes as 'highly intellectualized analyses... that do not easily lend themselves to understanding the organization as an active, unique, living entity' (Levinson, 2002).

His view is that a good assessment is comprehensive, covering a number of major areas with both quantitative and qualitative data collection that moves from fact to inference, and then to interpretation. His approach includes assessing what can be termed the body, mind and spirit of the organization, and includes looking at the relationship of the organization as an open system with other systems with which it interacts.

It is important to remember his advice. Organizational health is a multi-faceted, dynamic concept. In choosing to address it both from a preventive (proactive) perspective and from a problem-solving (reactive) perspective, careful choices should be made on the trade-offs between time, cost and quality of the assessment processes, with additional considerations of organizational fit and specific contextual criteria. There is no one right way to do an organizational health assessment; it is contingent on circumstances. For example a small engineering company may opt for an off-the-shelf organization health survey tool rather than employing a team from a major consulting company to come in and do an organizational health assessment 'project'. The important thing is to consciously agree what constitutes health for a particular organization, and how to continuously and appropriately assess its maintenance.

This book aims to provide a background and foundation to help make informed choices about organizational health, what to look for and where to go to get help on both preventive care and reactions to problems arising.

Exercise

Assess the 'heart health' of your organization

	Please indicate whether you agree or disagree with the following	Yes	No
1	Frequent communication between managers and subordinates is encouraged		
2	Open communication exists between managerial levels		
3	Employees are appropriately involved in organizational decision making		
4	Employees are proud to tell people where they work		

	Please indicate whether you agree or disagree with the following	Yes	No
5	An atmosphere of high personal trust exists in the organization		
6	High morale exists in the organization		
7	Employees are motivated		
8	A friendly atmosphere exists in the organization		
9	The organization has a respectable reputation		
10	Employees value the organization's reputation		
11	Employees act ethically		
12	A written code of ethics exists in the organization		
13	Employees feel valued and appreciated		
14	Appropriate recognition for achievement is common		
15	Organizational goals are usually achieved		
16	Employees can identify organizational goals		
17	Managers act in the best interests of the organization		
18	Managers are friendly and approachable		
19	A budget exists for training and development		
20	Resources are shared fairly in the organization		
Total the number of 'yes' ticks/check marks			

Score sheet:

	Diagnosis	Treatment
17–20 points	Good to fairly good – only have chest pain when under great stress	'Eat less fat in your diet.' In other words, start to consider cutting out some of the bureaucracy and barriers to communication; use new technologies. Recommendations: More exercise – use training and development programmes, engage in innovating.
13–16 points	Chest pain when there is minimal exertion	More of the above but do it sooner – no procrastination! Things could fall apart quickly. Put immediate effort into improving health. Re-evaluate training programmes, update recognition/evaluation procedures, create a code of ethics. Develop change and adaptability capacities.
9–12 points	Chest pain when at rest	Find out exactly what blockages are occurring; most likely need a bypass. In other words rework the organization design. Consider changes in top management and align the vision and practice of the organization.
5–8 points	Imminent heart failure	The heart is so weak it cannot carry out the functions necessary to survive. Only hope is transplantation. Need to consider extreme options – buyouts, liquidations, divestitures, merger.
0–4 points	Cardiac arrest	Charge the paddles – low probability that the heart will start beating again. A very slim chance that employees will re-motivate and want to continue working for this organization.

Key messages

- Organizational health care is analogous to human health care, but there are limitations to the analogy.

- Organizational health is not a 'nice to have' but an essential condition for an effective organization. Rigorous preventive health care approaches are required.

- Organizational health is maintained through addressing the whole system (mind, body, spirit) and assessing its state of health on a regular basis.

- Where a symptom of ill health appears, a single and simple instant 'treatment' should be avoided in favour of an investigation of any underlying root causes.

- There is no one right way of assessing and maintaining organizational health. What counts as health is related to the purpose and goals of a specific organization, although there are some common indicators across organizations.

References

Beckhard, R and Rueben, T (1977) *Organizational Transitions: Managing complex change*, Addison-Wesley, Reading, Mass

Bruhn, JG (2001) *Trust and the Health of Organizations*, KluwerAcademic/Plenum Publishers, New York

Bryant, A (2011) Fix the problem and, not just the symptoms, *New York Times*, 9 October [Online] http://www.nytimes.com/2011/10/09/business/joseph-jimenez-of-novartis-on-finding-the-core-of-a-problem.html?pagewanted=al (accessed 25 October 2011)

Butler, S (2011) Welcome to upside [Online] http://blog.ups.com/tag/tony-hsieh/ (accessed 11 November 2011)

Caulkin, S (2008) Gore-Tex gets made without managers, from *Guardian*, 1 November [Online] http://www.guardian.co.uk/business/2008/nov/02/gore-tex-textiles-terri-kelly (accessed 4 November 2011)

Cimilluca, D, Linebaugh, K, Miller, WJ and Fuhrmans, V (2011) Companies in Europe are pulling back, from *Wall Street Journal Online*, 31 October [Online] http://online.wsj.com/article/SB10001424052970204528204577008043494119510.html (accessed 4 November 2011)

Collins, J (2009) *How The Mighty Fall: And why some companies never give in*, Harper Collins, New York

Company, M (nd) [Online] http://www.mckglobal.com/Q/Reviews/Price_Hamel.html

Dothetest (2008) Test your awareness: do the test [Online] http://www.youtube.com/watch?v=Ahg6qcgoay4 (accessed 16 October 2011)

Economist online (2011) Lessons not learned [Online] http://www.economist.com/blogs/newsbook/2011/01/bp_and_deepwater_horizon_spill (accessed 11 November 2011)

Feilden, T (2010) A near miss for the North Sea oil industry [Online] http://www.bbc.co.uk/blogs/today/tomfeilden/2010/12/a_near_miss_for_the_north_sea.html (accessed 11 November 2011)

Financial Times (2011) An oil spill born of complacency, from FT.Com, 6 January [Online] http://www.ft.com/intl/cms/s/2159e888-19cd-11e0-b921-00144feab49a,Authorised=false.html#axzz1t6a5h8Mx (accessed 20 October 2011)

Govindarajan, V (2005) Is innovation in your organizational DNA? from *Fast Company*, October 10 [Online] http://www.fastcompany.com/resources/leadership/vgct/101005.html (accessed 16 October 2011)

Greiner, L (1998) Evolution and revolution as organizations grow, *Harvard Business Review*, May–June, 55–67

Hamel, GA (2010) *Building a Healthy Organization: A conversation between Gary Hamel and Colin Price*, McKinsey & Company, London

Kleiner, A (2011) The organization is alive, from *Alia Institute Fieldnotes* [Online] http://aliainstitute.org/blog/2011/03/24/the-organization-is-alive/ (accessed 25 October 2011)

Levinson, H (2002) *Organizational Assessment: A step by step guide to effective consulting*, American Psychological Association, Washington DC

Lyden, JA and Klingele, WE (2000) Supervising organizational health, *SuperVision*, 61(12), p 3

Maritime Law Staff (2010) Transocean withheld internal report that proved fatal for Deepwater Horizon 11 [Online] http://www.offshoreinjuries.com/blog/1268/transocean-withheld-internal-report-that-proved-fatal-for-deepwater-horizon-11/ (accessed 11 November 2011)

Morgan, G (1997) *Images of Organization*, Sage, London

National Cancer Institute (2010) Cancer staging [Online] http://www.cancer.gov/cancertopics/factsheet/detection/staging (accessed 12 November 2011)

National Oil Spill Commission (2011) National Commission on the BP Deepwater Horizon oil spill and offshore drilling [Online] http://www.oilspillcommission.gov/sites/default/files/documents/Advance%20Chapter%20on%20BP%20Well%20Blowout%20Investigation%20Released.pdf (accessed 11 November 2011)

NHS Choices (2010) Paula Radcliffe on asthma [Online] http://www.nhs.uk/Livewell/asthma/Pages/PaulaRadcliffe.aspx (accessed 11 November 2011)

Organizational Health Development and Diagnostic Corporation (2011) What is organizational health? [Online] http://www.organizationalhealth.com/assessment_what.php (accessed 20 October 2011)

Pocock, G and Richards, CD (2006) *Human Physiology: The basis of medicine*, 3rd edn, Oxford University Press, Oxford

Prevent Cancer Coalition (2003) Avoidable cancers [Online] http://www.preventcancer.com/avoidable/ (accessed 12 November 2011)

Reference MD (2007) Health promotion [Online] http://www.reference.md/files/D006/mD006293.html (accessed 23 October 2011)

Transocean (2011) Transocean mission and values [Online] http://www.deepwater.com/fw/main/Mission-Safety-Vision-Core-Values-138.html (accessed 11 November 2011)

Organizational structures

"Optimum organization [forms] must be derived from an analysis of the work to be done and the techniques and resources available.

(WILFRED BROWN, CHAIRMAN AND MANAGING DIRECTOR OF GLACIER METAL COMPANY (1939–65), QUOTED IN BENNIS, 1966)

Objectives

At the end of this chapter you will be able to:

- provide an overview of the four organizational structures through which work flows – the business model, the organization chart, the organizational network, the friendship and social network (see Glossary);
- discuss each one in more detail;
- present the idea that healthy organizational functioning requires insight into all four structures;
- give some symptoms of unhealthy structural functioning.

Having determined that organizational health is characterized by:

- effective performance or functioning;
- well-managed adaptation, change and growth;
- a strong sense of alignment interdependency and community;
- a spirit of energy, vibrancy and vigour, perhaps what the online shoe retailer Zappos defines as WOW.

Then what form should its organizing structures take? There are two principal formal structures to consider: the business model and the organization chart. Additionally there are two informal organizing structures: the organizational network and the social network.

Within these overlapping and interdependent structures work is organized and conducted in four ways in most organizations:

- Through the choices, decisions and consequences inherent in the business model.

- Through the formal organization, as shown on a chart that depicts hierarchies and formal relationships and includes (by virtue of job descriptions and grades of staff) formal allocation of accountabilities and authorities.

- Through the informal organizational work patterns that are revealed through organizational and network analysis and by observing the way people learn how to do their work in relationship with others. This includes networks of influence and sources of informal power and authority.

- Through the friendship and social networks that people develop in the course of their work that impact the way they feel about what they do and how they do it.

In a healthy organization these four elements of business model, formal organization, informal work organization, and informal social patterns combine and align in order to allow the work to flow effectively so as to achieve the business objectives. The functioning and effectiveness of this combination can be revealed by investigation and interpretation, essentially a diagnosis of what is going on. For example, it might be of value to discover why person A asks her supervisor to make a decision, but person B, in the same role but with a different supervisor, makes the decision herself – analysis is likely to prove that all four elements are involved in the difference.

Remember the human body analogy at this point – alignment comes when the business model (the genetic array), the formal organization (the skeleton), the informal work organization (the interactions and behaviours) and the social networks (how people feel and respond) are in harmony and the 'work' flows with optimum efficiency. Thus when Luciano Pavarotti, a world famous tenor and opera singer, died in 2007 one tribute noted that:

> No one matched Pavarotti at his best for sheer, prodigal outpouring of vocal beauty. And what he lacked in subtlety and polish he made up for in vitality, natural talent and entertainment value. In this sense Pavarotti the celebrity and

Pavarotti the artist were one. The same simplicity, verve and generosity of spirit that made him a walking media event shone through his resplendent voice.

(Porterfield, 2007)

In Pavarotti's case his 'work' – singing – flowed naturally through his formal and informal organizing structures.

Note, however, that these organizing structures are not the only contributors to health. Both humans and organizations can maintain good enough performance while experiencing aspects of ill health. For example a broken finger would not necessarily compromise Pavarotti's singing performance. One dysfunctional team may not bring down the organization, but in both instances the presenting symptom could be an indicator of a wider vulnerability.

The business model

Although there are varieties of definitions and depictions of business models, they all agree that a business model is more than a strategy or a focus on revenue generation. Essentially a business model is the 'what and how' of a business in terms of the choices and decisions made in relation to its specific operation. When someone starts a new company they develop its business model. And they do this by figuring out: Who is the customer for the product/service? What does this customer value? How can money be made in this business? How can value be delivered to the customer at an appropriate cost? Figure 2.1 shows one representation of a business model.

In this model the boxes represent the 'what' of the organization and require conscious choices and decisions to be made for each of them; for example, the box 'competences, activities and resources' requires choices and decisions around questions like: 'What are the main activities we operate to run our business model? On which key resources do they rely? To which value propositions, channels or relationships do they contribute?'

The arrows between the boxes represent the 'how' of the organization and include both 'hard' things like IT systems or explicit policies, and 'soft' things like leadership style or speed of decision making. Again, organizational members make choices and decisions around these. For example, the arrow from 'customer relationship' to 'offer' requires choices and decisions around soft questions like: 'How responsive will we be to customer feedback? Are we going to tell the customer or are we going to make choices and decisions by involving the customer? Will we treat all customers equally?'

FIGURE 2.1 Representation of a business model

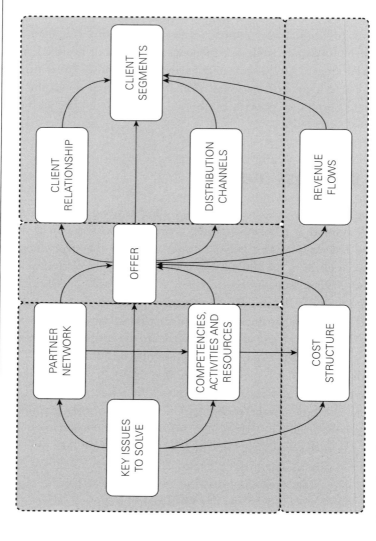

SOURCE: Alex Osterwalder http://www.slideshare.net/Alex.Osterwalder/business-model-innovation-matter

and hard questions like 'What IT system is the best customer relationship management system for our purposes? What packaging shall we offer our product in? What price point should we offer at?'

Think about Walmart, for example. The business model choices and decisions that Walmart makes about its offer, partner networks, distribution channels and so on, and the consequences of these choices, make the company distinctively Walmart and not Tesco or a similar competitor. So in the United States Walmart is noted for:

- low labour costs (it is a no-union company);
- an authoritarian structure;
- hyper-centralized managerial control;
- requiring workers promoted to the managerial ranks to move to a new store in a different location;
- workweeks around 50 hours or more, which can surge to 80 or 90 hours a week during holiday seasons;
- cutting out the middlemen and shifting costs and risks onto the manufacturer;
- bringing warehousing, distribution and trucking in-house;
- building new stores around distribution centres;
- harnessing retail information through high-tech barcode and product-tracking software;
- revolutionizing the relationship between merchant and vendors.

Walmart's business model choices and decisions mean that the customer gets the lowest possible price for a product, but there are consequences to the choices and decisions made. In Walmart's case it has 'developed a reputation as a rapacious, anti-labor-union, un-environmental "big box" destroyer of small towns and independent businesses' (Schell, 2011).

Healthy companies review their business models at regular intervals and adjust or even radically change them in the light of changes in their internal and external contexts. The Appendix provides a worksheet for exploring the business model elements in more detail.

Failure to review has significant consequences, as US telecoms company AT&T found out. Originally established in 1885 as the American Bell Telephone Company, in 2005 it was bought by SBC for around $16 billion. SBC was one of the 'baby bells' that was spun out of the company known as 'Ma Bell', as part of a 1984 court-ordered break-up. Keeping up the human/organization analogy a historian remarked: 'It ought to be humbling to any empire-builder to see what was once the greatest corporation in America be acquired by one of its offspring' (*Economist*, 2005).

The failure, at the time, of leaders of AT&T to change its business model in order to take advantage of new technologies such as wireless and the internet were cited as reasons for the takeover. But they are not alone in this failure as Clayton Christensen, of Harvard Business School and author of several books on innovation, said on hearing that AT&T been bought. 'It is a tragic fall [for AT&T] and I lament the passing, because it was a huge disruptive success in its day. The world is filled with companies that are marvellously innovative from a technical point of view, but completely unable to innovate on a business model' (*Economist*, 2005).

Six years on the new AT&T (following the purchase of the American Bell Telephone Company SBC changed its name to AT&T) was still in some difficulties. Fierce competitors such as cable companies and firms pitching cheap, pre-paid mobile deals that competed with AT&T's pricier, longer-term contracts were targeting its customers. 'All these firms are like a flesh-eating virus that spreads over telecoms companies' bodies,' said Mike Sapien of the consultancy Ovum (*Economist*, 2010). The environment had shifted but the failure to adapt and respond to these external context changes remained.

Generally speaking, companies that are more adept at rethinking their business model both pay close attention to the external environment – constantly horizon scanning for threats and opportunities constantly – and have the following attributes: (Grant Thornton, 2010)

- *Flexibility*: to evolve to business models where: a) products and services are able to be paid for on an as-needed basis (for example, in the IT world moving from the software licence model to the software as a service model); and b) companies can scale up or down without loss of business continuity.

- *Ability to deliver short-term cost savings and/or efficiency gains to customers*: to offer customers a greater level of granularity in the way products and services can be bought (for example Ryanair's menu of options compared with British Airway's all-in single-price approach).

- *Capacity to drive innovation*: to engage with those interested in participation in open-innovation (looking to people outside the organization to come up with new and/or improved product and service ideas).

- *Capability to enter new markets*: to look outside their traditional markets and be in a position to offer products and services tailored to customers in these new markets.

- *Collaborative ownership structures*: to achieve economies of scale and reduce competitive pressures.

- *Use of the digital (information and communication) economy*: to help reinvent what the company is capable of offering and how it offers it.

One way of developing the adeptness and attributes required was suggested by Peter Drucker. He called it 'Planned abandonment', saying that it is better to abandon a product, service, policy, rule or other organizational element much earlier than when it begins to cause problems. As a rule it is time to abandon when any of the three following conditions apply:

- The product, service, market, process, or whatever still has a few good years of life

- Its greatest virtue is that it is fully written off. Ask instead: 'What is it producing?'

- An old and declining product, service, market, process, etc is being maintained at the expense of new and growing products, services, markets, processes, etc.

Drucker suggested that the leadership team should regularly ask a series of questions aimed at pinpointing areas for abandonment. This is a good suggestion and one followed by Lenovo, a computer maker. The members of its team of nine leaders (down from two dozen at one time) are based in six cities and three continents, yet they meet every other month to review the business, typically spending three or four days together in a key market, visiting local stores and listening to partners, customers and employees (Salter, 2011).

The goal of these review meetings is to align the organization's goals, and take quick action where things are not working well. For example, following a leadership team visit to India Lenovo restructured its business model there to drive growth in segments like small and medium business (SMB), government and education, which were not getting much attention earlier. The company separated SMB, earlier part of its consumer division, to make it an independent business. It also created different teams to handle its government and education business, as these required a different focus. These decisions were made because, although it was the leading PC vendor in the enterprise space in India, success in that arena alone would not help to improve its share in India (Mishra, 2011).

Lenovo, which launched its first personal computer in 1990, has the goal of becoming the first global consumer brand to emerge from China, and its management team is willing and able to change the company's business model as required to meet this goal. For other organizations barriers to business model change are the skills of the management teams, and/or additionally the sheer complexity of the structures, processes, policies and working practices that for any long-established company have been in place over many years.

In a fascinating blog post, 'The collapse of complex business models', Clay Shirky (writer, consultant, lecturer) discusses the idea that an organization's failure to respond to stress in the environment is not a lack of will, it is simply that the organization cannot adapt. One of the examples he cites is AT&T, mentioned earlier. His suggestion is that the complexities of long-established organizations make them unable to change:

> In such systems, there is no way to make things a little bit simpler – the whole edifice becomes a huge, interlocking system not readily amenable to change... Under a situation of declining marginal returns collapse may be the most appropriate response... Furthermore, even when moderate adjustments could be made, they tend to be resisted, because any simplification discomfits elites.
> (Shirky, 2010)

Look back at the list of six attributes that make it easier to adapt a business model. Note that three of them relate to management skills: capability to enter new markets, use of the digital economy and capacity to drive innovation. (Chapter 5 discusses healthy development.) Three relate to complexities in business models: flexibility, ability to deliver efficiencies and collaborative ownership structures. But take the point that health is within a range of tolerances. High-performing organizations may not have all the attributes listed.

Pause for thought

How does a systems model of an organization differ from a business model? What is the intent of each?

How important is it for managers to have a clear grasp of what their organization's business model is?

What makes a business model more or less effective, and how can it be made more effective?

How can complexities in organizations be minimized and management skills maximized to avoid collapse?

The organization chart

Too frequently in the case of organizational problems arising, the first response is to look to the organization chart: that is, names of jobholders in boxes that show a formal reporting relationship between the jobholders. Figure 2.2 below illustrates six commonly seen types of organization chart.

When people are trying to decide the 'best' structure for their organization, they often forget that work has to flow through it, and that different structures have different attributes. For example, adaptability is poor in a traditional hierarchy but good in a network. Instead structure decisions are made based on personalities, politics and expediency. This is a mistake on three counts:

- It fails to explicitly recognize that structure choices impact organizational capabilities.

- Getting work done efficiently in order to meet organizational goals is, or should be, the purpose of the organizing frameworks and structures.

- It assumes that changing the organization chart alone will enable effective workflow.

On the first point – that structure choices impact organizational capabilities – Conway's law (see Glossary) suggests that the technical architecture of a computer system reflects the bureaucratic structure of the organization that produced it. Now consider Figure 2.3, which shows, tongue-in-cheek, the structures of six well-known technology firms.

As with all caricatures there is truth in the depiction. The system architectures – the organization capabilities – developed by the respective companies in fact reflect the structures shown in their organization charts. So, for example, Microsoft has the Windows Group, the Office Group and the XBox group, and their systems are isolated from each other. Although at one stage Office and Windows were 'joined at the hip', trust-busters made Microsoft erect a Chinese wall between the two organizations, so their architectures had to bifurcate.

It is likely that Apple's organization chart will change following the death of Steve Jobs (here represented by the dot in the middle) but at the time this chart was drawn up Apple controlled its systems – chips, software, hardware, content, sales channel – vertically to a far greater extent than any other company except perhaps Sony. Thus the organization chart reflects their system architecture.

FIGURE 2.2   Six common organization structures

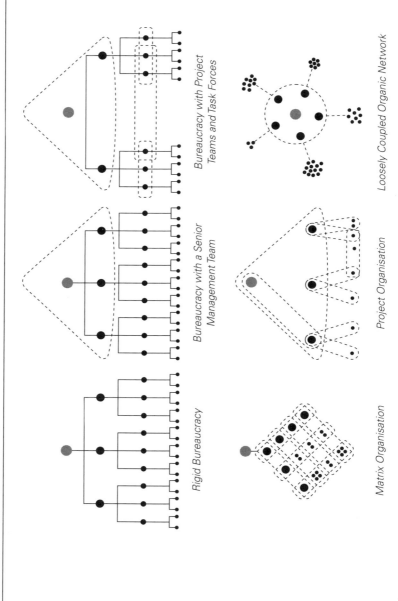

Rigid Bureaucracy

Bureaucracy with a Senior Management Team

Bureaucracy with Project Teams and Task Forces

Matrix Organisation

Project Organisation

Loosely Coupled Organic Network

SOURCE: Morgan, G. Imaginization (London, Sage, 1993) p161.

FIGURE 2.3   'Structures' of six technology companies

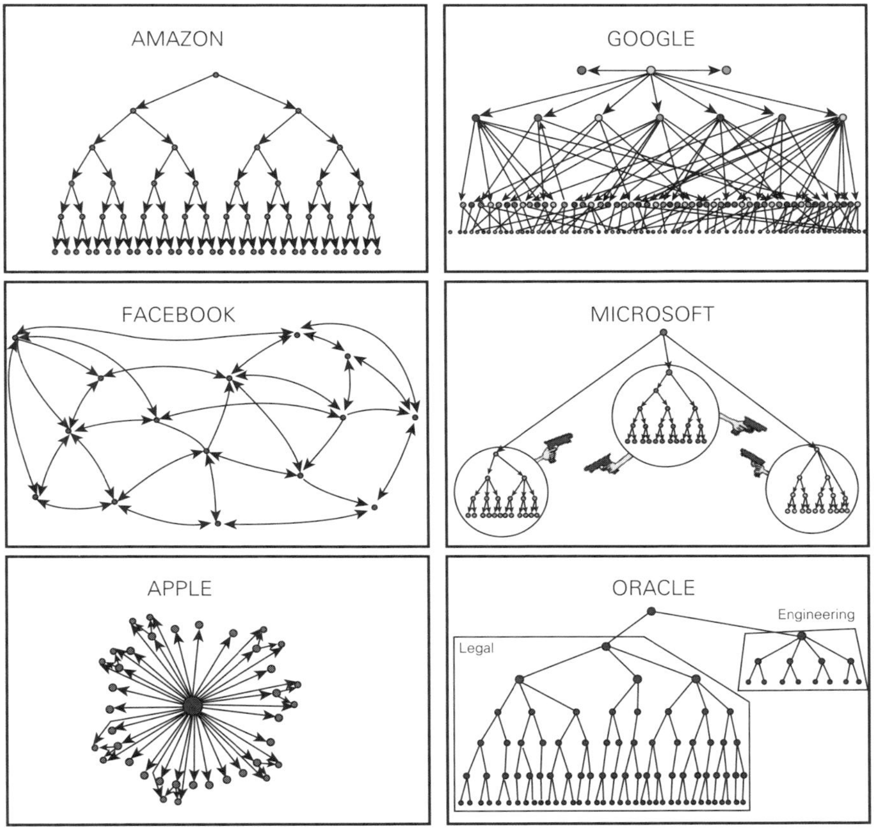

AMAZON

GOOGLE

FACEBOOK

MICROSOFT

APPLE

ORACLE

Engineering

Legal

SOURCE: Manu Cornet http://www.bonkersworld.net/images//2011.06.27_organizational_charts.png

Of course, it could be that the cartoonist knew the systems architectures of the companies and drew the structures to match – nevertheless the question the cartoon raises is worth considering. How far do structures (and by implication other organizing frameworks) affect the way products and services are designed and offered to customers?

On the second point – that getting work done efficiently in order to meet organizational goals is, or should be, the purpose of the organizing frameworks and structures – organization charts offer almost no insight into how work is done. Work occurs in what is commonly called the 'white space' in the chart – and can be mapped by organizational network analysis, and social network analysis. Figure 2.4 illustrates this.

FIGURE 2.4 Traditional organization chart v organization network map

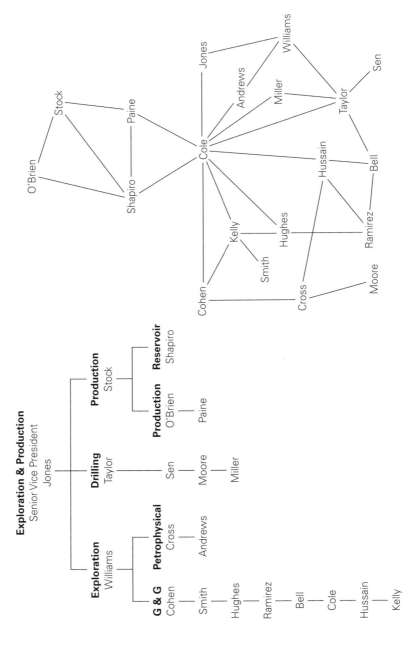

SOURCE: Rob Cross http://www.robcross.org/network_ona.htm

The organization chart on the left shows the formal reporting lines. The organizational network analysis chart on the right shows how work is getting done via information flows and collaboration. There is very little relationship between the two charts, which depict the same people through different perspectives.

The possibilities that technology now offer for charting the way work actually gets done in organizations and the advent of new business models raise the question about the future of the traditional organization chart. Is it of any real value? Three different but common scenarios make it a question worth thinking about.

- Take the way work gets done. In many organizations employees play multiple roles, for example working on project teams (perhaps more than one at a time) while contributing expertise and skills in a variety of forums, and they often work for more than one boss. In these cases, and even using dotted lines, it is not so easy to allocate them to a slot in an organization chart.

- Now consider the business model of a new organization. LiveOps, established in 2000, deploys cloud computing to virtualize its business services. It is a cloud-based call-centre service that manages a network of more than 20,000 independent at-home agents. Companies use the service on a pay-as-you-go model, either as a fully outsourced call centre or to augment their own. The technology enables an on-demand, scalable service to subscribers. The relationship of the stakeholders – LiveOps, the independent agents and the companies buying the services of the agents via Live Ops – is not easily depicted in a standard chart. Nevertheless the three parties together form an organization that delivers a service to a customer. Look at Amazon's Mechanical Turk for another example of a new business model.

- In other organizations, fully employed members of staff work side by side with contractors, consultants and temporary workers. It is difficult to argue this type of staff augmentation is not part of effective organizational functioning and success (why pay for their services if they do not contribute?) yet these people do not appear on a standard organization chart.

In all three instances – and others like them – organization chart development and maintenance could well be a redundancy that is better not introduced in the first instance, or if it is already established should be reviewed for its value. Is it adding value to spend time, effort and money to produce and maintain something that shows in broad terms the level of formal authority of various positions, their numbers and their presumed reporting relationships?

Sun Hydraulics, established in 1970 and profitable from the start, is an example of an organization that decided not to have an organization chart. Its website explains:

> Our workplace is as distinctive as our products, and provides just as many advantages. We have no job titles, no hierarchy, no formal job descriptions, organizational charts or departments. We have open offices, promoting open communication. This environment encourages innovation and helps develop a spirit of entrepreneurship throughout the organization. The result is a workforce inspired to satisfy every customer, no matter the challenge.
>
> (Sun Hydraulics, 2002–11)

W L Gore, also very financially successful, takes the same approach

> Gore has been a team-based, flat lattice organization that fosters personal initiative. There are no traditional organizational charts, no chains of command, nor predetermined channels of communication. (WL Gore and Associates, 2011)

Starbucks too has taken a rather non-traditional view of its organization chart (Figure 2.5), streamlining it radically for the purposes of educating employees that their prime boss is the customer, and that is who they 'report' to.

FIGURE 2.5   Starbucks' organization 'chart'

SOURCE: (Brand Autopsy, 2006) http://www.brandautopsy.com/2011/09/simplify_org_chart.htm In Tribal Knowledge, John Moorel

On the third point – thinking that changing the organization chart alone will enable effective workflow – if the decision is made that it is of value to spend time, effort and money to produce and maintain something that shows in broad terms the level of formal authority of various positions, their numbers and their presumed reporting relationships, then follow the seven principles outlined below for developing the structure and depicting it as an organization chart. Following these principles will allow for better integration with the other three organizing frameworks.

The start point is to determine the work flow, the activities and the work volume that need to be achieved to deliver the business strategy; from this the number of people and their grade levels can be gauged. Then:

- The structure must demonstratively deliver the strategic goals of the organization. Check that:
  - The structure enables the required combination of products, services and customer relationships to be delivered.
  - It minimizes costs.
  - It enables the organization to create added value.
- Departmental accountabilities must be clear. Check that:
  - Each element has clearly articulated responsibilities, accountabilities and performance measures.
  - Strategic deliverables have a clear owner.
  - Where there is shared ownership for a strategic deliverable, the structure maximizes co-ordination.
- The structure should be as flat as possible. Check that:
  - It is designed to a minimum number of organization levels.
  - Spans of control are reasonable and efficient.
- Avoid unnecessary duplication. Check that:
  - No other parts of the company perform this service.
  - Activities are located together to create economies of scale and centres of expertise.
  - Expertise and resources are located where they have optimal impact.
  - Customers (external or internal) will not experience duplication.
  - Activities that most need to be co-ordinated are located together.
- The structure should be flexible and responsive to change. Check that:
  - It copes with workload fluctuations (peaks and troughs) and variations in customer demand.
  - It will support predicted future growth and innovation.

- The structure demonstrates appropriate governance and risk standards. Check that:
  - It complies with the regulatory and financial governance framework within which it operates.
  - It has clearly documented risk and governance accountabilities.
  - It enables issues to be escalated swiftly and appropriately.
- The structure supports the development of key capabilities. Check that:
  - The business-critical career paths are clearly visible within the structure.
  - Any capability gaps created by the new structure are resolved.

Pause for thought

Has the formal organization structure chart had its day? Explain why/why not?

How valid is the assertion that the way the organization chart is configured, maintained and 'lived' influences, for better or worse, the design and development of the organization's products and services?

The organizational network

Review Figure 2.4 above. It shows, side by side, the formal structure (the organization chart) and the informal structure (revealed by organization network analysis) of the interactions that take place to get the work done. Among some of the interesting patterns it reveals is that one employee – Cole – is a hub for communication and information requests and that Jones – the head of the department – is rather isolated in his connections.

Organizationally this could mean that Jones is not fully participating in work flow and decision making, and that things could go wrong if Cole left or fell sick for a period of time. Neither of these possibilities is shown on a standard organization chart. The power of mapping organizational relationship networks in this way is multiple:

- They show how work gets done via organizational relationships, building on the commonly used phrase that, to be effective, organizations not only need 'the right people in the right place at the right time' but also that these people must have the right relationships.

- They illustrate that there is an asset value inherent in the informal relationships around work flow. In the network shown in Figure 2.4 it is likely that the organization is not getting full value from Jones because he is isolated, and that Cole's hub role is an organizational vulnerability – his loss would mean drops in productivity by his co-workers as they were dependent on him for information.

- They suggest how network structures, can impact, for better or worse, organizational improvement (eg knowledge management, strategic alliances, information flow) as well as individual development (eg mentoring and career development) (Storberg-Walker, 2007).

- They make it clear that artificially separating a thing (person, process or group) – as a formal structure chart does – from its system (the organization network) will produce a flawed understanding of the enterprise and preclude the ability to develop it. This is comparable to human bone health. Bones are not hard, unyielding substances which grow to a specific size then remain so until death, as might be assumed from looking at a picture of a skeleton. The skeletal system constantly remodels old bone tissue with new through a complex metabolic process involving minerals and vitamins. When all the elements of this system work properly there is bone homeostasis (that is, balance).

- They can serve to generate ideas and solve problems, frame issues, design interventions and pose questions that focus on the relations between organizational members, rather than relying on the more traditional exclusive focus on the characteristics of individuals, groups, processes or organizations. Team-assessment tools that concentrate on the characteristics of team members, their personality, style and/or their expertise are examples of this.

- They can be used to identify 'weak links' in information chains; build solidarity among disconnected groups; identify influential persons in the network to act as change agents; and nurture diverse connections between mentors and mentees, among other things (Storberg-Walker, 2007). In this respect social capital based on the relationship between people is built, as well as the individual human capital (see Glossary).

The friendship and social network

Perhaps oddly, friendship and social ties based on shared interests, trust and enjoyment of each other's company, rather than the instrumental organizational relationships formed to do the work, are rarely discussed as an organizing principle or framework when considering how work gets done in organizations. It may be that the notion of friendship and the social network as being an important framework when thinking about organizational health has been neglected because it is seen as a personal thing rather than an organizational or management thing. (How many managers discuss people's friendships and social networks when doing a performance review – unless it is to do with an obvious personality clash, or alternatively closeness that gets in the way of work performance?)

The way friendships develop could be one reason why they are not considered organizationally important: often they start in the parts of the organization that are not under management scrutiny – places like the smoking areas, the corridors, around the water coolers, and in the car pools and cafeterias. As such they may not be specifically related to a particular work flow – many friendships develop more randomly than within work groups, and they are not necessarily related to organization chart hierarchies. On this latter point however, there is some evidence that the 'shared interests' inherent in friendship involves fraternizing with people of a similar perceived status.

Yet the social network, built on friendly (or adversarial) interactions – although perhaps not crucial to effective functioning, as organizations can function well on collegiate relationships rather than friendships – is important to consider as an organizing framework for a number of reasons:

- Friendship and effective social relationships have an impact on individual well-being and the way people feel and experience their working life. This, in turn, can impact an individual's motivation, productivity, and overall mental and emotional health. Feeling part of a community brings health benefits, while feeling socially isolated can, among other things, engender hostility and seriously accelerate declines in health and well-being that are costly to an organization.

- Social capital – that is the reciprocity, co-operation and collective goodwill derived from connection with others in the community but in a relationship disconnected from getting the work done – contributes to organizational value in terms of ability to attract and retain people, share knowledge and strengthen the culture. Think of the number of people who, when asked why they stay with a specific organization, will answer 'because of the people in it'.

- National and international organizations now employ well-being as an indicator of societal progress, and organizations are increasingly concerned with measuring this aspect of their performance. The Gallup organization, for example, in their Q12 survey of employee satisfaction asks, as one of the 12 questions: 'Do you have a best friend at work?' It explains the reason for including it as follows: 'The evolution of quality relationships is very normal and an important part of a healthy workplace. In the best workplaces, employers recognize that people want to forge quality relationships with their co-workers, and that company allegiance can be built from such relationships.'

- Healthy friendships and social networks are built on mutual trust, and it is from this attribute that collaboration, innovation and adaptive capacity can be developed – think, for example, of Hewlett and Packard, Ben and Jerry's or Google, all companies initiated in the friendship of individuals.

In the 1980s McMillan and Chavis defined community as 'a feeling that members have of belonging, a feeling that members matter to one another and to the group, and a shared faith the members' needs will be met through their commitment to be together'. This definition could equally be applied today in the context of someone's social network. At its best a social network is a community that creates, again in McMillan and Chavis's terms:

- *Feelings of membership*: feelings of belonging to, and identifying with, the community.

- *Feelings of influence*: feelings of having influence on, and being influenced by, the community.

- *Integration and fulfilment of needs*: feelings of being supported by others in the community while also supporting them.

- *Shared emotional connection*: feelings of relationships, shared history and a 'spirit' of community (McMillan and Chavis, 1986).

Organizational life is coloured, for good or ill, by the quality, extent and nature of the friendships, social ties and communities that people form within it. Thus it is appropriate to suggest that organizations make efforts to understand the influence and experiences of people's social networks in order to design organization development interventions that will encourage and increase social capital overall and hence of organizational/individual benefit.

Pause for thought

What is the value of considering social networks as an element of the organizing structures of an enterprise?

How much, if at all, should organizations involve themselves in the social networks of their members? Why should they/should they not do this?

Insight into all four structures

To determine whether an organization is structurally healthy it is necessary to gain insight into the four structures of business model, organization chart, organizational relationships and friendship networks, and the quality of the interactions between them. This sounds a lot easier than it is. First, most organization structures are too complex in operation to readily be understood. Second, they manifest differently in different parts of the organization. Third, they are in a continuous state of flux. And fourth, determining what is 'in' the structures and what is 'out' of the structures in order to gain the insight is a complicating factor.

Nevertheless, insight into the structures is necessary in order to take structural actions to keep the business running effectively. This is shown by the type of questions people ask about structures. For example, prior to a training course on organization structures participants were asked an open question: 'What topics do you want this training programme to address?' Intriguingly, each response could be categorized into one of the four structures discussed, as the table below illustrates, and each area that was mentioned hints at a changing organizational environment. Note that participants use the word 'structure' in all four contexts.

Business model – about explaining customer-focused value creation, performance and competitive advantage

- How to align the structure with the business strategy to deliver results
- What are the merits of centralization versus decentralization (or global and local) for business performance?
- How can we implement a multiple merger of organizations with different legal and governance structures that will succeed when one of the partners is significantly larger, has a much larger turnover, has different legal status, and is much more complex in structure?

Organization chart – about explaining hierarchies, roles, and accountability levels

- What are the pros and cons of various structures for organizational responsiveness?
- How can we design a structure that allows for career development of technical specialists and not just managers?
- What is the process to be followed when reviewing the organization's structure to enable streamlining and efficiency gains?

Organizational network – about explaining the flow of work through the individual players

- What are the key risks and consequences in organization restructuring and what should be put in place to mitigate these?
- How do we keep employees working productively during the restructure process?
- How can we challenge any organization changes that do not have a justifiable business reason for undertaking?

Social network – about explaining the friendships and personal communities that oil the organizational wheels

- How can we manage personal adversity caused by organization structure changes?
- How do we help people maintain social ties when structure changes might mean they have to relocate?
- What does 'having a best friend at work' mean in terms of structure decisions?

Getting the necessary insight involves conscious activity. It requires first establishing a baseline of the four components, next assessing and interpreting how they interact, and then continuing to observe and test what is going on both qualitatively (how people are feeling about working in the organization) and quantitatively (how well the organization is performing and meeting strategic objectives). With these insights action can be taken if things seem out of kilter.

To establish the baseline start by asking these nine questions about the business model (Figure 2.1).

1　Is this working to deliver our offering in a competitive way?
2　Is there clarity about who is being offered our product/service, and who is likely to buy it?
3　Do we have the right communication and distribution channels to bring our offering to the target customers?
4　Are we organized to develop good relationships with customers?
5　Are we leveraging our core competencies (and allowing activities that can be performed by anybody to go to the lowest bidder)?
6　Do we know where our organizational sources of value are located?
7　Are our value-creating sources configured to deliver effectively?
8　Are we operating effectively with our partners and stakeholders?
9　Are our sourcing, pricing and spending decisions giving us healthy cash flows?

Move on to examine the organizational network. One way is to use specific software designed to do this, and another is to do a more traditional survey. Such a survey was conducted by one organization that wanted to find out who the sustainability subject matter experts were in order to provide better customer service, spur innovation on products and services, and increase efficiencies by putting people working on like projects in touch with each other. The exercise was initiated with the following e-mail:

We are launching a survey to build an organization-wide network of sustainability subject matter experts (SME).

The purpose of this survey is to identify the people you go to for answers about environmental and sustainability matters. Your feedback will help us identify personnel from across the organization that hold technical and historical knowledge about several specific sustainability subject matter areas.

Our customers rely on our organization to help them be as sustainable as possible, especially during this budget-constrained time period. To meet our customers' demand, we need all staff to be able to answer sustainability-related questions. By taking this survey, you will help identify the staff that you rely on for sustainability information.

This 'organizational mapping' network is different from most subject matter expertise listings you have seen. To build this network, we are asking staff to identify who they go to within the organization when they have a particular sustainability-related question.

By identifying the colleagues that you rely on to answer your sustainability questions, we increase our total shared knowledge by connecting our staff to fellow employees across business lines, services and geographic locations. Once we gather the names of the experts, we will create a tool that not only allows these experts to find each other, but helps others within the organization to find them.

The survey is broad and covers seven sustainability-related categories. When prompted, please enter the first and last name of associates that you would contact for answers to environmental and sustainability questions. These associates can be from anywhere across the organization. Think broadly about the experts whose advice you seek and include those in Service Centres, Operations and in Property Management at the field level.

Thank you for the fantastic support you continue to provide to our customers.

Move on to see how the organization chart supports the questions raised in the business model assessment, and the patterns revealed in the organizational network mapping. Then consider undertaking a social network analysis (being mindful of the ethical implications of this sort of activity). The value of this activity comes from gaining information that has the potential to identify how to align the network with organizational goals. This is more important than it might seem. Social exchanges and the knowledge they transmit have an effect on organizational performance and perception.

Take the example of store assistants in Marks and Spencer. In 2002, a period in the organization's life cycle when things were particularly tough and the company had got a lot of bad press, assistants reported that they would not wear their M&S uniforms on the bus home for fear of what people said to them; as they travelled by bus, however, they talked about the conditions in the stores and others could overhear. Both factors contributed to a downward spiral in individual and organizational performance. As one researcher pointed out, knowledge is the discrete asset of social networks and must be managed and used to be effective. Just as the bloodstream carries blood, the social network carries knowledge and is redundant without it (Warner, 2004).

Once the baseline is established, the next step is assessing and interpreting how the networks interplay. Again this is not straightforward as the interplay is not rigid or stable, but ongoing and dynamic. Healthy structures are ones which have harmony in and across all four dimensions. And that means paying attention to their individual and collective functioning.

Symptoms of unhealthy structural functioning

There are various ways of discerning the symptoms of healthy and unhealthy structural functioning. Two in use are qualitative types of 'field studies' using techniques drawn from ethnography and anthropology.

Here is a small but telling example from an employee:

> I left my organization because I was asked to work from home. At first I liked it but then I began to feel isolated. My manager wasn't good at making us feel like team members and I wasn't sure whether or not I could take certain customer-related decisions. Sadly, I lost touch with most of the casual social contacts I'd made when I worked in the office. Having lunch with people you are friendly with and bump into every day is easy. Ringing them up to specially arrange to meet them because we're all working out of our homes isn't the same. I found that I didn't feel as confident about my work – I wasn't building the same level of trust with my colleagues when I couldn't see them face to face so often. And I wasn't sure where I fitted into the big picture or what my career paths might be. I decided to find another company that didn't do homeworking and joined that. One of my friends from the previous company joined too.

In this example, the business model, the organization chart, the organizational network and the social network are all hinted at in one employee's experience. *Homeworking* is a business-model choice, *career paths* are evident in organization charts, *managers' ability to keep work flowing* effectively is part of the organizational network, and the *friends to go to lunch with* are part of the social network.

Ethnographers take notice of the types of patterns these stories tell (although one story is not sufficient to make a judgment on); economists and accountants put them alongside a more formal analysis and interpretation of hard data. These two approaches working hand in glove make for a fairly good platform on which to base decisions about changes. So in this particular instance, the ethnographic story gathering might lead to checking sales figures and customer satisfaction (business model), looking at job roles and accountabilities (organization chart), manager interactions in work flow (organizational networks), and employee satisfaction (social network). With these in hand, decisions can be made on whether and how to intervene either to do more of any healthy activity or address unhealthy ones.

Additionally there are some specific signals of organization ill health that are worth bearing in mind. Common ones are:

- Organizational politics and power plays where people are playing games of one kind or another, or playing people off against one another.

- 'Turf protection' where people are holding onto what they think is 'theirs'. This can lead to duplication of activity – for example if several departments all insist they need their own communications team.

- A need for providing obvious status symbols such as job titles, parking spaces and the like that suggest a level of performance and productivity rather than demonstrating the actual level of performance and productivity.

- Rewarding people with a different role at the expense of the workflow or the efficiency of the structure. Structures are more efficient if they are designed around roles not individuals.

- Saying one thing and doing another (eg holding a participative experience and then telling people what to do).

- Putting in organizational layers in some parts and not others.

- People being unclear on their decision-making level, accountabilities and authorities.

- Disrupting the social and organizational networks when changes are introduced.

- Asking for more staff through an inability to estimate work volume/content accurately and to streamline work.

Pause for thought

Who in the organization should have responsibility for keeping an eye on the health of the four structures?

What are the types of activities that this role holder would undertake?

What is the justification, rationale and business case for having this role?

Exercise

Think about the following questions related to an organization's business model:

Strategy
- What are the top five strategic drivers that influence today's business strategy (eg shareholder needs, public perception of brand)?
- What are the top five strategic drivers that are likely to influence the business strategy in the coming two years?
- What are the business vision, strategy and objectives currently being pursued?
- Are there other strategic options being considered in the light of the current or future drivers?
- If yes, describe any changes to business vision, strategy and objectives.

Business model
- Describe the current business model (use Figure 2.1 for the elements on which to base the description), using the worksheet in the Appendix.
- Does this business model need to be changed to achieve the current or immediate future (within two years) business strategy? Think about (Grant Thornton, 2010):
  - Assumptions: Review those made when the model was last discussed.
  - Focus: Is it too internal or on the right customers?
  - Customers: Are their needs being satisfied as they become more value conscious, and more demanding, or are competitors taking them?
  - Markets: Are the markets right – product/service/ geographic and/or are there new growth opportunities to be exploited?
  - Technologies: What new technologies might be used to stay ahead of competitors?
  - Competitors: What are the competitors doing? Are they focused more on innovation and growth than cost-cutting?
  - Funding structure: Is it still appropriate or are there alternatives available?

- Resources: How flexible is the organization in adapting to environmental and context changes?
- Financial performance: How cash generative is the business? Could margins be improved? What opportunities exist to improve operational efficiency?
- Talent: Are the right people being acquired, identified and nurtured? Are the right leadership and people in place to take the strategy forward?
- Relationships: Are relationships with customers, staff, suppliers, stakeholders being protected? Are communications with and to them transparent?

Examine the answers. Do they suggest that the business model should be changed? Then how will it change and what degree of change is required? What impact will business model changes have on the organization chart, the organizational network and the social network?

If this exercise suggests that the model does not need to change, then why is this the case and when will the situation be reviewed? What impact will not changing the business model have on the organization chart, the organizational network and the social network?

Key messages

- Four elements of business model, formal organization, informal work organization and informal social patterns combine and align in order to allow the work to flow effectively to achieve the business objectives.

- Different organizational structures (represented by organization charts) have different attributes. There is no one right structure, and organization charts offer almost no insight into how work is done.

- Friendship and social ties are rarely discussed as an organizing principle or framework when considering how work gets done in organizations.

- Check the healthiness of structures by using a combination of qualitative methods using techniques drawn from ethnography and anthropology and analysis of quantitative data, eg customer satisfaction scores.

References

Bennis, W (1966) *Changing Organizations*, McGraw Hill, New York

Brand Autopsy (2006) Radically simplify your organization chart [Online] http://www.brandautopsy.com/2011/09/simplify_org_chart.html (accessed 20 November 2011)

Drucker, PF (2001) *Leading in a Time of Change Viewer's Workbook*, Peter F Drucker Foundation for Nonprofit Management, New York

Economist (2005) The fall of a corporate queen, *The Economist*, 3 February [Online] http://www.economist.com/node/3632638 (accessed 16 November 2011)

Economist (2010, June 10) Of atrophying flesh and phones, *The Economist*, 10 June [Online] http://www.economist.com/node/16326374 (accessed 16 November 2011)

Grant Thornton (2010) Retrench or refresh? Do existing business models still deliver the goods [Online] http://www.grant-thornton.co.uk/thinking/innovation/images/uploads/New_World_Report.pdf (accessed 16 November 2011)

McMillan, D and Chavis, D (1986) Sense of community: a definition and theory, *Journal of Community Psychology*, 14, pp 6–23

Mishra, BR (2011, June) Lenovo rejigs business model in India for next phase of growth [Online] http://www.business-standard.com/india/news/lenovo-rejigs-business-model-in-india-for-next-phasegrowth/437999/ (accessed 19 November 2011)

Porterfield, C (2007) Pavarotti: a voice for the ages [Online] http://www.time.com/time/arts/article/0,8599,1659419,00.html (accessed 16 November 2011)

Salter, C (2011) Protect and attack: Lenovo's new strategy [Online] http://www.fastcompany.com/magazine/161/lenovo (accessed 19 November 2011)

Schell, O (2011) How Walmart is changing China, *Atlantic Magazine*, December, [Online] http://www.theatlantic.com/magazine/archive/2011/12/how-walmart-is-changing-china/8709/ (accessed 16 November 2011)

Shirky, C (2010) The collapse of complex business models [Online] http://www.shirky.com/weblog/2010/04/the-collapse-of-complex-business-models/ (accessed 16 November 2011)

Storberg-Walker, J (2007) Social networks as a conceptual and empirical tool to understand and 'do' HR, *Advances in Developing Human Resources*, 9 (3), pp 291–311

Sun Hydraulics (2002–11) Welcome to Sun [Online] http://www.sunhydraulics.com/cmsnet/aboutus.aspx?lang_id=1 (accessed 20 November 2011)

WL Gore and Associates (2011) A team-based, flat lattice organization [Online] http://www.gore.com/en_xx/aboutus/culture/index.html (accessed 20 November 2011)

Warner, MA (2004) *Managing in Virtual Organizations*, Thomson, London

Systems and processes

"Institutions will try to preserve the problem to which they are the solution. **(CLAY SHIRKY)**

Objectives

At the end of this chapter you will be able to:

- present and discuss the relationship between the systems and processes of an organization;
- describe four types of high-level systems and explain the concepts of complex adaptive systems;
- explain work process flows and the human factors that facilitate or hinder the flows;
- identify some indicators of healthy and unhealthy systems and processes.

Think once again about a human body. In its entirety it is a whole complex, adaptive system. But it functions through the myriad interdependencies and interactions between its various subsystems including:

- the circulatory system;
- the digestive system;
- the endocrine system;
- the immune system;
- the nervous system;
- the reproductive system;
- the respiratory system.

Organizations are similar in that they are a whole system (look back to Figure 1.1 in Chapter 1) but effective functioning of the whole organizational system depends on the viability of the subsystems that support it. Asked to list organizational subsystems people mostly come up with the various IT software systems that carry the workflow, for example:

- HR systems (Oracle, SAP) etc;
- financial systems;
- management information systems (MIS);
- operating systems;
- distribution systems;
- purchasing systems;
- supply chain systems.

Their lists depend on the type of organization and industry they are working in, although most have the common support function systems (IT, HR, MIS and financial). This emphasis on the IT systems probably arises because they are easy to define and talk about, and in many organizations the IT systems are among the main vehicles in which the operational processes are 'transported'. Thus thinking of organizational systems as predominantly IT based makes sense, and is fine up to a point.

It is fine up to a point because IT systems represent only a subtype of one of four types of systems that are discussed in the next section. Organizations that do not acknowledge or invest in the other systems are risking problems arising.

However, let us stay with IT systems for the moment as they serve to illustrate the relationship between a system and a process. If a system goes down the process or processes it carries cannot flow. The three-day BlackBerry system crash in October 2011 is one example of systems failure that had process (and reputation) repercussions. A server update at the UK headquarters of Research In Motion (RIM), the BlackBerry company, went wrong, causing service outage. This meant that millions of users worldwide were unable to receive or send e-mails or to browse the web: their communications processes froze. One user, Lord Alan Sugar, creator of one of the first really large British PC businesses, Amstrad, was reported as saying: 'All my companies use BBs, everyone is so reliant on getting e-mail on the move, people don't know if they are coming or going [with this outage]. It will cause massive damage to their [BlackBerry's] image. Corporate users must be going bananas.'

Adding insult to injury, RIM 'said barely anything to explain the problem, issuing brief statements until Stephen Bates, its UK and Ireland chief executive, told a group of developers on Wednesday morning: 'We thought we had found the problem [that caused the outage] but had not. We are working around the clock to get to the bottom of the problem' (Arthur, 2011).

In this BlackBerry example, the failure of RIM, the provider of the IT system to other companies, resulted in the disruption of the internal and external communications processes of those companies. This demonstrates interconnectivity and interdependence at multiple levels: of the IT systems to the processes, of the BlackBerry organizational system to its customers' systems, of the communications processes within BlackBerry to the outside world, and of the communications processes of the companies that could no longer use BlackBerries to communicate.

Again an analogy can be made with the human body. In healthy adults the way the digestive process 'works' varies between people, depending on their diet, their metabolism and so on, but their digestive systems have the same system 'components' as Figure 3.1 illustrates.

However, the digestive system does not stand alone; the way food is processed and absorbed in the journey through the digestive system is related to the functioning of all other body systems and the processes they carry.

Comparing organizational process flows and systems diagrams (Ross, 1994) illustrates the difference between the two, as shown in Table 3.1. This

TABLE 3.1   Comparison of process and system flows

Process	System
Show flow of activities in a straight line	Show cause and effect in a circle
The labels are verbs and tasks	The labels are nouns and variables
The arrows indicate sequence	The arrows indicate influence or causality
A change in one activity does not necessarily affect other activities	A change in one element produces a change in all variables
Tends to represent a static picture	Always represents a dynamic picture

SOURCE: Hoyle, 2009.

FIGURE 3.1 Human digestive system

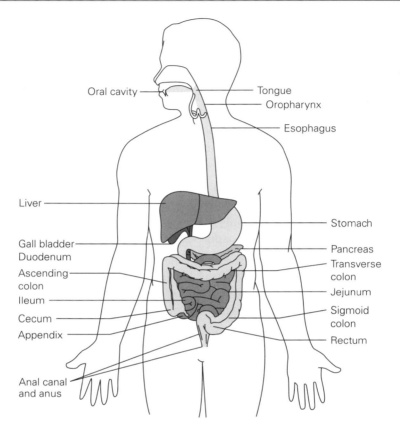

SOURCE: AMA's *Current Procedural Terminology*, Revised 1998 Edition. CPT is a trademark of the American Medical Association. http://www.ama-assn.org/ama/pub/physician-resources/patient-education-materials/atlas-of-human-body/digestive-system.page

table illustrates that, although processes and systems are frequently confused, they are different but complementary and interrelated. Studying the billing process and the way it flows through the billing systems may help lead to efficiency gains in billings but it will not give insight into the way that the billing process affects and is affected by other critical processes and systems in the company (Ross, 1994).

How important is it to understand the difference between a process and a system to foster effective organizational performance?

Where does a system begin and end?

By what other means can processes flow if a system collapses: are there bypass systems?

Four types of system

One approach that enables a higher-level discussion of systems (ie beyond a system as IT software) is to consider the notion that there are four basic types of system, depending on whether the parts of the system and the whole system can make choices and be purposeful. This concept of purposeful systems was developed by Russell Ackoff, an academic and formerly Wharton Professor Emeritus, and explained in his book (authored with Fred Emery) *Purposeful Systems: An interdisciplinary analysis of individual and social behavior as a system of purposeful events* (ACASA, 2011). Figure 3.2 illustrates the four types of system he discusses.

FIGURE 3.2   The four types of systems

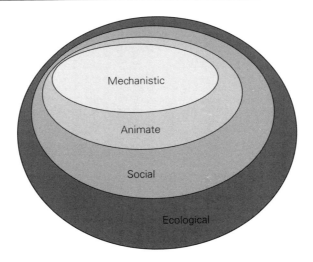

SOURCE: AcoffCollaboratory for the Advancement of the Systems Approach
http://www.acasa.upenn.edu/4sys.htm

TABLE 3.2 System types

Type of system model	System parts	Whole system	Example	Open or closed system
Mechanistic (Not purposeful)	No choice eg fuel injector in car	No choice eg the car that houses the fuel injector	Machines eg cars and their parts	Closed if their behavior is unaffected by any external conditions or events; open if they are affected.
Animate (Purposeful)	No choice eg the lungs of a person	Choice eg the functioning human being	People	Open ie they must interact with their environments in order to survive.
Social (Purposeful)	Choice eg local governments including parts at least some of which are animate, hence have purposes of their own, and (3) are a part of one or more larger (containing) systems that may have purposes of their own and may contain other social systems	Choice	Corporations	Open eg a local government is part of a state government, which in turn, is part of a national government. Social systems can be and usually are nested.
Ecological (Not purposeful)	Choice as they incorporate animate and social systems	No choice at the whole systems level (eg climate warming)	Nature	Open eg the purposeful use by people (animate and social) of fluoro-carbons as a propellant (mechanistic) and the emissions of power plants that affect the ozone layer.

These four systems form a hierarchy, with the outside ecological system being the highest order. The animate, social and ecological systems can include whole systems or parts of other systems of the same or a lower type, but not of a higher type; for example, social systems (eg society) may incorporate animate systems (people) and mechanistic systems (machines), but a mechanistic system cannot incorporate either an animate or social system. Ecological systems can incorporate systems of all the other types. Only animate and social systems can be said to be purposeful. That is, by their choices they can produce: a) the same outcome in different ways in the same environment; and b) different outcomes in the same and different environments (ACASA, 2011). Table 3.2 expands on this explanation.

If this all sounds too theoretical, academic and difficult to grasp read the following story:

> About two years ago, after a lifetime of running, aerobics, yoga, tennis and everything else you can think of to keep fit, I found myself suddenly limping, in a lot of pain and losing my quality of life. When I went to my family doctor, he told me to get a hip replacement. He said it just like that: 'time for a hip replacement.' It might as well have been: 'replace the spark plugs.'
>
> I was not keen on surgery as I knew a lot about alignment. After all, the 'hip bone's connected to the thigh bone, the thigh bone's connected to the knee bone,' and they are all connected to the spine. So I sought a surgeon who could help me with the hip replacement while not destroying the subtle alignment I had created in my spine and back muscles through yoga.
>
> I found a surgeon I trusted and went through the surgery – I chose to have a titanium joint fitted. However, the recovery wasn't easy. Then I found a local support group with great people I could talk with about the emotional ups and downs. It was great as the group was part of a wider national network so we could always reach out for more information or advice. (Hardaway, 2007)

Now look at Table 3.3.

This example shows the four types of systems in evidence at an individual level. Within organizations the same hierarchy and relationships between the four overarching systems are present, as the following example illustrates:

> In 2011 the UK government made the decision to halt the implementation of a computerized patient record system planned to cover the entire UK National Health Service. A government spokesperson said that: 'It was meant to be a very helpful thing for NHS staff and patients but instead has become this amazingly top-heavy, hideously expensive programme [£12.7 billion]. The problem is, it didn't deliver. It was too ambitious, the technology kept changing, and loads and loads of money has been put into it. It's wasted a lot of money that should have been spent on nurses and improving patient care, and not on big international IT companies.'

TABLE 3.3 System types applied

Type of system model	System parts	Whole system	Open or closed system (See Glossary)
Mechanistic (Not purposeful)	**No choice** Artificial hip joint Diseased natural hip joint	**No choice** N/A Impact of diseased joint on rest of body	Closed
Animate (Purposeful)	**No choice** Artificial hip joint Diseased natural hip joint	**Choice** Choice to take hip replacement surgery to regain quality of life. Impact on rest of body including skeletal alignment	Open
Social (Purposeful)	**Choice** Surgery in hospital Group support	**Choice** Wider hospital system Network support group organization	Open
Ecological (Not purposeful)	**Choice** about type of replacement (metal, plastic, ceramic)	**No choice** about impact on environment of titanium mining	Open

The decision to cancel the programme came after government ministers received advice from the Cabinet Office's major projects authority, which assesses the value for money of major public expenditure. Instead of an enterprise-wide patient records system, providers of NHS care such as hospitals and GP surgeries will strike IT deals locally and regionally to get the best programmes they can afford (Campbell, 2011).

In this example the patient record system is an example of a mechanistic system. The IT implementation team is an example of the animate system. The NHS and the government are parts of the social system. And the ecological system is present in the choices made around things like the environmental impact of the travel of IT consultants to sites, the physical materials used in the development of the system and so on.

Although it may seem complex and over-the-top there is value in thinking about these four systems in relation to an organization, as in every organizations all four systems are present. As stated earlier, there is a tendency to think about organizational systems only at the mechanistic level – which an IT software system is – but as the examples show it is critical to consider the interconnectivity between systems because choices related to one system (or parts of a system) have consequences in other systems (or parts of them).

As a recap, look back at the BlackBerry example: in this the server is the mechanistic system, the individual users are the animate systems, the companies that have made policy decisions to communicate via BlackBerries and Research in Motion are the social systems, and the choices made about handset materials, use of radio frequency transmitters and so on are the ecological system.

The BlackBerry example and the other two examples (hip replacement and the UK's National Health Service) all show that the organizational systems involved are responding in concert to what is going on in their environment. That is they (the people acting in and for the systems) are making decisions and choices around the responses, and they are responding in line with their structures, prior knowledge and experience, and other constraints and boundaries.

Responding to what are effectively their 'rules' whether explicit or implicit, demonstrates that organizations are what are known as 'complex adaptive systems'. That is 'systems composed of interacting agents described in terms of rules. The agents adapt by changing their rules as experience accumulates' (Holland, 1995). In practice, this means that when something happens in the environment that reduces the organization's ability to meet its goals, the organization responds by changing either its own state or the environment in order to continue meeting the goals efficiently; this capability is 'adaptiveness'.

This adaptiveness is evident in the examples given above: BlackBerry users resorted to their personal iPhones to communicate, while the person who had the hip replacement adapted her lifestyle to a reduced range of motion,

TABLE 3.4   Concepts of complex adaptive systems

Concept	Description	Example
Agent	Individual actors or basic entities of action	People, objects, concepts
• Attribute	Internal states of agents	Expertise, wealth, age
• Behavioural rule	Schemata that govern attributes and behaviors of agents	Political one-upmanship, employment policies
Interaction	Mutually adaptive behaviors	Co-operation, team norming
• Connection	Relational links among agents	Friendship, LinkedIn Networks
• Flow	Movement of resources	Goods distribution, knowledge sharing
Environment	Medium for agents to operate on and interact with	Landscape, social context
• Structure	Topography of an environment and its relationship to agents	Resource exchange between the environment and its agents.

Adapted from (Nan, 2011)

and the NHS handed responsibility for patient record keeping to local agents. See Table 3.4 that summarizes the concepts of complex adaptive systems.

Systems interactions

Although each of the four types of systems comprise subsystems (as noted IT systems[1] are a subset of mechanistic systems) that vary depending on the enterprise and its products and services, it is important to be aware that subsystems are interrelated both within and between the four types. Looking back at the business model (Figure 2.1) helps to understand the systems and their interactions. It shows that systems are not independent of one another:

when performing as they should, they produce a synergistic, powerful and multiplier effect on the whole that is greater than the sum of the individual subsystems. As Ervin Laszlo, writer and Nobel Peace Prize nominee, pointed out 'the concept of wholeness defines the character of the system as such, in contrast to the character of its parts in isolation. A whole possesses such characteristics that are not possessed by its parts singly; the whole is therefore, other than the simple sum of its parts (Laszlo, 1972).

Here's an example of the multiplier effect of the four systems working in concert:

> In 2008 Starbucks, feeling it had lost its position as leader in the coffee
> industry and the brand had become 'somewhat blurred', started to introduce
> the innovative Clover coffee machines (mechanistic system) into some of its
> coffee shops (social system). The feature of the machine is that rather than
> brewing coffee by the pot, the Clover brews each cup individually with freshly
> ground beans. The temperature, amount of water and brewing time can all be
> programmed and tailored to a particular bean, to suit the tastes of a consumer
> (animate system).
>
> Coffee tasters (animate system) were fairly unimpressed by the performance
> of the Clover, noting that the machine is only as good as the coffee beans
> (ecological system) put in it. Since the Starbucks purchasing system buys coffee
> in mass quantities, its supply system is unable to deliver fresh bags of beans very
> quickly, and the quality control system is sometimes inadequate: 'By the time
> the customer experiences it, the beans have been blended and have been sitting
> in a bag for six weeks. Anything special about the Clover system coffee is lost'.
>
> (Honan, 2008)

In this example, the connection between the systems becomes evident. Changing parts of one system – for example the coffee beans used, or the supply chain length – will have an impact, for better or worse, on the other systems and on the whole quintessential 'Starbucks' experience' that the company seeks to give its customers. So, remember that changes made to one part of a system or subsystem can have an overall effect on the whole that is very different from that which it has on the subsystem itself.

Plato, writing in 380 BC, expressed this notion in human systems terms, saying that:

> as you ought not to attempt to cure the eyes without the head, or the head
> without the body, so neither ought you to attempt to cure the body without
> the soul; and this is the reason why the cure of many diseases is unknown
> to the physicians of Hellas, because they are ignorant of the whole, which
> ought to be studied also; for the part can never be well unless the whole is
> well (Plato).

How can systems theories and concepts be made 'accessible' and useful without becoming oversimplified?

What are some organizational benefits of applying systems theories and concepts in things like organization design projects, restructurings and organization development work?

Processes

As mentioned earlier, a process is the work that flows through a system in a logical order. Each of these processes can be 'mapped': that is expressed visually as diagrams that show a sequenced flow of activities and information using a specific symbol set and following a set of rules that makes the process scalable (in other words, the map can encompass all parts of a process at whatever level of detail is selected by the user). Process mapping using these symbol and rule conventions is robust as it can be applied to any flow of work in virtually any kind of organization. Additionally it is verifiable: it can describe existing processes as they are, and any map can be audited or checked against the actual flow of materials and information and the behaviour of jobholders to determine its accuracy (Kmetz, 2010).

Look at the simple process map (Figure 3.3) that shows some of the conventional symbols used (rectangle, oval, diamond), the logical sequence of activity, and a decision point: time to eat? This could be made more detailed, for example by expanding the 'shower' activity into sub-activities like 'turn on tap', etc. and it could be checked for accuracy.

Returning to the Starbucks' Clover coffee machine example – the machine is the system. The way the coffee is processed through it is the work. The process (this time in words not a process map) is as follows:

1 A barista selects dose, water temperature and steep time.
2 A piston pulls down the filter platform while freshly ground coffee is poured into the chamber.
3 Hot water flows into the chamber.
4 The barista briskly stirs the grounds with a metal whisk, and the water and beans steep for several seconds.
5 The piston rises, creating a vacuum that separates the brew from the grounds, then lowers, forcing the coffee out of a nozzle below.
6 The piston rises to the surface again, pushing up a disc of grounds, which are squeegeed away.

FIGURE 3.3   Simple process map

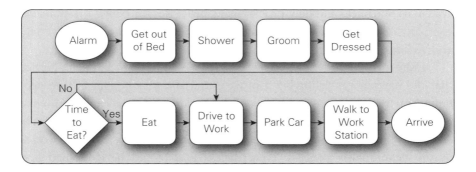

Getting a good cup of coffee depends on several factors. As previously mentioned the type of beans are one, the roasting process another, the choices and decisions the barista makes in working the process are a third. Additionally, getting a quality drink includes accurately programming the temperature, amount of water and brewing time to a particular bean and then following the serving protocols.

Here a tester describes the experience of ordering a cup of Clover-brewed coffee:

> A young barista in training tells me they're out of the first two specialty coffees I request and suggests instead Starbucks' everyday blend, called Pike Place. She just takes some previously ground coffee, without measuring the quantity, and puts it into the machine although the required procedure is to weigh and then grind the beans for each cup. I watch to see if she reprogrammes the brew time and temperature for the chosen coffee. But she doesn't – again showing she doesn't know the process. During brewing, the barista stirs the grounds into the Clover with a clunky rubber spatula – not a metal whisk – and pours the concoction into a crummy paper cup. I smell, I sip, I inhale. I experience nothing special. Is it the beans? My palate? The rubber spatula? The barista's inexperience? I don't know but there is room for improvement here. I wish I'd just ordered the standard cup of coffee at a quarter the price. (Adapted from Honan, 2008)

Now begin to wonder what is going on in the process flow. The barista is handling the mechanical system (the Clover machine) well enough – in that a cup of coffee emerges at the end – but she is less adept in the animate system where she is making decisions in relation to the coffee preparation process and she may be unaware of the social system impacts of her decisions. Nevertheless both the barista's decision-making process and the process for sustaining a good customer experience in order to differentiate Starbucks from other coffee shops could both be mapped.

Just to carry the link between systems and process to a conclusion, this barista and the coffee tester are both likely to be aware of the ecological system as Starbucks publicly proclaims its processes for being a responsible company on a range of issues (environmental, ethical, community, diversity and wellness).

To improve the tester's experience what would have to happen? Notice that the barista was following a process that she may not have been very familiar with, but had a rough idea of. It would be relatively easy to invoke the training process and train her to use the Clover machine more effectively – though this would not solve any issues with the supply chain processes or the bean-quality process. Nevertheless both could be examined and improved. And this illustrates a more general point, that most business process assessment focuses on improving or replacing existing processes, activities that are long standing and usually well understood, as in this case of coffee from bean to cup in customer's hand.

Yet experience suggests that it is often the processes that organizations do not have but need that offer the greatest potential for adding value. And the rapid advances in information and communications technology (ICT) make considering new processes a necessity for most organizations. For example, take a company that has a Twitter account. In November 2009 a report (Weber Shandwick, 2009) was published that stated there were 50 million users of Twitter worldwide, offering huge opportunities for companies to engage with customers, build new relationships and create a new pool of advocates talking positively about their brands. At that point the study found that:

> 73 per cent of Fortune 100 companies registered a total of 540 Twitter accounts. However, about three-quarters (76 per cent) of those accounts did not post tweets very often, and more than half (52 per cent) were not actively engaged. (This was measured by engagement metrics such as numbers of links, hashtags, references and retweets.)
>
> In addition, 50 per cent of the Fortune 100 accounts had fewer than 500 followers, a small number in relation to the size and reach of a major corporation. Another 15 per cent were inactive; of those, 11 per cent were merely placeholder accounts – unused accounts to protect corporate names against so-called brand-jacking on Twitter – and 4 per cent were abandoned after being used for a specific event. This misses the opportunity that Twitter offers as a valuable communications channel and strategic social network.

The report recommended a four-part Twittervention to help companies get high value from their Twitter accounts. Table 3.5 lists the recommendations in the left column and the process implications in the right.

TABLE 3.5 Twittervention: recommendations and process implications

Recommendations	Process implications
Create a company-wide engagement strategy; a set of guidelines with best practices	Process for engaging the right company spokespeople in offering opinions and encouraging discussions Process for developing Twitter guidelines (may be covered by social media policies that many companies have)
Demonstrate a consistent and comprehensive brand presence	Process for demonstrating brand presence
Build a dialogue that paves the way to new relationships with customers and advocates	Process for reaching out to their communities of customers and advocates and responding to tweets
Generate loyalty among new and existing communities	Process for building relationships with new customers and looking for untapped supporters. (Likely to be different from any existing customer relationship building/management process)

A year later, in September 2011, Twitter announced Twitter Web Analytics, a tool that helps website owners understand how much traffic they receive from Twitter and the effectiveness of Twitter integrations on their sites. They said that the product provided three key benefits:

- 'understanding how much of your website content is being shared across the twitter network;
- seeing the amount of traffic twitter sends to your site;
- measuring the effectiveness of your Tweet Button integration'.

(Golda, 2011)

Now consider whether a company with a Twitter account would benefit from acting on the recommendations of the report and additionally introducing a new process, or processes, for harvesting and acting on the metrics that this service provides.

Pause for thought

How can companies know which current processes are redundant, which need to be updated, and which need to be introduced?

What is the value of process mapping?

The human factor

Returning to the coffee-making example, the role of the barista is critical to the outcome of a good cup of coffee. Apparently she did not understand the correct process and adapted it according to her means. Understanding a process flow, its place in the overall system and its impacts is critical to both working it effectively and improving it.

An American doctor makes the point that: 'Cystoscopies, gastroscopies, biopsies. Doctors can do three or four of those and make five or six hundred dollars in a single day but we get nothing when we use our time to understand the lives of our patients' (Jones, 2011). Understanding the lives of the patient may make a big difference to the assessment and treatment plan a doctor prescribes, but there are reasons why doctors, perhaps unthinkingly, follow the process. Another doctor (Esselstyn, 2008) offers reasons for this:

- Over the past 100 years, the mechanical treatment of disease has increasingly dominated the medical profession in the United States. Surgery is the prototype, and its dramatic progress – light-years removed from the cathartics, bloodletting, and amputations that dominated medicine in previous centuries – is nothing short of breathtaking.

- Mechanical medicine is romantic and dramatic, a natural magnet for media attention; dramatic interventions engage the national imagination for months on end.

- There has been little incentive for physicians to study alternate ways to manage disease, as doctors are not rewarded for educating patients about the merits of truly healthy lifestyles. Thus the mechanical/procedural approach continues to dominate the profession even though it offers little to the unsuspecting millions about to become the next victims of disease.

- There is huge vested interest from stakeholders, including pharmaceutical companies, in maintaining the status quo.

Take the analogy back to organizational processes and a similar mindset prevails. First, the processes are often 'mechanical' in that they are developed and mapped with little input from, or in isolation from, the people working in the process. Second, there is little incentive to change the process (indeed sometimes people are penalized for doing so). Third, there are infrequent studies or reviews of alternate ways of delivering the process, and fourth, there are vested interests at play in maintaining the status quo (who wants 'their' processes to be reviewed when that may involve streamlining and perhaps job losses?). As an example, organization members who read the Twittervention report could decide to do nothing in response to it, maintaining the status quo, or they could decide they needed to make significant changes to their processes, including adopting new ones, to optimize their Twitter investment.

These four points underscore the fact that although processes and procedures can be mapped and protocols determined, they can, for the most part, only be actioned by people. And:

> human systems are complex and are fundamentally different from machine-type systems. Human behaviour is not predictable and people are capable of changing their rules of interaction, thus changing expected outcomes. They are able to self-organize, to influence each other and be influenced in turn, and this reciprocal influence can change ideas, behaviour, ways of thinking, working and relating – that is, humans are able to co-evolve, to self-organize and to create something new that is emergent in the sense that it could not have been predicted at the outset. They create intricate networks of relationships sustained through communication and other forms of feedback, with varying degrees of inter-dependence. Although heavily influenced by their history and culture they can transcend both when necessary. When they meet a constraint they are able to explore the space of possibilities and find a different way of doing things, ie they are creative and innovative. (Mitleton-Kelly, 2004)

This means that process flows will get disrupted by people making decisions that are right for that moment – so the barista will offer a different choice of coffee if the ones required by the process are not available. Sometimes people will decide to override the process altogether and just do something 'their way', and sometimes the fear of overriding it will lead them to make odd choices, lampooned in the office wisdom of David Brent where he noted that: 'Process and procedure are the last hiding place of people without the wit and wisdom to do their job properly.'

But what is the middle ground between inappropriate process override and sticking to the process so punctiliously that things still go wrong? One way is to help employees develop enough work process knowledge that they will be able to individually and collectively solve problems at work and help improve organizational performance.

Work process knowledge is the 'active knowledge which is directly useful for performance at work. It is constructed in the workplace, typically while solving problems, and doing so often involves synthesizing codified knowledge eg theory learnt in the classroom, or procedures set out in manuals with experiential knowledge acquired on the job' (Boreham, 2004).

To make the knowledge directly useful, individuals have to know how their own immediate tasks interconnect with operations carried out in other parts of the overall system. It is not sufficient to know only their set of tasks and activities. The experience of Ben Sliney, Federal Aviation Administration's national operations manager at the time of the 11 September 2001 terrorist attack on the World Trade Center, illustrates this:

> Sliney was only a few hours into his new job as a national operations manager with the Federal Aviation Administration when terrorists guided planes like missiles into the World Trade Center's twin towers and the Pentagon on the morning of 11 September 2001.
>
> 'When I saw the size of the fire and flames coming out of that building, I knew it was no way that was a small aircraft that hit the building,' Sliney said. 'Small planes bounce off buildings.'
>
> An air traffic controller with the FAA on and off since 1969, Sliney said he didn't hesitate to make his next move. He ordered a national ground stop, halting all take-offs nationwide. 'I was confident I had the authority to do that,' he said. 'It was a natural thing.'
>
> The veteran air traffic controller... said he was 'very experienced' to make the crucial call. In fact, it's a call that has landed him a lot of notoriety and praise. Sliney said he constantly relayed information to his superiors, but didn't get any feedback because communication lines were overloaded.
>
> (Sweeney, 2011)

This example shows that Sliney used his work process knowledge at a whole-systems level and understood the processes of the organization as a whole. He had to know what the potential impact of his decision to interrupt the normal air traffic processes would be and to judge whether to take the risks as they balanced against the rewards. But although the write-up implies he was making this decision using only his own experience, in fact he is likely to have made it in close contact and collaboration with his peers and colleagues, his positional power ultimately holding him accountable for the decision. Using the social and collective competence vested in the employees and developed in a culture that encourages collaboration, 'intrapreneurship' and cross-boundary activity is a healthy and valuable way of improving processes and/or developing new ones.

Amazon is an organization that positively encourages this kind of cross-boundary thinking. Jeff Bezos, CEO, talks about the importance of collaborative experimentation processes, stating that, 'I encourage our employees to experiment. In fact, we have a group called Web Lab that is charged with constantly experimenting with the user interface on the website to figure out improvements for the customer experience' (Dyer, 2011).

The other side of the coin shows some companies taking advantage of new technologies to replace humans with robots. There is a risk to this – could a robot, in a similar situation, have made the decisions that Sliney did? And there is also a reward: the processes are operated more predictably and more cheaply. Taiwan's Foxconn Group is one company that between 2011 and 2015 plans to introduce more robots into its workforce:

> Taiwan's Foxconn Technology Group, known for assembling Apple's iPhones and iPads in China, plans to use more robots, with one report saying the company will use one million of them in the next three years, to cope with rising labour costs. This is an increase from about 10,000 robots in use in 2011 and an expected 300,000 in 2012. Commenting on the Foxconn announcement one reporter noted, 'Foxconn's move highlights an increasing trend toward automation among Chinese companies as labour issues such as high-profile strikes and workers' suicides plague firms in sectors from vehicles to technology'.
>
> (*Daily Mail Reporter*, 2011)

Pause for thought

What is the benefit of employees knowing what part they play in the overall work process flow?

How would/would not helping employees develop their decision-making processes support organizational health?

What processes beyond decision making are at play in the 'animate' system and the social system?

System and process health

Earlier in this chapter, four types of system (mechanistic, animate, social and ecological) were discussed. For the whole system to be healthy, the four systems and their subsystems also need to be healthy. Additionally the processes that flow through them, and the various interactions and inter-dependencies, have to be healthy. The question then is what constitutes system and process health and how it can be maintained? In some respects it is easier to identify what organizational system and process health is not than what it is. And Scott Adams, the Dilbert cartoon originator, is a maestro at this as the cartoon below (Figure 3.4) demonstrates.

Beyond its amusement value, the strip shows the connection between a single system and a process, and also the interconnections between systems and processes. It also illustrates the things that happen when something in the system fails and there is no adequate workaround, and the difficulties experienced when people do not know how the system works. These factors are important to bear in mind when assessing the health of an organization's systems, and hold true for process health as well.

As mentioned, taking preventive action is a healthier approach than solving issues when problems arise: much as is the case in the convention for individuals to have regular health checks to find out whether blood pressure, heart rate, cholesterol levels and so on are within normal ranges, indicating effective system and process function and whether there are any early warning signals related to these.

The thing is not to have blind faith in the efficacy of the standard, off-the-shelf preventive health check to surface current or potential health issues, either for individuals or organizations. On the human health check, scientific experts and practising medical personnel hold widely divergent views of the annual physicals and their value. One research paper states that there is no strong evidence base for a one-off annual health check, and there is no consensus on what it should include if one is done. A better health outcome is likely to be achieved by preventive care linked to evidence-based high-value activities (for example checking for and treating cardiovascular risk factors, preventable or curable cancers) and tailored to the patient's lifestyle, prior history and other individual factors leading to a personalized prevention plan (Darves, 2010).

This mindset of tailored preventive care is equally useful in organizations. There are numerous organizational health assessments available off the shelf and a scan of them shows that they each focus on different things,

FIGURE 3.4   Dilbert

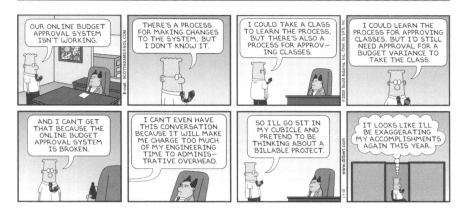

which makes choosing the 'right' survey difficult. And when it comes to assessing the health of systems and processes, they are not always tackled as separate aspects to assess in relation to the whole. Of course this might be appropriate, but it might not give enough information for more focused action to be taken in regard to malfunctioning systems and processes.

So instead of reaching for a survey with which to assess organizational health, a different approach is to employ 'watchful waiting' – that is, relatively lax observation with late, reactive action if issues arise – and/or 'active surveillance' that involves close monitoring with early, more proactive action if warning symptoms start to appear in the processes and systems. Determining where to focus either watchful waiting or active surveillance on the various systems and processes depends on the business model and business strategy. An example illustrates:

> The US Centers for Medicare and Medicaid (CMS) – a government agency – estimated that in 2010 it lost approximately $70 billion in fraudulent claims, which is a fraud loss of somewhere between 10 per cent and 30 per cent – the percentage is not known as there is no valid way of measuring it. Reasons cited for the high losses include inability to quickly look up billings in the system, no methods for checking anomalies or spikes in the system, and insufficient collaboration between investigators and data analysts. Compare this with credit card companies who have very sophisticated methods, using pattern recognition programs for detecting fraudulent activity and are able to take immediate action if they see anything suspicious. (Korten, 2011)

In this example CMS is using watchful waiting and making late, slow responses to fraud, resulting in a very high fraud rate. This is explained, in part, by the fact that CMS's business model is designed to process medical claims effectively (which it does), but not to spend resources on fraud. On the other hand, credit card companies, who would go out of business with high fraud rates, are using active surveillance systems to identify fraud. In 2010 CyberSource, a major credit card payment gateway, reported a drop in average percentage of online revenues lost to payment fraud to 1.2 per cent, from 1.4 per cent in 2008.

In most organizations there are some systems where it is fine to use 'watch and wait' techniques, and others where it is essential to use active surveillance. As stated, this depends on the organization in question. Those where active surveillance might be more appropriate are the systems that are directly related to delivering the products and services effectively and where immediate and effective responses to customers are required. Apple, discovered this in its development of Siri – the voice recognition system on the iPhone. The system struggled with strong regional accents, and Apple was bombarded with complaints from people with heavy accents. Their response was to tell users that the system is designed to adapt over time and has system features that will help; additionally they put more resources into speeding up the process for improving Siri:

> There's another important feature of Siri that makes it likely to get better at accents quite soon: its mobile, cloud-based nature... Siri is constantly collecting data not just on your accent, but on the accents of hundreds or thousands of people who sound like you. 'In a cloud-based system like Siri, most of these systems are adaptive systems, the more people use it, the smarter it gets. We're going to get more data and have the ability to get more refined views of different accents, and over time it's just going to get more and more accurate'.
>
> (Zax, 2011)

Deciding which approach – watchful waiting or active surveillance – to apply to which system requires skilled systems thinkers/practitioners and it helps if they practise most of the 13 habits shown in Figure 3.5.

These habits are equally useful for process assessors and it would be a mistake to think that there are 'experts' in either process or system assessments. In practice anyone in the organization should have the power to recommend improvements, or suggest retiring or introducing processes and systems.

Given all the process improvement programmes on the market, assessing process health offers more choices of method than assessing system health. Most of the popular process improvement methods – six sigma, lean

FIGURE 3.5   Habits of systems thinkers

Seeks to understand the big picture

Observes how elements within systems change over time, generating patterns and trends

Recognizes that a system's structure generates its behavior

Identifies the circular nature of complex cause and effect relationships

Habits of a Systems Thinker

Changes perspectives to increase understanding

Surfaces and tests assumptions

Considers an issue fully and resists the urge to come to a quick conclusion

Considers how mental models affect current reality and the future

Uses understanding of system structure to identify possible leverage actions

Considers both short and long-term consequences of actions

Finds where unintended consequences emerge

Recognizes the impact of time delays when exploring cause and effect relationships

Checks results and changes actions if needed: "successive approximation"

©2010 Systems Thinking in Schools, Waters Foundation

SOURCE: The Waters Foundation
http://www.watersfoundation.org/index.cfm?fuseaction=search.habits

thinking, theory of constraints, total quality management, Toyota production system, just-in-time – involve looking for opportunities for continuous improvement.

Thus there is a range of analytical tools available in the various programmes that help identify business process dysfunction. But even without using the analytical tools, symptoms of malfunctioning processes are spottable by looking for issues, or what are sometimes known as 'process anti-patterns'. A few of the commonest anti-patterns are shown in Table 3.6.

TABLE 3.6   Process anti-patterns

Anti-pattern description	Symptoms	Causes
Two heads are better than one	Excessive checking.	Lack of trust. Arbitrary fragmentation of process. Unnecessary controls.
Yesterday's news	Excessive time taken to complete process.	Too many actors and controls.
Haven't I seen you somewhere before?	Excessive transfer and rekeying of data.	Lack of Information Management. Lack of system integration. Reliance on paper processing.
Belt and braces	Too much stock or too many staff at certain times.	Lack of Information Management. Lack of system integration. Reliance on paper processing.
Play it again Sam	Unnecessary reworking.	Too many actors involved. Reluctance to accept best practice. 'Not invented here' syndrome.
One size fits all	Unable to cope with range of client needs.	Lack of client focus. Working practices haven't kept up with changing requirements. Trying to 'pave cow paths'.

TABLE 3.6   *continued*

Anti-pattern description	Symptoms	Causes
Whose line is it anyway?	Clients passed between departments to complete process.	Lack of client focus. No-one accepting responsibility for client satisfaction.
Superman's day off	Knowledge resides in individuals.	Lack of communication. Reliance on old unsupported technology.
Not my fault	Blame Culture	Lack of leadership. Responsibility and authority separated. Lack of staff development.
Running to stand still	All of the above & frequent organisational restructures.	Lack of strategy & leadership. Institution constantly in firefighting mode.

Adapted from JISC InfoNet, 2011

Exercise

Systems assessment

Using the template below:

1   With a specific organization in mind, think about business systems in four categories: operational/technical systems, management/HR systems, financial systems and energy systems. Note that these appear within and across the four overarching systems discussed earlier (mechanistic, animate, social, ecological).

2   For each of these four, list key systems within them and then do a SWOT analysis on each of the systems listed.

3   Finally answer the two system improvement questions.

Category	Key systems and subsystems	Strengths, weaknesses, opportunities, threats	Improvement questions
Operational/ technical systems	eg Information systems	Strength: Well designed to monitor and predict the changing needs of the customer.	For each of these, what are the three most important system problems/ opportunities that if addressed would significantly improve profitability or organizational effectiveness? Why? What actions will you take on these? When?
Management/ HR systems	eg Compensation systems	Opportunity: Design to reward employees for excellent service to customers	
Financial systems			
Energy systems			

Processes assessment

Below are 13 statements about business processes. Use these as a basis for identifying process issues and opportunities linked to the delivery of the business strategy.

1 Our organization recognizes the key processes that deliver our business performance.

2 Our core cross functional processes are proactively managed in our business.

3 Our business results are improving due to strong standard process methods and good local expertise.

4 Our attention is focused on customer needs to ensure effective delivery.

5 We work towards continual business performance improvement through focusing on our processes.

6   Our key processes are designed and their purpose is understood 'end to end': across functions, suppliers and customers.

7   Our key managers have clear accountabilities for individual key processes and for the impact of the process performance on business performance.

8   There are good business and process metrics being kept alive and being actively used to manage and improve our business.

9   All staff are engaged in continual improvement of their processes through teamwork, structured change methods and good use of metrics.

10   Workers get ongoing feedback about process performance and are recognized for good results.

11   Our IT, HR and finance systems and other infrastructure are designed to support our key business processes.

12   There is a sufficient focus on process details to eliminate most inefficiencies, waste and rework.

13   Our processes are fast, well designed, smooth running and evenly paced, and use standardized procedures. They eliminate idle time, mistakes, unnecessary movement, bottlenecks, downtime and inventory build-up.

Key messages

- There are four interrelated high-level organizational systems (mechanical, animate, social, ecological).
- With each of these are systems and subsystems that again are interconnected and interdependent.
- The systems act as vehicles for carrying processes.
- Human factors intervene to foster or hinder system and process effectiveness, depending on decisions and choices made.
- System and process health can be assessed by 'watchful waiting' and/or 'active surveillance' depending on context and circumstances.

Note

1   Here 'IT systems' excludes the developing technology field of artificial intelligence and intelligent systems.

References

ACASA (2011) Ackoff collaboratory: types of systems [Online] http://www.acasa.upenn.edu/4sys.htm (accessed 17 December 2011)

Arthur, CA (2011) Satisfaction with BlackBerry crumbles as server problems keep users in dark [Online] http://www.guardian.co.uk/technology/2011/oct/12/blackberry-server-problems-users (accessed 24 December 2011)

Boreham, N (2004, September) Collective competence and work process knowledge [Online] http://www.cedefop.europa.eu/etv/upload/projects_networks/paperBase/BorNi04.pdf (accessed 26 December 2011)

Campbell, D (2011) NHS told to abandon delayed IT project, from *Guardian*, 21 November [Online] http://www.guardian.co.uk/society/2011/sep/22/nhs-it-project-abandoned (accessed 18 December 2011)

Daily Mail Reporter (2011) Apple factory finds answer to worker suicides... replace staff with one million robots, from *Daily Mail Reporter*, 2 August [Online] http://www.dailymail.co.uk/sciencetech/article-2021251/Foxconn-Apple-factorys-answer-worker-suicides-replace-staff-1m-robots.html (accessed 27 December 2011)

Darves, B (2010) Rethinking the value of the annual exam [Online] http://www.acpinternist.org/archives/2010/01/annual.htm (accessed 28 December 2011)

Dyer, J (2011) The DNA: people, processes, and philosophies of innovative companies [Online] http://www.fastcompany.com/article/innovators-dna-clayton-christensen-jeff-dyer-hal-gregersen (accessed 27 December 2011)

Esselstyn, C (2008) Prevent and reverse heart disease [Online] http://www.amazon.com/Prevent-Reverse-Heart-Disease-Nutrition-Based/dp/1583333002/ref=sr_1_1?ie=UTF8&qid=1324937001&sr=8-1#reader_1583333002 (accessed 26 December 2011)

Golda, C (2011) Introducing Twitter web analytics [Online] https://dev.twitter.com/blog/introducing-twitter-web-analytics (accessed 26 December 2011)

Hardaway, F (2007) EmpowerHer: my hip replacement story after a lifetime of running, aerobics, yoga & tennis [Online] http://www.empowher.com/community/share/my-hip-replacement-story-after-lifetime-running-aerobics-yoga-tennis (accessed 17 December 2011)

Holland, J (1995) *Hidden Order*, Addison-Wesley, Redwood City

Honan, M (2008) The coffee fix: can the $11,000 Clover machine save Starbucks? [Online] http://www.wired.com/gadgets/miscellaneous/magazine/16-08/mf_clover?currentPage=all (accessed 24 December 2011)

Hoyle, D (2009) Systems and processes: is there a difference? [Online] http://www.thecqi.org/Documents/community/South%20Western/Wessex%20Branch/Systems%20and%20Processes%20article%20by%20David%20Hoyle%20Oct09%20(2)pdf (accessed 17 December 2011)

JISC InfoNet (2011) Process improvement [Online] http://www.jiscinfonet.ac.uk/infokits/process-improvement/dysfunction (accessed 28 December 2011)

Jones, D (2011) Dr David Jones quotes [Online] http://thinkexist.com/quotation/cystoscopies_gastroscopies_biopsies-they_can_do/203389.html (accessed 26 December 2011)

Kmetz, JL (2010) Mapping workflows and managing knowledge
[Online] http://www.buec.udel.edu/kmetzj/business_consulting/WFMA%20
brief.pdf (accessed 25 December 2011)

Korten, T (2011) The $70 billion scam, *Fast Company*, December, 146–56

Laszlo, E (1972) *Introduction to Systems Philosophy*, Gordon and Breach,
New York

Mitleton-Kelly, E (2004) Co-evolutionary integration: a complexity perspective on
mergers and acquisitions [Online] http://www.triarchypress.com/pages/articles/
Co-evolutionary-Integration-a-complexity-perspective-on-ma.pdf
(accessed 26 December 2011)

Nan, N (2011) Capturing bottom-up information technology use, *MIS Quarterly*,
35 (2), pp 505–32

Plato (nd) Charmides or temperance [Online]
http://classics.mit.edu/Plato/charmides.html (accessed 24 December 2011)

Ross, R (1994) *Systems Thinking with Process Mapping: A natural combination in
Fifth Discipline fieldbook*, Doubleday, New York

Sweeney, DT (2011) On hectic first day, FAA manager shut down all US flights
[Online] http://www.thetimesnews.com/articles/job-47662-manager-sliney.html
(accessed 27 December 2011)

Waters Foundation (2010) Systems thinking for schools [Online]
http://www.watersfoundation.org/index.cfm?fuseaction=search.habits
(accessed 28 December 2011)

Weber Shandwick (2009, November) Do Fortune 100 companies need a
twittervention? [Online] http://www.webershandwick.com/resources/ws/flash/
Twittervention_Study.pdf (accessed 27 December 2011)

Zax, D (2011) Siri, why can't you understand me? [Online]
http://www.fastcompany.com/1799374/siri-why-cant-you-understand-me
(accessed 28 December 2011)

Control

> *Who is the Fat Controller? Who is in charge? Where does the buck stop? The truth is that no one knows. Until that matter is sorted out... I do not believe that we shall make a great deal of progress.* **(LORD GREAVES, HANSARD, 2001)**

Objectives

At the end of this chapter you will be able to:

- identify the different types of control used in organizations;
- explain the differences between formal and informal controls and their appropriate use;
- discuss the role of leaders in organizational control;
- debate the changing nature of organizational control in relation to organizational health.

Sometimes there is confusion between 'power' and 'control': they are different. Power is the ability of someone to impose their will even against resistance from others and results primarily from position in a social structure, although there are others sources of power: for example, someone who controls access to resources may have little positional power but is able to use their resource power.

Control is manifested in things like formal rules such as those that give authority to supervisors in an organization and thus grant them power to control the behaviour of others. But formal rules are not the only methods of control; there are a whole variety of control mechanisms – think of the automatic switch that cuts off the electricity supply when the water in a kettle has reached boiling point, or the regulators in a human body that keep body temperature pretty much constant at 37 Celsius. And think too about the informal control mechanisms that keep people conforming to 'the way we do things around here'. Herb Kelleher, a former CEO of South Western Airlines, makes the point on this:

> A financial analyst once asked me if I was afraid of losing control of our organization. I told him I've never had control and I never wanted it. If you create an environment where the people truly participate, you don't need control. They know what needs to be done, and they do it. And the more that people will devote themselves to your cause on a voluntary basis, a willing basis, the fewer hierarchs and control mechanisms you need.

Control, then, is both the purposeful or automatic deployment of various mechanisms that act to guide organizations down a path that keeps them moving towards achievement of their business strategy and goals, and the informal protocols and unwritten norms that keep people in organizations working towards the goals.

Any discussion on organizational control, though, cannot be divorced from a discussion on leadership controls and leaders' use of control mechanisms, because leadership style and choice matters in terms of organizational health. Compare Herb Kelleher's comment on leadership control with John Chambers, CEO of Cisco, who says: 'I'm a command-and-control guy. It clearly has worked well for me. I say, turn right, 66,600 people turn right' (*McKinsey Quarterly*, 2009).

So, this chapter looks at control from three perspectives:

- the formal controls that are used within organizations to keep performance and productivity in line with goals;
- the informal cultural controls that keep people in line with organizational norms and mores;
- the controls that formal and informal leaders use that have an impact on organizational performance and productivity.

Note that responses to the many, many external compliance controls required from governments, professional associations, insurance companies, shareholders and so on are largely outside the scope of this chapter, although they are touched upon at points. Also outside the scope is any consideration of financial control systems – both traditional and newer.

Given that the noun 'control' has at least 11 meanings and the verb 'control' has eight, a useful discussion of healthy organizational control has to begin with some boundary setting around the word as it is played out inside organizations. Relating the various meanings of control to each of the four system types (Chapter 3), helps with this.

Table 4.1 shows the range and variety of controls available for organizational use, categorized by system type. Also given are some signs of healthy controls and symptoms of unhealthy controls.

Notice that at first sight most of the familiar management and organizational controls seem to be within the animate and social systems. But think again – office buildings, factories, manufacturing plants, IT systems and so on are all using mechanistic control systems, and things like light, temperature, air quality and noise levels all have an impact on the healthy functioning of an organization as one study found:

> Chilly workers not only make more errors but cooler temperatures could increase a worker's hourly labor cost by 10 per cent, estimates Alan Hedge, professor of design and environmental analysis and director of Cornell's Human Factors and Ergonomics Laboratory. When the office temperature in a month-long study increased from 68 to 77 degrees Fahrenheit, typing errors fell by 44 per cent and typing output jumped 150 per cent. Hedge's study was exploring the link between changes in the physical environment and work performance. (*Cornell News*, 2004)

And within the ecological system, control choices that organizations make – say on carbon emissions, or chemical waste disposal – have a profound effect on the wider environment, as the film *Erin Brockovich* so clearly depicts. This is a true story about an electricity company that was improperly and illegally dumping hexavalent chromium, a deadly toxic waste, and by doing this poisoning the land and the residents in the area.

At their best the controls keep the organization running in a healthy way, that is, a way that results in:

- effective performance or functioning;
- well-managed adaptation, change and growth;
- a strong sense of alignment, interdependency and community;
- a spirit of energy, vibrancy and vigour.

But if controls are left unmonitored or deployed poorly or thoughtlessly then there are likely to be unfortunate repercussions. Apple Inc found this out in 2010 when it appeared that worker conditions, including long working hours and highly regimented operations in one of the Chinese factories owned by Foxconn that supplied its parts, were implicated in a rash of worker suicides at the plant. In the wave of adverse publicity that hit Apple and in the face of international criticism of plant conditions Terry Gou, Chairman of Foxconn Technology, said 'We're reviewing everything. We will leave no stone unturned and we'll make sure to find a way to reduce these suicide tendencies' (Barboza, 2010).

TABLE 4.1 Range and variety of organizational controls

System type	Meanings of word 'control'	Examples of control type	Healthy signs	Unhealthy symptoms
Mechanistic	Regulation or maintenance of a function or action or reflex etc. eg blood flow. A mechanism that controls the operation of a machine.	Valves Shut off mechanisms Regulators	System runs smoothly. System shuts down appropriately.	System runs in fits and starts. System shuts off or slows inappropriately.
Animate	Power to direct or determine a relation or constraint of one entity (thing or person or group) by another. Discipline in personal and social activities. Control (others or oneself) or influence skillfully, usually to one's advantage.	Checklists Exercise of various types of power (resource, positional, information, etc.) Goal or objective setting Individual performance reviews Feedback Position in organization hierarchy Pay scales and career progression Compensation and reward systems Self-discipline Surveillance and measurement systems Language and vocabulary used	Controls are felt as fair and equitable. People feel trusted and respected in the organization and that their voice is heard. Stress is within manageable tolerances. People know what to do, how to do it, and have the tools and skills to do it. People are rewarded and recognized for contribution. People feel they have freedom to act. Communication is inclusive. There is clarity of role function. People feel psychological empowerment.	People are overly controlled (micro managed) People feel fear and anxiety Dysfunctional behaviors are evident (bullying, bursts of anger, destructive conflict, abusiveness). There is punishment for non-conformance. Counting keystrokes. Communication is coercive. Data manipulation. Job related stress.

TABLE 4.1 *continued*

System type	Meanings of word 'control'	Examples of control type	Healthy signs	Unhealthy symptoms
Social	The activity of managing or exerting control over something The state that exists when one person or group has power over another The economic policy of controlling or limiting or curbing prices or wages etc. exercise authoritative control or power over	Policies, procedures, regulations 'Red tape' in various forms Laws, executive orders, mandates Codes of practice Surveillance and measurement systems Language and vocabulary used Accounting practices (budgeting, costing)	There is a sense of directedness with plan and order. Policies/rules/etc. are clear and the reasons for them understood. There is a sense of fair play and tolerance for a wide spectrum of opinion and citizenship.	There is a sense of things gone awry eg 'Health and Safety gone mad'. There is intolerance for certain groups or affiliations. Groups of people are victimized or hounded for their beliefs or actions. 'Gaming' the system. Intergroup conflict
Ecological	(Physiology) regulation or maintenance of a function or action or reflex etc.	Bottom-up control, of the nutrient supply to the primary producers that ultimately controls how ecosystems function. Top-down control: predation and grazing by higher trophic levels on lower trophic levels ultimately controls ecosystem function (Regents of the University of Michigan, 2008)	System is resilient and adaptive. It is able to thrive as circumstances change.	System has no resilience and cannot return to equilibrium. Eg American 'dust bowl'

Making choices about controls that will enable organizational health is not straightforward. There are many complicating factors, including different schools of thought on what matters, and constant knowledge and technology expansion and change leading to what was received wisdom at one point being outdated the next.

In much the same way, making personal choices about controls for maintaining individual health is complicated. The example of stretching before athletic exercise that was the norm at one point and recommended to control muscle damage illustrates this:

> Science, however, has moved on. Researchers now believe that some of the more entrenched elements of many athletes' warm-up regimens are not only a waste of time but actually bad for you. The old presumption that holding a stretch for 20 to 30 seconds – known as static stretching – primes muscles for a workout is dead wrong. (Reynolds, 2008)

Much of today's organizational control theory is based on the work of William Ouchi. In his classic paper 'A conceptual framework for the design of organizational control mechanisms' (Ouchi, 1979) he discusses two questions: What are the mechanisms through which an organization can be managed so that it moves towards its objectives? How can the design of these mechanisms be improved, and what are the limits of each basic design? His findings developed into the now dominant model of organizational control. But as in the stretching example, Ouchi's model is giving way because it has two key limitations, as another researcher has pointed out. First, the model is too simple, in that it predicts that control mechanisms are determined by the type of task but does not predict what the outcomes of the chosen control mechanisms are on performance. And second, his work is based on a single control method for a specific context. In practice organizations use a combination or a portfolio of control methods to maintain or develop performance, choosing from a basket of possibilities depending on context, tasks and outcomes required (Liu, 2010).

Other recent research takes this further and questions the whole basis of management control. The suggestion is that commonly used controls derive from an era of bureaucratic and hierarchical organizations that is not relevant today as organizations become flatter, more flexible and more networked. Some reasons for taking another look at traditional management controls are:

- Costs expended by organizations to operate the administrative mechanisms to monitor, evaluate and sanction member behaviour consume scarce resources without adding value.

- Controls on employee behaviour can be negative if they result in loss of commitment and shirking.

- As work flows are regulated more by technology itself, the activities in which operating employees engage are becoming increasingly less routinized and more tied to discretion.

- Control needs to be taken over by those closest to the problem/work.

- Information and communication technologies enable real time facilitation of the work teams and the social networks surrounding them, offering an alternative to formal control: that is informal or soft control.

- Bureaucracies are breaking down in the current era. Globalization, mass customization and hyper-competition, have led organizations to become flatter and increasingly virtual.

- Linked to this, organization system boundaries have become more porous, many organizations participate in webs of partnerships (suppliers, customers, competitors, etc). In these contexts responsibility is taken by whoever has the appropriate expertise.

This post-bureaucratic thinking is seen in the actions taken by John Chambers, Chairman and CEO of Cisco. He recognized that his command-and-control style mentioned earlier '[is] not the future. The future's going to be all around collaboration and teamwork, with a structured process behind it.' So starting in 2006, he reorganized the company via a system of councils and boards made up of managers from different functions. Both were supported by 'working groups' created as needed. Reporting on this, *The Economist* (2009) said: 'Given its track record with other institutional innovations such as acquisitions and outsourcing, Cisco has a good chance of coming to exemplify a new world of "co-ordinate and cultivate" in the same way that GE stood for 'command and control.'

Cisco's story is an interesting one to follow because as operating circumstances change so do the control mechanisms they are using. In 2011 the company went through another major reorganization, having discovered that its unique structure brought with it its own bureaucracy with some managers serving on up to 14 of the councils and boards that comprised the structure. Explaining, Chambers said:

> Cisco has driven transformational change before, and we are again transitioning to the next stage of the company's evolution. Today, the market is driving toward simplification and it's why the network matters. Our role as the

leading network platform provider is strong, we have great customers, talent and expertise – and we know how to bring innovation to every aspect of the network. It's time to simplify the way we execute our strategy, and today's announcement is a key step forward. (Cisco Press Release, 2011)

Whether the switch from formal 'hard' control through rules, policies, technological monitoring (eg time cards) and regulation is more effective in delivering results and more organizationally healthy than the informal 'soft' control managed through subtly requiring conformance to organizational norms is a moot point. Again this is similar to the controls practised by individuals seeking to stay healthy. They might monitor their cholesterol level by a 'hard control' – the numbers – and use a 'soft control' of making, and sticking to, a resolution not to eat anything high in saturated fat and trans-fat like ice cream that elevates cholesterol levels. In practice, most organizations (as individuals aiming to stay healthy) operate a blend of hard and soft controls to keep things on track. Here's what a newcomer's boss said of a senior new joiner to an organization:

> Mike has adaptive ability – he can pick things up quickly and flex his style as needed. But he's had to change the way he operates. He's learning to debate and discuss – you can't command and control people in this organization – he'll be spat out if he does. But he is able to read when he needs to do things differently. He had a win the other day when he showed people the customer satisfaction scores and asked for their suggestions on how to improve them. Previously he would have just told them what they had to do.

This short example illustrates the formal and informal controls going hand in hand but also implies several questions: what combinations of controls are 'right' and in what circumstances, how do individuals learn to flex their control style, and why should they? Making these judgment calls is an art form that calls for reflective leadership and teamworking. But briefly, it is safe to say that some controls are chosen, some are imposed, some arise from the history and experience of the organizational members, and some are custom and practice.

On this last it is evident that national cultural norms have a part to play in attitudes to organizational controls. As an example, in 2005 Lenovo, a Chinese PC company, bought IBM's PC business for $1.75 billion. At the time things did not go so well. Lenovo's leadership team did not speak English and had no multicultural experience. There was also a significant cultural divide. In one story told Liu, Lenovo's Chairman used to insist that late arrivals to a meeting stand in the corner, 'a punishment he imposed even on himself' (Salter, 2011).

As mentioned earlier, control requirements are often mandated from external sources. An example is the Sarbanes–Oxley Act, introduced in the United States in 2002, which was designed to address flaws in the way companies reported their financials. Companies had to comply with this law, and this meant that in the years after it was enacted they had to create and operate control systems to meet certification standards.

In summary, theories about traditional management controls that derived from the 'machine era' of command and control are giving way to different forms of controls that are more appropriate for faster, flexible, more networked organizations looking to control through co-ordination and cultivation. Most organizations operate a portfolio of hard and soft controls, across the four systems of mechanistic, animate, social and ecological; the mix in the portfolio is partly contingent on external context and partly on factors such as business strategy, technology choices, organizational structure and size, culture and leadership choices.

Pause for thought

What are management controls for?

How are control mechanisms chosen, or are they?

What are the characteristics of 'good' organizational control?

Formal control

Gary Hamel, an academic and consultant, in his book *The Future of Management*, questions whether readers have ever asked themselves what foundational principles underlie their views on how to organize and manage. He suggests that most managers are probably as 'unaware of their managerial DNA as they are of their biological DNA', and explains that modern management practices are rooted in the early 1900s problem of how to get the highest operational efficiency and reliability in very large, predominantly manufacturing enterprises (Hamel, 2007). This problem was 'solved' by Frederick Winslow Taylor, who in 1911 published his paper 'The principles of scientific management'. In this he describes the most prominent single element in modern scientific management as:

The task idea. The work of every workman is fully planned out by the management at least one day in advance, and each man receives in most cases complete written instructions, describing in detail the task which he is to accomplish, as well as the means to be used in doing the work. And the work planned in advance in this way constitutes a task which is to be solved, as explained above, not by the workman alone, but in almost all cases by the joint effort of the workman and the management. This task specifies not only what is to be done but how it is to be done and the exact time allowed for doing it.

(Taylor, 1911)

The way of getting to a fully planned out task involved the manager 'gathering together all of the traditional knowledge which in the past has been possessed by the workmen and then of classifying, tabulating, and reducing this knowledge to rules, laws, and formula'.

Many of the formal organizational controls evident today are rooted in these scientific management principles of standardization, specialization, hierarchy, alignment, planning and control, and the use of extrinsic rewards to shape human behaviour. Table 4.2 illustrates the goal of each principle with a current example.

Returning to the point that controls that derive from an era of bureaucratic and hierarchical organizations may not be relevant today is worth another look on two counts.

First, there are many hierarchical and bureaucratic, predominantly manufacturing organizations in the world today. It happens that they are more likely to be in emerging markets than established markets where significant union struggles during the 20th century led to sufficient formal legislative controls being put in place to keep workers from harm. In the UK and United States, for example, these controls cover contracts of employment, a minimum wage, working time, health and safety, anti-discrimination, unfair dismissal, child labour and labour (trade) unions.

In emerging markets, factory and working conditions today effectively mirror those of the last century in the Western world. Controls do not always exist, or do not have teeth if they do. An example illustrates:

Li Qi-bing had been working for 12 hours without a break making plastic flowers, when a machine sliced his leg off below the knee. He said: 'the factory hadn't bought insurance for us.' The outcome of the accident was that he was sacked with no compensation. A local lawyer gave three reasons for the high industrial injury rate in the city where this factory is situated: a) the equipment is old and there is no effective factory inspectorate; b) workers work very long hours without a break; c) there is lack of adequate government regulation and control. (Mason, 2008)

TABLE 4.2 Scientific management principles, goals and examples

Scientific management principle	Goal	Current control example
Standardization	Minimize variances from the standard	Building regulations to ensure people with disabilities can access them
Specialization	Reduce complexity and accelerate learning	Certifications precluding non-certificate holders from practicing
Goal alignment	Ensure individual work efforts are in line with organization's goals	Performance appraisals Budgeting, costing
Hierarchy	Maintain control over a broad scope of operations	Job levels and descriptions that include authorities and accountabilities
Planning and control	Enabling tracking of progress against plan and level of predictability of operation	Programme management methodologies Six sigma
Extrinsic rewards	Motivate personnel and encourage compliance with policies and standards	Bonus payments given if certain conditions are met

SOURCE: Adapted from Hamel, 2007.

Formal legislative and regulatory controls to protect workers' conditions and livelihoods serve as basic and necessary factors in any workplace anywhere in the world, and the urgency with which this is required is reflected in the work of many labour unions and other forums, including the International Labor Organization, which is working to ensure 'Decent Work' across four domains – creating jobs, guaranteeing rights at work, extending social protection and promoting social dialogue – all involving formal controls.

FIGURE 4.1   Organizational hierarchy of needs

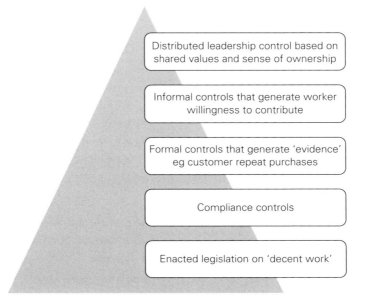

Distributed leadership control based on
shared values and sense of ownership

Informal controls that generate worker
willingness to contribute

Formal controls that generate 'evidence'
eg customer repeat purchases

Compliance controls

Enacted legislation on 'decent work'

SOURCE: Naomi Stanford, 2012.

It seems then that an equivalent of Maslow's hierarchy of needs is a helpful way of thinking about management controls. Figure 4.1 above illustrates this. In a healthy organization the bedrock of its culture is properly enacted 'Decent Work' types of legislation.

Second there is an argument that formal controls play a positive psychological part in worker well-being. With these in place workers 'know where they stand', which reduces role ambiguity and enables people to get on with the job while feeling at least relatively safe. Additionally being able to see (and show) where they stand increases an individual's sense of impact, competence and self-determination. Douglas Edwards, Google employee number 59, and employed as one of their first marketing managers, describes a world without these formal controls:

'[Google's] founders are okay with a loose shag bag of marketing folks who are ready to execute on their whims but a real marketing department with a VP, proper organization, funding, and a strategy is not a priority,' I was told by [my boss] Cindy. As a result, our world was without form and confusion was on the faces of those who dwelled in it. 'Who's working on letterhead? Who handles sponsorship requests?' I asked Cindy. Were these areas that fell into my domain?

> I was seeking something more than organizational clarity. I wanted to be sure there was some substance to my job... 'No structure, no foundation, no control', is how Heather Cairns, Google's HR lead at the time, remembers the company's early days. (Edwards, 2011)

The fine line is getting the formal controls balanced: formal controls that are too lax or non-existent can have damaging consequences for both organizations and individuals, as the examples given in this section illustrate. Conversely formal controls that are too tight and overly prescriptive can hamstring organizational success.

As with anything there is a middle ground on formal control. Being overly bureaucratic, or 'health and safety gone mad' as the UK phrase goes, means that things tip into ill health. Two, previously mentioned, symptoms of formal control ill health are:

- Costs expended by organizations to operate the administrative mechanisms to monitor, evaluate and sanction member behaviour consume scarce resources without adding value.

- Employee behaviour turns negative or passive aggressive. A heavy reliance on time cards for example means that employees will not work outside that agreed commitment.

The extract below from a government department e-mail regarding 'proper procedures related to the restoration of annual leave' is an example of organizational overkill on formal control that is likely to result in both of the above symptoms being evident.

> All restored annual leave requests must be approved by the Head of Service or Staff Office, the Regional Manager, or their designee. The written memorandum, with appropriate accompanying documentation, should be sent to the Director, National Payroll Branch through the appropriate Servicing Human Resources Director. The written memorandum must include: 1) The calendar date the leave was approved by the official having authority to approve leave; 2) The date(s) during which the leave was scheduled for use and the amount of leave (days/hours) that was scheduled; 3) The facts and circumstances that precluded the use of annual leave at the time it was scheduled and why it could not be rescheduled; 4) The beginning and ending dates for the exigency of public business; and 5) Written documentation of the annual leave request. An NP–35 may be used as documentary evidence.

Beyond the formal explicit controls that include codes of behaviour, policies, rules and tracking of organizational progress against various metrics there are rapidly increasing numbers of more behind-the-scenes electronic surveillance and monitoring devices used by organizations. Devices used include ID card swiping on electronically operated doors, video cameras, keystroke pattern monitoring, phone call and voice mail recordings, and GPS tracking systems in cars and mobile phones. All these yield extremely powerful information that can be used creatively or destructively. Legislation on the privacy rights of employees and the rights of employers to undertake this surveillance is in a state of flux because of the difficulty of staying abreast of new technologies.

In a healthy organization employees know what surveillance techniques are being used and for what purposes, they have a voice in determining the design and implementation of surveillance systems, and they have access to their individual data mine (Schumacher, 2011).

Informal control

W L Gore and Associates is a US manufacturer of fabrics and related materials. It operates without a hierarchy, has a voluntary turnover rate of only 5 per cent, and is financially very successful. Informal controls are built around social relationships, shared responsibility and, in Bill Gore's words, 'fun'. Gore has a distinctively 'theory Y' attitude to the people in its workforce. 'Theory X and Y', developed by Douglas McGregor in 1960, describes two ends of a continuum, where Theory X is an attitude of control and management by fear, underpinned by a belief that people are inherently lazy when it comes to working productively. Theory Y on the other hand develops from the perspective that given the right conditions workers are self-motivated, keen to do a good job and happy to work hard. Controls still operate in Theory Y organizations but they are more likely to be imposed and regulated by the workgroup members than by people with positional power in a hierarchy (McGregor, 2005).

And this is the case at Gore where there are no job titles, no managers and no job descriptions, just associates and leaders. Associates adhere to four basic guiding principles articulated by Bill Gore:

- fairness to each other and everyone with whom they come in contact;
- freedom to encourage, help and allow other associates to grow in knowledge, skill and scope of responsibility;
- the ability to make one's own commitments and keep them;
- consultation with other associates before undertaking actions that could impact the reputation of the company.

Another fascinating example of an almost pure form of Theory Y organization is the 'Occupy' organization that became visible in the latter half of 2011. Describing itself as a 'leaderless resistance movement', the organization gained global reach with presence in many of the world's cities. The major theme of the Occupy movement on both sides of the Atlantic was the income inequality between the top 1 per cent of the population and the rest.

Occupy camps, usually within a week or so of establishment, became what the *Financial Times* described as functioning micro-societies, with work-teams, operating for the most part from tents, offering medical, technical, meditation, education, catering – usually dispensing free food – and media support and expertise. Camps were organized using a non-binding, consensus-based, collective decision-making tool known as a 'people's assembly' (see Resources). A by-product of the movement was a string of innovative technology services.

Pixar, the company that designs and makes animated films, is another, more mainstream organization that flourishes on a bias towards informal rather than formal controls. Ed Catmull, co-founder of the enterprise, explains their innovative success as follows:

> I believe our adherence to a set of principles and practices for managing creative talent and risk is responsible. Pixar is a community in the true sense of the word. We think that lasting relationships matter, and we share some basic beliefs: Talent is rare. Management's job is not to prevent risk but to build the capability to recover when failures occur. It must be safe to tell the truth.
>   The company resists the notion of formal controls saying that 'the easiest way to deal with numerous problems is to trust people to work out the difficulties directly with each other without having to check for permission'.
>
> (Catmull, 2008)

On the face of it informal controls operated through culture, norms and trust seem to be a 'healthier' way to operate. But trust is a very difficult concept to operationalize in organizations and there are often subtle, and sometimes not so subtle, pressures to conform to established norms, with penalties for non-conformance. Numerous studies (the Asch conformity experiments conducted in the 1950s are the classic) have shown the way people succumb to group pressures to conform even if that conformity is in conflict with their own previously held values, and wider societal and/or organizational values.

Another part of the subtlety of informal control lies in the language used; rather than 'getting' people to work in a different way they can be 'invited', or 'encouraged'. Words like 'empowerment' and 'commitment' somehow seem less controlling than 'authority' and 'requirement'. Similarly, 'guidance notes' and 'frameworks' appear to give more leeway than 'rules' or 'policies'.

Again connecting individual health with organizational health, a study released in August 2011 provides scientific evidence of the specific individual neurobiological mechanism that lies behind social conformity. 'Overall, the results suggest that some of the most commonly cited sources of social influence – such as normative group pressure, cognitive dissonance and advice – in fact generally share the same fundamental neurobiological mechanisms' (Rotterdam School of Management, Erasmus University, 2011). An outcome of this research could be that individuals could take drugs to immunize themselves to group pressure. Musing on this the UK's *Daily Telegraph* reports that, 'Such drugs would be controversial, however, as they could be used by companies hoping to make their employees more reliable or to help control rebellious individuals' (*Daily Telegraph*, 2011).

Pause for thought

Are surveillance style technologies and subtle team coercion just different forms of formal bureaucratic control?

How far does a combination of formal and informal control support business strategy delivery in organizations?

How compatible is the use of formal and informal controls with building trust in organizations?

Leadership control

Countless theories of leadership exist as academics and practitioners try to codify and document what makes a great leader. The eight commonly cited theories are shown in Table 4.3. Some of these compete with others, some have so far stood the test of time, and others have been criticized. Adding further to the leadership debates are myriad questions about effective leadership; for example, what are desirable leadership competences and capabilities, are there gender and cultural differences in leader success, and what sources of power do leaders use?

Both the theories and the questions are based on the model of a single powerful leader in a bureaucratic hierarchy who operates through command and control. And although this type of organization is rapidly morphing as

TABLE 4.3   Common leadership theories

Theory	Headline	Main theorist
Great man theory	Leaders are born not made	Thomas Carlyle (in 1840s)
Trait theory	Leaders have specific attributes or clusters of attributes that others do not have	Gordon Allport Raymond Cattell Hans Eysenck
Behavioural theory	Leaders are made not born	B F Skinner
Contingency/ situational theory	The situation and context determines the leader's style and response	Frederick Fiedler P Hersy and KH Blanchard
Transactional theory	Leadership vested in a system of rewards and punishments	Max Weber
Transformational	Leaders inspire followers	James McGregor Burns, Bernard M Bass
Leader Member Exchange (LMX theory)	Focuses on the amount of interaction between a leader and a subordinate	F Dansereau, G Graen and W J Haga
Participative leadership theory	Leader does not make autocratic decision but seeks involvement from others	Kurt Lewin Rensis Likert

organizations move to flatter, more flexible forms, Rosabeth Moss-Kanter, an academic and management theorist, is confident in her assertions that:

> Yes, command-and-control structures are being shaken up in favor of more empowered people who are treated as part of the team and included in communication and decisions. Yes, hierarchies are being flattened and the

vertical dimension of organizations de-emphasized in favor of the horizontal. Yes, crowds can possess wisdom above and beyond the intelligence or perspective of individuals. But no, that does not mean the end of a division of labor, identification of decision-making authority, and individual accountability.

(Kanter, 2011)

Assuming Moss-Kanter is correct, and she is one among many academics and researchers who do think this, then it follows that traditional models of leadership have to change and evolve in order to align with new models of organization shape and form. In fact, there are signs of this happening. Peter Senge, Senior Lecturer at MIT, talks now about the subject of 'collective or shared leadership'. He notes that complex systems have complex methods of distributed control as all living organisms do. In this regard he cites the example of the bodily controls that leap into play if someone cuts their finger.

He rejects the 'great men, who do great things' – the leaders are born not made leadership model of previous decades (think Jack Welch, Walt Disney, Henry Ford) – in favour of a much broader leadership base that is distributed among individuals who share a common set of values and feel a sense of ownership and accountability for the overall success of the organization. And Terri Kelly, CEO of W L Gore, endorses this perspective, saying: 'the capacity of the organization increases when it distributes the leadership load to competent leaders on the ground who can make the best knowledge-based decisions' (Kelly, 2010).

This 'distributed leadership' model is also at play in Wholefoods, a supermarket chain. Front line employees make decisions on what to stock. There is peer pressure rather than management pressure to perform, team members select or reject new hires, everyone knows what everyone else gets paid, and senior executives limit their pay to 19 times the average wage (*Financial Times*, 2008).

Distributed leadership is typified by three characteristics:

- Leadership is visible from those not in formally identified leadership roles – they can be 'thought leaders', or subject matter experts, or informal leaders, and take the lead in various ways.

- Leadership appears at all levels of the organization. There can be bottom-up and front line leadership as well as top-down leadership.

- Leadership activities are not confined to specific functions or roles within an organization and they can appear in people outside the organization as well as inside it (for example a software vendor who takes the lead in the internal marketing of the product).

Be aware, however, that distributed leadership does not mean there is a vacuum at the top of the organization. Terri Kelly, CEO of W L Gore, is a typical example of a strong focal point leader who supports and sustains the distributed leadership model. Her role still requires her to step in to:

- make key decisions that keep the firm achieving its strategy and aligned with external demands;
- ensure that local decisions are not getting in the way of economies of scope and scale;
- speed up decision making if and when more collaborative and consensus-based approaches require short circuiting (Ancona, 2010).

Neither does distributed leadership mean a kind of free-for-all or bizarre anarchy – healthy distributed leadership organizations have in place support-ing structures and processes, together with protective controls, risk mitigation and guiding principles. As Kelly points out 'a critical role of leaders [in a distributed leadership model] is to instill the right values and just enough structure to enable the entire organization to flourish' (Kelly, 2010).

This statement squares with one of the better (and many) definitions of leadership:

> Leadership is a process of giving purpose (meaningful direction) to collective effort, and causing willing effort to be expended to achieve purpose.
> (Jacobs and Jaques, 1990: 281)

And it is a definition apt for any leader – informal or formal, top or front line – but it is a demanding brief to follow as the story of Howard Schulz illustrates. Howard Schultz joined Starbucks in 1982 as director of retail operations and marketing and became CEO in 1987, growing the company from 17 stores then to 2,498 in 2000 when he handed the CEO role to Orin Smith and became Chairman and chief global strategist. Smith retired in 2005 and Jim Donald became CEO.

> Two years later, during the depths of the 2007 recession Starbucks nearly drowned in its caramel macchiato. After decades of breakneck expansion under Mr. Schultz, tight-fisted consumers abandoned it. The company's sales and share price sank so low that insiders worried Starbucks might become a takeover target. (Miller, 2011)

So in 2008, by which point there were 15,001 stores worldwide, Schultz returned to the CEO role with what he called a 'transformational agenda' that included wooing back customers, remodelling some stores and closing 900 others (predominantly in the United States), streamlining the supply chain and changing out members of the executive team.

In his several decades of leading Starbucks, he provides a good example of a leader who embodies both healthy and unhealthy leadership attributes.

Healthy leadership

Taking Starbucks through the 'transformational agenda' had the effect, according to one commentator of leaving 'Mr. Schultz a changed man. Starbucks, these people say, is no longer "The Howard Schultz Show". The adjective that many use to characterize his new self is "humble" – a word that few would have applied to him before.' And Schultz says of himself that 'he can no longer run Starbucks through the Cult of Howard... he readily acknowledges that he badly misread the economy and underestimated the extent to which his customers would pull back during the recession' (Miller, 2011).

In leading through this traumatic period in Starbucks' history, Schultz learned to listen to his executives and take their advice. In December 2008 during an executive rehearsal for a meeting with Wall Street Schultz kept interrupting. 'Vivek Varma, who had recently joined Starbucks as head of public affairs, told him that he should leave. No one could remember anyone talking like that to Mr Schultz. But he left' (Miller, 2011).

A different example of the adoption of healthier leadership habits concerns the roll-out out of Starbucks' instant coffee Via in January 2009.

> Market research was showing that skeptical customers needed a lesson about instant coffee. Some executives worried that a big rollout might flop. Ms Gass and a few others told Mr Schultz that Starbucks should delay Via and introduce it in two cities before going national.
> 'That was hard for him,' Ms Gass says. But rather than overrule his executives, as he might have in the past, Mr. Schultz agreed. It turned out to be the right decision. After testing Via in Seattle and Chicago, Starbucks rewrote the plan for a nationwide introduction. (Miller, 2011)

In Schultz's words: 'What leadership means is the courage it takes to talk about things that, in the past, perhaps we wouldn't have, because I'm not right all the time.'

One aspect of Schultz's leadership that has remained constant during his tenure is being fanatical about Starbucks. He remains obsessive about the details. One customer tells the story of how he e-mailed Schultz to say that coffee lids in a particular outlet leaked coffee onto his shirt. Schultz's almost instant reply was that he was 'On it'. And his employees have respect and trust him on that score.

Unhealthy leadership

In the years 1987 to 2000, when Schultz was growing Starbucks from a small US West Coast chain to a global multi-billion dollar business described, by Rupert Everett, a UK actor, in a neat ill-health analogy as 'a cancer' (*Mail Online*, 2006), he had an in-company reputation for being an iconoclast, measuring success on his own terms.

He had many hates – research and development among them: A former executive recalls what happened to anyone with the temerity to suggest doing more research. 'Everybody would cringe and say: "You're new, aren't you?" Howard would say: "We're not P&G."' He's on record as saying 'I despise research. I think it's a crutch.' Advertising was another thing he was not interested in, and he did not care much for cost control either.

The fact that Starbucks was immensely successful hid some of the symptoms of ill health that Schultz should have been paying attention to. With hindsight he remarked: 'We got swept up.' Schultz says: 'We stopped asking: How can we do better? We had a sense of entitlement' (Berfield, 2009).

Whilst it is dangerous to overgeneralize from the specific, reading the stories of Schultz's leadership, chronicled in several books, and also in videos, and articles (see Resources) reveal some common indicators of healthy and unhealthy centralized leadership, whether this operates in a command and control, or a collaborate and cultivate (distributed) leadership model.

Leadership: positive health indicators

- demonstrating a strong desire to learn, grow and change;
- showing the ability to read and then internalize all the information people are giving about an organization's leadership and then practising to get it right;
- being willing to take the hard hits and difficult conversations and see them as valuable learning;
- listening to what people are saying;
- standing up to a strong set of humanistic values.

Leadership: negative health indicators

- leading through command, control, and coercion;
- being volatile, unreliable, and/or untrustworthy;
- having scant ability to gain the trust of others;
- passing the buck, scapegoating or blaming others rather than taking responsibility;
- encouraging 'yes men', and not continually encouraging people to challenge the process.

Leaders at all levels are accountable for the performance of their organization. They have to have the skills, courage and attributes to set a good course, think independently, value criticism, and flex their skills to meet all the various situations and challenges that come their way. They have to do this without losing the trust and respect of their colleagues and customers. Effective leading demands that a leader has a strong sense of self, but not an egotistical approach.

Pause for thought

How much of the leader's role is to control the processes and how much to serve as a facilitator of organizational success?

How true is it to say that leadership literature and research has not kept pace with the shift in organizational forms (from bureaucratic hierarchies to more flat and flexible networks)?

What is the evidence that distributing leadership is the way forward for organizations?

Exercise

It is a Herculean task to balance formal, informal and leadership controls so that they work effectively as a total control system that effectively regulates and keeps in balance the organization. Unlike the human body's distributed control systems, which have evolved to perform what is called 'homeostasis' (ie maintain physical and chemical settings to keep body cells, tissues, organs and organ systems working smoothly), organizations are not living organisms in that way; yet still the concept of homeostasis is relevant.

Gary Hamel, in his book, *The Future of Management* (2007) offers five organizing principles that enable organizations to be 'highly adaptable and fully human' and by definition achieve homeostasis. These principles are:

- life/variety;

- markets/flexibility;

- democracy/activism;

- faith/meaning;

- offices/serendipity.

He presents an exercise, adapted below, that helps an organization move from a traditional command and control mindset towards a 'co-ordinate and cultivate' mindset. Briefly the exercise is a series of face-to-face workshops and discussions held with leaders and employees across the organization. Alternatively it could be a single large-scale collaboration using a collaborative technology. The exercise asks participants questions and seeks actionable answers in each of the five areas:

- *Life/variety*: How would you introduce a greater diversity of data, viewpoints and opinions into the organization? How would you design the organizational controls so that they facilitate rather than frustrate the continual development of new strategic options and encourage relentless experimentation?

- *Markets/flexibility*: How would you redesign the organizational controls so that they exploit the wisdom of the market, rather than just the wisdom of the experts? How might these be used to help speed up the reallocation of resources from legacy programmes to new initiatives? How could we make it easier for innovators to get the resources they need to advance their ideas?

- *Democracy/activism*: How would you change the organizational controls so that they encourage, rather than discourage, dissenting voices? How would you make the organization more responsive to the needs and concerns of those working on the front lines? How do we give folks on the ground a bigger voice in shaping policy and strategy?

- *Faith/meaning*: How would you use control devices to help focus on the higher-order goals our company claims to serve (or should be serving)? How could these help employees to identify and connect with the goals they care about personally?

- *Offices/serendipity*: How could the space be redesigned and controlled in a way that would help our organization to become an (even more) exciting and vibrant place to work and a magnet for creative talent? How could the space controls be used to facilitate the collision of new ideas?

Key messages

- There is not a single, universal management control system that serves all organizations in all circumstances.
- The effectiveness of control systems is contingent upon the particular circumstances faced by the organization. Formal, informal and leadership controls act together to either create or destroy organizational homeostasis (that is, balance and effective functioning). Enron is an example of the balance between these three being lost, which led to the organization's collapse.

References

Ancona, D (2010) It's not all about you [Online] http://blogs.hbr.org/imagining-the-future-of-leadership/2010/04/its-not-all-about-me-its-all-a.html (accessed 14 January 2012)

Barboza, D (2010) Electronics maker promises review after suicides [Online] http://www.nytimes.com/2010/05/27/technology/27suicide.html?pagewanted=all (accessed 30 December 2011)

Baxter, JW (2012) Power, influence, and diversity in organizations, *Annals of the American Academy of Political and Social Science*, 639 (1), pp 49–70

BBC (nd) Science: human body and mind – pancreas [Online] http://www.bbc.co.uk/science/humanbody/body/factfiles/pancreas/pancreas.shtml (accessed 30 December 2011)

Berfield, S (2009) Starbucks: Howard Schultz vs Howard Schultz, from *Bloomberg Businessweek*, 6 August [Online] http://www.businessweek.com/magazine/content/09_33/b4143028813542_page_2.htm (accessed 27 April 2012)

Catmull, E (2008) How Pixar fosters collective creativity, *Harvard Business Review*, September, pp 65–72

Cisco Press Release (2011) Cisco announces streamlined operating model [Online] http://newsroom.cisco.com/press-release-content?type=webcontent&articleId=752727 (accessed 8 January 2012)

Cornell News (2004) Study links warm offices to fewer typing errors and higher productivity [Online] http://www.news.cornell.edu/releases/Oct04/temp.productivity.ssl.html (accessed 7 January 2012)

Daily Telegraph (2011) Scientists find they can control how people react to group pressure, 3 September [Online] http://www.telegraph.co.uk/science/science-news/8739376/Scientists-find-they-can-control-how-people-react-to-group-pressure.html (accessed 14 January 2012)

Economist (2009) Reshaping Cisco: The world according to Chambers, *Economist*, August 27, [Online] http://www.economist.com/node/14303574 (accessed 16 November 2011)

Edwards, D (2011) *I'm Feeling Lucky: The confessions of Google employee number 59*, Harcourt Mifflin Houghton, New York

Financial Times (2008) The chaos theory of leadership, 2 December [Online] http://www.ft.com/intl/cms/s/0/4f20ec38-c012-11dd-9222-0000779fd18c.html#axzz1jSgIZQYW (accessed 14 January 2012)

Hamel, G (2007) *The Future of Management*, Harvard Business School Press, Boston

Hansard (2001) Lords sitting: Railtrack, 5 April, 6.46 pm [Online] http://hansard.millbanksystems.com/lords/2001/apr/05/railtrack (accessed 30 December 2011)

Jacobs, TO and Jaques, E (1990) Military executive leadership, in *Measures of Leadership*, KE Clark and MB Clark (eds), Center for Creative Leadership, Greensboro, NC

Kanter, RM (2011) Cisco and a cautionary tale about teams [Online] http://blogs.hbr.org/kanter/2011/05/cisco-and-a-cautionary-tale-ab.html (accessed 14 January 2012)

Kelly, T (2010) No more heroes: distributed leadership [Online] http://www.managementexchange.com/blog/no-more-heroes (accessed 14 January 2012)

Liu, L (2010) A normative theory of organizational control: main and interaction effects of control modes on performance, 18th European Conference on Information Systems [Online] http://is2.lse.ac.uk/asp/aspecis/20100031.pdf (accessed 15 January 2011)

Long, CP (2002) Three controls are better than one: a computational model of complex control systems, *Computational and Mathematical Organization Theory*, 8 (3), pp 197–200

Mail Online (2006) Actor Everett labels Starbucks a 'cancer', 18 August [Online] http://www.dailymail.co.uk/news/article-401223/Actor-Everett-labels-Starbucks-cancer.html (accessed 27 April 2012)

Mason, P (2008) *Live Working or Die Fighting*, Vintage, London

McGregor, D (2005) *The Human Side of the Enterprise: Annotated edition*, McGraw Hill, New York

McKinsey Quarterly (2009) McKinsey conversations with global leaders: John Chambers of Cisco, from *McKinsey Quarterly*, July [Online] http://www.mckinseyquarterly.com/McKinsey_conversations_with_global_leaders_John_Chambers_of_Cisco_2400 (accessed 14 January 2012)

Miller, CC (2011) A changed Starbucks: a changed CEO, from *New York Times*, 12 March [Online] http://www.nytimes.com/2011/03/13/business/13coffee.html?pagewanted=all

Ouchi, W (1979) A conceptual framework for the design of organizational control mechanisms, *Management Science*, 25 (9), pp 833–48

Regents of the University of Michigan (2008, October 31) The concept of the ecosystem [Online] http://www.globalchange.umich.edu/globalchange1/current/lectures/kling/ecosystem/ecosystem.html (accessed 27 April 2012)

Reynolds, G (2008) Stretching: the truth [Online] http://www.nytimes.com/2008/11/02/sports/playmagazine/112pewarm.html (accessed 14 January 2012)

Rotterdam School of Management, Erasmus University (2011) New research reveals the neurobiological mechanism behind herd behaviour [Online] http://www.rsm.nl/home/faculty/Research%20News?p_item_id=7105950 (accessed 15 January 2012)

Salter, C (2011) Protect and attack, *Fast Company*, December, pp 116–21

Schumacher, S (2011) What employees should know about electronic performance monitoring, *ESSAI*, 8 (1), pp 138–44

Taylor, FW (1911) *Principles of Scientific Management*, Chapter 2 [Online] http://nationalhumanitiescenter.org/pds/gilded/progress/text3/taylor.pdf (accessed 15 January 2011)

Developing well-being

"*[Development] requires a resilient mindset and ability to change, adapt, re-conceptualize and engage in deep listening with humility, and to get out of your comfort zone.*

(JOHN SEELY BROWN)

Objectives

At the end of this chapter you will be able to:

- describe the differences between 'healthy' and 'effective' organizations;
- define the relationship between organizational 'health' and 'well-being';
- choose appropriate approaches to support organizational change;
- support management capability to develop social networks and community.

The Corporation, a clever, thoughtful and provocative film, describes how in the United States in the mid-1800s the corporation emerged as a legal 'person'. This concept (the characteristic of a non-living entity regarded by law as having the status of personhood) is found not just in the United States but in almost all legal systems, and lends itself to the notion that corporations have a personality. The film uses diagnostic criteria of the World Health Organization and some standard diagnostic tools (Hare, 2003) of psychiatrists and psychologists to assess the personality of a corporation, revealing that the operational principles of the corporation give it a highly anti-social personality: 'it is self-interested, inherently amoral,

FIGURE 5.1   Organization as pyschopath

SOURCE: The Corporation http://hellocoolworld.com/media/TheCorporation/house_party_logo.jpg

callous and deceitful; it breaches social and legal standards to get its way; it does not suffer from guilt, yet it can mimic the human qualities of empathy, caring and altruism.' The conclusion is that the corporation is a psychopath (Figure 5.1).

The legal concept of 'personhood' reinforces the analogy of an organization as a human being with a personality that can be assessed (as the film demonstrates). Integral to personality are the mind and spirit, attributes referred to in Bruhn's definition of organizational health detailed in Chapter 1 (Bruhn, 2001); in summary:

- Mind refers to how underlying beliefs, goals, policies, and procedures are implemented, 'how conflict is handled, how change is managed, how members are treated, and how the organization learns'.

- 'Spirit is the core or heart of an organization... what makes it vibrant, and gives it vigor. It is measurable by observation.'

Whether all corporations are psychopathic, and whether this is an inevitability given the legal frameworks that they operate within, is a matter of debate, opinion and reflection.

However, it may be as an unconscious hedge against organizational psychopathic traits that a whole industry of 'organization development' (OD) has emerged that is concerned with the mind and spirit of an organization. Pinpointing the date of the birth of OD is not easy. Generally it is put at the end of the Second World War – mid-1940s – coming at a time when there was a need to reorganize, rebuild and manage in a new and different world, but it was not until Richard Beckhard's book *Organization Development: Strategies and models* was published in 1969 that the phrase 'organizational development' became mainstream. At this point Beckhard defined OD as:

> an effort planned, organization-wide, and managed from the top, to increase organization effectiveness and health through planned interventions in the organization's processes, using behavioural-science knowledge'. (Beckhard, 1969)

However, as organizations move away from the command-and-control, bureaucratic and hierarchical systems towards more collaborative, participative and networked forms, many OD practitioners feel a more appropriate definition of OD is that it is:

> a dynamic values-based approach to systems change in organizations and communities; it strives to build the capacity to achieve and sustain a new desired state that benefits the organization or community and the world around them [and] helps to create and sustain a healthy effective human system as an interdependent part of its larger environment.
> (Organization Development Network, 2011)

Both definitions include two words which cause confusion: 'healthy' and 'effective'. To clarify: an organization can successfully achieve its business goals, or in other words be effective. But it can do that without being healthy. Again Foxconn, mentioned in Chapters 3 and 4 illustrates this. The company meets its business goals in manufacturing parts for Apple, Sony, Nintendo and HP, among many others, but has had a history of suicides at its factories. In 2010 18 workers threw themselves from the top of the company's buildings, with 14 deaths. Several reports from inside Foxconn factories have suggested that while the company is more advanced than many of its competitors, it is run in a 'military' fashion that many workers cannot cope with. At Foxconn's flagship plant in Longhua, 5 per cent of its workers, or 24,000 people, quit every month (Moore, 2012).

Foxconn is 'effective' by one measure – meeting its customer's parts requirements – and in this respect its mechanistic systems and controls may be judged as 'healthy' but its mind and spirit, the human aspects, vested in the values, beliefs, social systems, community interactions and so on are clearly unhealthy.

FIGURE 5.2   Organization effectiveness and health

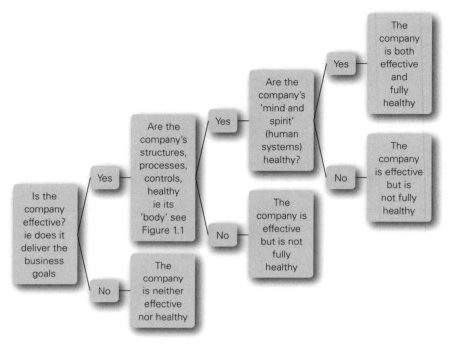

SOURCE: Naomi Stanford, 2012.

To be fully healthy an organization needs 'body, mind and spirit' to be evidently working interdependently and harmoniously. Figure 5.2 illustrates the flow and relationships between effectiveness, and health.

Along with many other organizations that recognize that organizational effectiveness on its own does not imply organization health, Apple said it conducted 229 audits at different factories during 2011 and found various cases of non-compliance with labour rights. In the supplier responsibility report is the comment that 'Apple is committed to driving the highest standards for social responsibility throughout our supply base. We require that our suppliers provide safe working conditions, treat workers with dignity and respect, and use environmentally responsible manufacturing processes wherever Apple products are made' (Apple, 2012).

Beyond the distinction between health and effectiveness, people want to know what the difference is between 'organizational health' and 'organizational well-being'. This too is a useful question to ask because often health and well-being are used interchangeably, which works well most of the time.

However, for managers and HR practitioners it helps to think of the two things as different but interdependent. Returning to the analogy of an organization's body, mind and spirit and now thinking about this in human terms, it is evident that someone can be physically healthy yet low-spirited and lacking in self-belief and esteem. As an example, in a memoir written when the writer Nigel Nicolson was 68 (he lived to be 87) he summed himself up:

> The two great deficiencies in my make-up are lack of judgment, and an incapacity to feel deeply, in anger or in love. A mushiness of temperament, a short-cut mind, indolence, no power to execute, a copy-cat mind, poverty of intellect and spirit, constantly wishing myself more rich in scope, self-indulgent, and selfish were it not that I take pains not to appear so, my generosity fake, my gentleness an excuse for lack of vigour. It's not a pretty self-portrait.
>
> (Nicolson, 2010)

Another person can be physically healthy and emotionally buoyant and purposeful. Here is Steve Jobs talking in 2005 about getting fired from Apple earlier in his career:

> I didn't see it then, but it turned out that getting fired from Apple was the best thing that could have ever happened to me. The heaviness of being successful was replaced by the lightness of being a beginner again, less sure about everything. It freed me to enter one of the most creative periods of my life... I'm convinced that the only thing that kept me going was that I loved what I did. You've got to find what you love. And that is as true for your work as it is for your lovers. Your work is going to fill a large part of your life, and the only way to be truly satisfied is to do what you believe is great work. And the only way to do great work is to love what you do. (Jobs, 2005)

The mind and spirit aspects of an individual or organization constitute 'well-being'. The word 'health' covers the totality of body, mind, and spirit.

This explanation becomes clearer when looking again at the systems diagrams presented in Chapter 1 (Figures 1.1 and 1.2). They represent the 'body' of the organization and the body of the individual. Notice that what they lack is any representation of 'mind' and 'spirit', the aspects that give the organization and individual their 'personalities' – part of what differentiates one enterprise or human being from another. Positively enabling, developing or facilitating the mind and spirit aspects of either an organization or an individual leads to 'well-being', which is one of the components of overall health and one which fosters motivated performance.

The story of the key-cutters told in Chapter 1 reinforces the concept of 'well-being' as an integral component of organizational health. Concluding that story is the question 'so how is it that two stores, part of the same organization, in the same city have opposite approaches to their work and to their customer service?' On the face of it they look alike, have the same metaphorical DNA, and a customer expects the same sort of experience in each store. In fact, however, they function as two distinct organizations. So it is with identical twins: they may look indistinguishable but their minds and spirits differ.

The Minnesota Study of Twins Reared Apart is a fascinating research study of sets of identical twins over two decades (1979–2000), explaining how identical twins can be so similar in many respects but different in others the researcher says: 'If you think of our DNA as an immense piano keyboard and our genes as keys – each key symbolizing a segment of DNA responsible for a particular note, or trait, and all the keys combining to make us who we are – then epigenetic processes determine when and how each key can be struck, changing the tune being played.' (Simply put epigenetic means resulting from external rather than genetic influences.)

Identical twins George and Donald, according to their grandfather Freeman Dyson, 'not only have the same genes but also have the same environment and upbringing. And yet they are no more alike in personality than twins reared by two different sets of parents in two different homes' (Harris, 2002).

So it is with organizations; they may be part of the same enterprise, and have the same DNA, but their different divisions and business units may have very different 'personalities'. Developing the well-being of the whole enterprise means acknowledging that different parts of it may need different development activities, and that it is ok for different parts of the enterprise to have these different personalities as long as they are healthy and contributing to overall organization performance.

So whilst the three previous chapters on Structures, Systems and Processes, and Controls have discussed the 'body' aspects of the organization, this chapter turns to the mind and spirit aspects that contribute to the organization's 'personality'. It considers the development of individual (animate system), social (social system) and community (ecological system) well-being that collectively contribute to overall organizational health.

Pause for thought

If an organization is healthy, is it by definition effective?

What stands in the way of effective organizations becoming healthy organizations?

What is the organizational value of distinguishing between health, well-being and effectiveness?

Developing individual well-being

The way people feel, or their well-being, can account for more than a quarter of the differences observed in research into individuals' performance at work. Workplace well-being is therefore receiving increasing attention, as it may have economic implications for the organization if workers are under-performing or unhappy. The Gallup Organization, for example in 2008, introduced into the UK, United States and Germany the Gallup-Healthways Wellbeing Index, which tracks on a daily basis how citizens evaluate their lives, both now and as they expect it to be in five years' time, on the Cantril Self-Anchoring Striving Scale, where '0' represents the worst possible life and '10' represents the best possible life. Respondents are classified by Gallup as 'thriving' if they rate their current life a 7 or higher and their future life an 8 or higher. Respondents are classified as 'suffering' if they rate their current life 0 to 4 and their future life 0 to 4. Those who are neither 'thriving' nor 'suffering' are classified as 'struggling' (Gallup Healthways, 2008). Figure 5.3 illustrates this.

FIGURE 5.3   Cantril self-anchoring scale

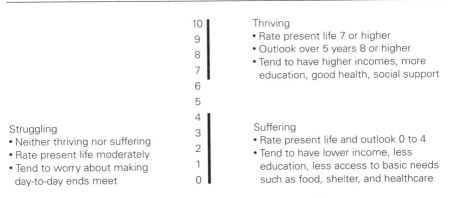

SOURCE: Well being index http://www.well-beingindex.com/overviewUk.asp

Gallup-Healthways' website notes that: 'Public and private sector leaders use data on life evaluation, physical health, emotional health, healthy behavior, work environment, and basic access to develop and prioritize strategies to help their communities thrive and grow.'

Over the past decade, the emerging discipline of Health and Productivity Management (HPM) has shown that health and productivity are inextricably linked (Loeppke, 2007). In response to this and other reports on the connections between health and productivity, organizations are looking at myriad ways of supporting the development of the mental, physical and emotional health of their employees. Take a look at the benefits offered by any multinational employer, usually shown on their 'careers with us' page. Typically they include:

- learning and development opportunities;
- career development plans;
- employee assistance programmes (EAPs);
- health and fitness (wellness) programmes;
- balancing work and family commitments (flexible working opportunities);
- reward and recognition schemes;
- transport plans or benefits;
- medical, dental and vision insurance;
- retirement savings plans.

All these are essentially aimed at safeguarding employee well-being in order to maintain employee motivation and productivity. These benefits packages are part of the explicit contractual arrangements an employer makes with an employee; they are sometimes well received and are sometimes underused.

EAPs, for example, usually include free, voluntary, short-term counselling and referral for various issues affecting employee mental and emotional well-being, such as alcohol and other substance abuse, stress, grief, family problems and psychological disorders. Sometimes employees feel a certain stigma in approaching them, but when they do such programmes can be very helpful:

Mark was a long-time employee. Bright, motivated and positive, he was always a solid performer. All that changed when his marriage broke down after 15 years. Suddenly Mark found it hard to concentrate at work. He made mistakes. He stopped taking care of himself. He lost weight and had trouble sleeping. He started taking more days off work. His co-workers noticed, and one of them suggested he contact the company's EAP programme. Mark commented on his situation:

'After my marriage came apart, everything in my life was turned upside down. I was living in an empty apartment. I was worried all the time. My daughter, Claire, started getting into trouble at school. I knew she was upset but I didn't know what to do. I felt so lost. It was hard for me to turn to the system and ask for help. But I finally did and I'm glad. I worked with a counsellor over several months; it made a real difference. I'm not out of the woods and I know things are still going to be difficult but I am finally able to focus at work, feel healthy and be myself again'. (Family Services Employee Assistance Programs, nd)

Wellness programmes include physical fitness information and resources, nutrition and healthy eating guidance, and sometimes medical support, for example for flu vaccinations. The Scotts MiracleGro company's CEO, Jim Hagedorn, worried about the costs of his unfit workforce – in 2003 half of the 6,000 employees were overweight or morbidly obese and a quarter of them smoked; to mitigate the costs of time off, loss of productivity, and health cover, introduced a wellness programme, LiveTotal Health. Hagedorn acts as a role model and fierce advocate for the programme taking it on himself to motivate employees.

> He walks around the site joking, slapping guts, and exhorting people to work out. The nudging begets peer pressure. Gym rats earn special pins they display on ID badge lanyards; these have become a coveted status object. Competition for trips to Hawaii, free massages and facials, and other cash and prizes is fierce. One group of employees started having lunch together every day to keep each other from peeling out of the parking lot for a smoke. Doughnuts have disappeared. 'The message is: If you're not trying to do something to make yourself better, then you're going to pay more'.
>
> (*Bloomberg Business Week*, 2007)

Both EAPs and Wellness programmes are voluntary. Employees can opt in or out of them, and that is one of several obstacles to their success. The US 2004 National Worksite Health Promotion Survey found that lack of employee interest accounted for 63.5 per cent of the reasons that these programmes did not achieve their goals for health and there are many reasons given for why employees choose to avoid them. For example:

- The purpose of the programme is not clearly explained.
- The benefits to the company and how these directly affect the employees is not explained.
- Lower-level management cannot convey the advantages of the programme to the employees under their authority.
- Employees are angry and distrustful of the employer.
- Employees feel forced to relinquish control over their own health to the company, resulting in a perceived violation of their rights (Bates, 2009).

All these suggest that much greater emphasis should be placed on involving employees in the design and communication of the programmes (the value of involvement is discussed in more detail below), building trust that programmes are in the employees' interests as well as the organization's, and publicizing the benefits of take-up to individuals. These types of actions would make the uptake higher and the likelihood of realizing the organizational investment benefits greater.

Strangely, two things that are rarely seen in the formal benefits list but which have a significant bearing on employee health and well-being are:

- how the organization's managers manage: ie the style, expectations and controls they use;
- the extent of involvement, participation and voice people have in the way the organization is run as it changes.

Sometimes these appear in employee stories of 'what it's like working for us' as a recruitment pull, but it is worth considering whether style of management and extent of employee involvement should be formally recognized and invested in as an explicit and integral part of the employment contract between employers and employees.

Management style and expectations

Generally, employees are looking for managers who clearly communicate expectations, give them meaningful assignments, treat them with respect, listen to them, and give them ongoing supportive and encouraging feedback. Both over-controlling managers who use threats as a way to motivate employees, and organizations that do not appear to value individuals' contributions, frustrate individuals' basic needs for autonomy, control and relatedness (how people relate to others). Several studies have shown how 'Considerate behaviour on behalf of the leader, structures initiated with consideration for the employee, and transformational behaviours (communication of a vision, intellectual stimulation, consideration of individual employees) have all been found to be related to good employee health, job satisfaction and productivity' (Nyberg, 2009). Here's what one admin assistant said about her supportive boss:

> My boss is a dynamo. She works very long hours and does very detailed and technical work, but she never forgets to tell me how much she appreciates me. If I have stayed on long after my regular eight-hour day she thanks me profusely and has even treated me to dinner. She often will come to me with photocopying jobs, and upon finding me busy with other people's work, she just rolls up her sleeves and does it herself – she's not above doing menial tasks! She is a real

team player, and sees our work as 'our work' rather than a division of duties. I love working with her. (EmployeeSurveys.com, nd)

On the other hand 'perceived abusive, passive-avoidant and laissez-faire leadership has been found to be associated with increased psychological distress, and lack of social support in combination with job strain has been shown to be related to elevated risks for cardiovascular disease and increased levels of sickness absence' (Nyberg, 2009). Here's an example of stress experienced by one employee at the hands of his manager:

> My boss, the advertising director, was nuts. We sales reps never knew what to expect from her from one day to the next. For example, one day she would bound through the office, telling us that we were obviously working hard, revenue was up and we were marvelous sales people. The next day (or in some instances just a few hours later) she would scowl and tell us all that we were lousy sales reps with no professionalism or skill and that she could never accomplish the things she wanted to accomplish with such an inferior sales team. I got so stressed I decided to leave.
>
> (EmployeeSurveys.com, nd)

In the first example above the notion of 'our work' indicates much more of a team-based management style, and one which suits the increasingly changing nature of work. GE is one organization that is moving away from managerial hierarchy towards self-managed teams. This style of organization allows for, and encourages, high degrees of participation, engagement and involvement – all key factors in positive and healthy organizational performance. Reckitt Benckiser, a UK-based health and home products company, is another; its CEO, Bart Becht, when asked, 'How much of your success is due to your unique business culture?' answered:

> A lot. We try to give our people considerable responsibility from virtually day one so that they develop a sense of ownership. We also try to develop a spirit of entrepreneurship unlike a lot of other big companies where it gets stifled. We actively encourage people to come up with new ideas. We are very focused on achieving results, but we don't punish people for failure just because a new idea doesn't happen to work. (German Retail Blog, 2009)

Yet many organizations, rather than rapidly relinquish traditional command and mechanisms in favour of cultivate and collaborate styles, or recognizing the need to reconfigure to meet new realities, cling on to what is known, perhaps hiding behind the well-worn phrase 'people resist change' without thinking too much about it. In fact, people can and do change all the time.

Involvement and change

Human stories of people making major life changes are commonplace and popular. For example, in just one issue of a UK magazine there are the stories of someone 'who could barely swim when she was in her 40s. Now [50+] she's not just competing in triathlons – she's winning them'; someone else who 'walked away from a six-figure salary to teach prisoners to bake bread'; a third person who 'was made redundant and used it to kick-start a whole new life'; and the story of Martine Wright who lost both her legs in a terrorist bomb attack in London in 2005, and is now on a volleyball team that is training to compete in the 2012 Paralympics (*Good Housekeeping*, 2012).

In order to maintain competitiveness, handle disruptive technologies and generally adapt to the external context individuals, it behoves organizations to disprove the myth that people resist change. Instead they need to use the available knowledge about behaviour, involvement and participation that demonstrates over and over again that when individuals have a sense of their own power and agency in a changing situation they can act positively on it. A research article (Woodward, 2004) gives some useful pointers on this, saying:

> In the changing workplace, employees are continually evaluating what is going on and what the significance for them is. They assess whether changes have any relevance for their well-being, and if so, in what ways. Such evaluations are of two kinds: A primary appraisal: What will I gain? What will I lose? What are the potential benefits or harm to me? Is what is happening irrelevant, can I ignore it? A secondary appraisal asks: What can I do to overcome or prevent the negative effects? What can I do to improve my prospects for benefiting from change? What coping options might be worth adopting? What are the likely consequences? Will I accomplish what I want to achieve?

Newer and primarily online organizations, for example Zappos, Mashable or Zynga, give other insights into how to organize to enable employee participation, involvement. However, there are examples in this book of older organizations with expertise in participative management – W L Gore is one, previously mentioned – that are worth learning from.

Additionally, there are many common-sense approaches organizations can take, even without reconfigurations or restructurings, that enable individual employees to relish rather than resist change. Table 5.1 lists some of these, with case examples of how to action the approach.

TABLE 5.1   Approaches to handling change

Effective approaches to handling change (Adapted from Woodward, 2004)	Virtual working example of approach in practice
Giving employees the resources to make change	A drive to increase virtual working means providing the technology tools to do that. 'Working remotely was really difficult until the VPN upgrade.'
Enhancing employees' sense of 'autonomy and control'	Allowing individual employees to choose how much and when to work virtually. 'My son was sick and I had to change my work hours to fit with the hospital visiting schedule, which meant working from home a lot more.'
Supporting employees in developing capability and competence to meet the changed situation	Offering accessible, always available, and engaging training and development activity in using virtual working tools – instant messaging, video conference, tethering BlackBerries as modems, etc. 'Our training now comes in ten-minute bite-sized packets, designed to respond to our queries. It's really good.'
Acknowledging employee success in meeting the requirements of the new situation	Publicly recognizing someone who has successfully learned how to use a new technology and passed on some tips to others. 'I organized a virtual Christmas party which was a real success. My manager sent a lovely thank-you note to me, copying in everyone.'
Helping those leading change to be more aware of their role in employees' acceptance of change process	Providing guidance and tip sheets on how managers can involve their workforce in making decisions about successful virtual working. 'I hadn't managed remote workers before. Now I get a weekly tip sheet on some aspect and I'm getting much more confident.'
Supporting and developing personal change management competence in those formally charged with leading change in the workforce	Running coaching sessions or peer-to-peer conversations about the impact of moving from office-based working to virtual working on management style and control. 'All of the Business Unit managers meet on a teleconf call monthly to share notes and lessons on how the change process is going – it's a big project and we need to keep in sync and keep on learning together.'

Beyond the types of interventions mentioned, organizations can look to the rapidly expanding field of neuroscience to help them gain an understanding of how the brain responds to change, how changes in behaviour can be nudged, and how neuroscience is informing traditional change management (see Resources).

Pause for thought

Should organizations relinquish management to employees (ie allow self-management)?

Do people resist change or embrace change?

How much is individual mental and emotional health an organizational responsibility?

How useful is neuroscience knowledge in supporting organizational change?

Developing social well-being

As well as supporting individual employees in developing their own mental, emotional and physical health and well-being, organizations also have a significant role to play in fostering social well-being – that is, enabling individuals to develop strong social networks of relationships and ties.

Researchers have found that the strength of an individual's social group is positively related to productivity and organizational commitment (Waber *et al*, 2010). Additionally, close friendships in general prove good for people's physiological health. As the Gallup organization reports:

> Relationships serve as a buffer during tough times, which in turn improves our cardiovascular functioning and decreases stress levels. On the other hand, people with very few social ties have nearly twice the risk of dying from heart disease and are twice as likely to catch colds – even though they are less likely to have the exposure to germs that comes from frequent social contact. (Rath, 2010)

Additionally, having a network of supportive relationships contributes to psychological well-being. Specifically a network gives people a sense of belonging and security, and feelings of self-worth. A Zappos' employee talks about this:

> Gone are the days of worrying that if I socialize throughout the day I will be considered unmotivated... Here at Zappos you are required to visit with your peers as part of your annual culture review. As I result, I've bonded with those

people who ultimately help me get my job done in a quick and efficient manner as they are personally vested in me. Gone are the days of running out of the office because I'd had enough of the people I worked with – now I can't imagine life without my team. Gone is a life I knew. And I am so grateful.

(Zappos.com, 2008)

So, strong social interactions are known to be important contributors to individual productivity, and to physiological and psychological health, while denying social interaction, as in the practice of putting prisoners into solitary confinement as a punishment, has been shown to cause serious psychological and sometimes physiological ill effects, in some cases within a matter of days (International Psychological Trauma Symposium, 2008).

In their book *Social Commitments in a Depersonalized World*, Edward Lawler, Shane Thye and Jeongkoo Yoon develop their theory around social commitment. The core of this is that:

if the tasks or activities around which people interact generate a strong sense of shared responsibility, they are likely to interpret their individual feelings as jointly produced in concert with others, and therefore they are likely to attribute those feelings to salient social units... The result is stronger person-to-group commitments and patterns of behavior that reflect such affective ties.

(Lawler, Thye and Yoon, 2009)

Their argument is based around four propositions:

- The greater the non-separability of individuals' contributions to task success or failure, the stronger the perceptions of shared responsibility.

- The stronger the perceptions of shared responsibility for success or failure at a joint task, the more inclined actors are to attribute the resulting emotions to social units (small groups, organizations, communities).

- Social-unit attributions of positive emotions strengthen social commitments to the unit, whereas social-unit attributions of negative emotions weaken social commitments.

- People are more likely to stay with, invest in and sacrifice for social units to which they have stronger social commitments.

Put more simply, this means that people who have a common task to do for which they are jointly responsible commit themselves to the group. This group loyalty can have both negative and positive outcomes. A soldier who participated in the 1968 My Lai massacre during the Vietnam War explains the darker side of group cohesion:

When you are in an infantry company, in an isolated environment like this, the rules of that company are foremost. They are the things that really count. The laws back home do not make any difference. What people think of you does not matter. What matters is what people here and now think about what you are doing. What matters is how the people around you are going to see you. Killing a bunch of civilians in this way – babies, women, old men, people who were unarmed, helpless was wrong. Every American would know that. And yet this company, sitting out here isolated in this one place, did not see it that way. I am sure they did not. This group of people was all that mattered. It was the whole world. What they thought was right was right. And what they thought was wrong was wrong. The definitions for things were turned around. Courage was seen as stupidity. Cowardice was cunning and wariness, and cruelty and brutality were seen sometimes as heroic. That is what it eventually turned into.

(Bilton, 1992)

On the other hand it can be positive, at least for the organization, as Douglas Edwards author of 'I'm feeling lucky: I was Google employee no 59' explains so well:

From the beginning, Google demanded the total immersion of the true believer. All the successful start-ups in that period had this cultish quality: Yahoo, Netscape and Amazon were all run on charismatic lines, 'but at Google I think it was perhaps a bit more intense than that'. As a marketing person, he came to feel he embodied the brand in some way. 'Everything I owned for a while had the Google logo: umbrellas, towels, T-shirts, boxer shorts... it was on every pen I picked up and every piece of paper. Google did, in some ways, take over my sense of who I was.'

Many of those who joined at the start who have now left the company have tried to replicate that feeling ever since, as venture capitalists. 'They want to recapture that lightning in a bottle,' he says, 'by starting new companies'.

(Adams, 2011)

Strong social interactions are characterized by the parties involved having the skills and abilities to:

- accept that people are different and that a diversity of views and opinions builds organizational strength;

- co-operate with others in matters of work or social activity;

- sensitively assert their real thoughts and opinions in a way that respects others;

- be open and confident about themselves, their vulnerabilities and their strengths;

- listen attentively to others and respond without judgment or harshness;

- empathize with colleagues – be able to understand how they are feeling;
- respect other people regardless of differences of opinion.

Reckitt Benckiser, mentioned earlier, is one organization that actively develops and encourages these social skills that foster healthy conflict, innovation and business success. Again CEO Bart Becht comments:

> We work in groups all the time, so team spirit is also very much part of our culture. We firmly believe that by having people from different backgrounds we get new ideas on the table much quicker than other companies. We have a very strong multinational team and what we have accomplished is a team effort. If I have 10 people with different backgrounds in a room they're not going to agree. As long as I have constructive conflict, by the end of the discussion they're going to come up with a perspective which is very different. That's what I want. (German Retail Blog, 2009)

In some organizations social networks are discouraged or do not thrive. There are various reasons for this, and Table 5.2 lists some of these, together with case examples and some mitigating actions.

TABLE 5.2   Social network health

Some reasons why social networks are discouraged or do not thrive	Example	Sample mitigating action
Over-reliance on structure and rules.	'We're not allowed to talk to each other except on break times. So if we have a query it gets hard.'	Re-examine the value of the rules which encourage compliance when set against the value of relaxing rules in favour of commitment.
Distant, one-sided relationships between managers and staff.	'My manager sits in his office all day. He's just not interested in coming out and seeing how we're doing or having a chat with us as a group.' (See Resources for Seven Neurotic Styles of Management)	Develop management skills that enable employees to respond positively to the statements 'My supervisor seems to care about me as a person.' and 'My opinions seem to count.' (Two of the Gallup Q12 statements – see Resources)

TABLE 5.2   *continued*

Some reasons why social networks are discouraged or do not thrive	Example	Sample mitigating action
Excuses or blame when things go wrong or mistakes are made.	'He blamed us for not debugging the software but he's the one who does the final checking. Now we're all looking over our shoulders.'	Publicize examples of positive lessons learned from mistakes made demonstrating how the mistake ultimately benefits the organization.
Caring more for the organization's survival than for its mission.	'We've lost sight of the fact that we're here to serve the citizens. It's all about saving jobs now. We're scared of getting laid off.'	Develop employee pride in the mission/purpose of the company. Help employees feel that their job is important to mission success.
Trying to make the person fit the organization rather than appropriately fitting the organization to the person.	'I came here because they wanted my skills and expertise but I'm getting isolated by my team because I have different views on how to handle things from them.'	Groupthink has negative outcomes. Look for examples that demonstrate the value of diversity in the workforce and communicate them.
Inability or refusal to trust.	'We don't believe it when they say there'll be no job losses in the change they want to involve us in.'	Be open. Tell the facts about difficult situations. Ensure people have all the information they need to make their own choices.
Working the system.	'We've got people on this team who won't do anything more than what they're contracted to do. They're just not team players.'	Develop flexible, informal, and continuous performance review and management systems. Encourage feedback amongst team members.

Adapted from: Bailey, 2006

Technology is now enabling very close observation of face-to-face social working interactions with a view to improving their timing and quality. A team at Massachusetts Institute of Technology, for example, has created a wearable 'Sociometric Badge' that has advanced sensing, processing and feedback capabilities. The badge is capable of:

- Recognizing common daily human activities (such as sitting, standing, walking and running).

- Extracting speech features in real time to capture non-linguistic social signals such as interest and excitement, the amount of influence each person has on another in a social interaction, and unconscious back-and-forth interjections, while ignoring the words themselves in order to assuage privacy concerns.

- Performing indoor user localization by measuring received signal strength, which allows for detection of people in close physical proximity.

- Communicating with Bluetooth-enabled devices to study user behaviour and detect people in close proximity.

- Capturing face-to-face interaction time using an infrared (IR) sensor that can detect when two people wearing badges are facing each other.

In one experiment, by using the data captured the researchers were able to change the break structure of call centre employees, and by doing this increased the strength of the employees' social ties and also 'by extension increased their productivity and job satisfaction all at no cost to the organization' (Waber *et al*, 2010).

In other organizations the changing nature of work is challenging conventional methods of social interaction building. Virtual working, for example, puts a greater responsibility on managers and employees to build in the mechanisms of informal meeting and collaboration that happen naturally with physical proximity. Researchers suggest that there are four things to bear in mind in building social interactions among virtual team members (Hart, 2002):

- Close personal relationships are built one message at a time, using a variety of online communication channels.

- Communication content between team members with strong personal relationships is not personal. Interestingly, those who reported the strongest relationships with co-workers exchanged far more task-related communications that those who reported weaker relationships – in the latter the communication content was mainly personal.

- In strong personal relationships communication is frequent, short and simple. It is limited to exchange of information with little in the way of friendly exchange. An IM inquiry, 'What day is the team meeting this week?' illustrates this.

- Relationships in virtual teams are developed and strengthened through a proactive effort to solve problems that occur in the course of doing the work.

What this means for managers of virtual teams is shown in Table 5.3.

Remember too that virtual workers need to take their own steps to guard against getting isolated both from their team members and other social interaction. For overall mental and emotional health, the amount of time spent socializing matters. Gallup data suggests that people need six hours a day of social time to thrive. This includes all kinds of communication with others (e-mail, voice, face to face, IM and so on).

Developing community well-being

Paralleling the development of systems theory and advances in technology has come the development of organizations not as independent units but as part of a wider business ecosystem – or community – characterized by a co-operative approach to developing businesses within a competitive 'space'. P&G, for example, in 2001 established Connect + Develop. Their website explains:

> Historically, P&G relied on internal capabilities and those of a network of trusted suppliers to invent, develop and deliver new products and services to the market. We did not actively seek to connect with potential external partners. Similarly, the P&G products, technologies and know-how we developed were used almost solely for the manufacture and sale of P&G's core products. Beyond this, we seldom licensed them to other companies. Times have changed, and the world is more connected. In the areas in which we do business, there are millions of scientists, engineers and other companies globally. Why not collaborate with them? We now embrace open innovation, and we call our approach 'Connect + Develop'.
>
> Today, open innovation at P&G works both ways – inbound and outbound – and encompasses everything from trademarks to packaging, marketing models to engineering, and business services to design... We are interested in all types of high-quality, on-strategy business partners, from individual inventors or entrepreneurs to smaller companies and those listed in the FORTUNE 500 – even competitors. We have a lot to offer [our] business partners, and believe that together, we can create more value than we ever could alone.

TABLE 5.3   Facilitating social interaction in virtual teams

Facilitating social interaction in virtual teams	Examples of how to do this
Facilitating conversations and communication about the work.	Schedule regular conference/video call check-ins in everyone's calendar. Make sure everyone knows how to use Instant Messaging and follows mutually agreed protocols for using this. Have in mind a specific task related problem or issue that needs addressing that everyone can weigh in on.
Providing forums for sharing learning.	Design work so that people have to work together. Develop work roles, task structures, and accountability systems in a way that generates shared responsibility.
Staying alert to team member interactions and participation.	Notice the frequency and type of communication between team members. Aim to encourage frequent, short, and simple information based interactions directed towards problem solving.
Focusing first on getting the tasks done rather than building camaraderie.	Present team members with tasks to be done as joint problem solving generates a common language, shared meaning, and new knowledge. Save the personal/social information for face to face interactions or allow it to emerge between team members as they learn to trust each other through their abilities to collectively get the tasks done.
Encouraging frequent communication with team members.	Broker communication between team members. Eg 'Kim might be able to help. Give her a call.' Point out how the communication between x and y results in a positive outcome that might not have happened if the exchange had not taken place.

However the value generated from these business ecosystems should not be thought of purely in terms of financial value to the participants but in the wider context of 'public goods' or wider benefits which include (Moore, 2005):

- Creating a system of complementary capabilities and organizations that is greater than would be created by organizations acting independently. Describing Project Masiluleke, a collaboration between frog, iTeach, Praekelt Foundation and Pop!Tech, to leverage mobile-phone technology to raise AIDS-services awareness in South Africa, Robert Fabricant (VP Creative Design, frog) makes the point that 'the biggest success so far has been the collaboration itself. We have watched partners like iTeach bring design to the very center of what they do. We have worked together to help them transform community outreach workers into skilled design researchers. iTeach now runs rigorous usability tests on everything from traditional healer-referral forms to the HIV self-test' (Fabricant, 2011).

- Being able to identify in a market 'space' developing products and services that did not exist before and would not have been easily identified or identifiable without the business ecosystem. One example of this is the collaborative project between Nokia and Oxfam which, via OpenIdeo's 2011 innovation challenge, asked the global online community for its best ideas about how to improve maternal health with the help of mobile phones (Nerenberg, 2011).

- Developing the ecosystem that encourages critical contributions requires learning to work co-operatively, fostering an environment (including legal and economic processes), and structuring the eco-system in a way that shapes the future and moves society forward in particular directions. Patagonia, a specialized eco-friendly retailer of outdoor gear, has teamed up with Walmart to help that retail giant green its supply chain. Since 2008 it has been working with Walmart to develop a sustainability index for its products. Walmart is aiming to place a scorecard on its store goods, rating products on eco-friendliness and social impact (Burke, 2010).

- Innovating faster and more furiously to stay ahead of other business ecosystems, which again can work for the greater good. Take the Myelin Repair Foundation, a non-profit organization seeking a cure for multiple sclerosis. Working faster and in a very different way from big pharmaceutical companies, it is focusing on collaboration at every stage of the research and development process. The organization works on the premise that, 'A cure is not going to come from a single target, a single lab, a single researcher. It's only going to come from bringing researchers together to share their data in real time and bringing industry into the fold' (Svoboda, 2010).

Developing the health of business ecosystems requires:

- Determining with participating parties the value to each within the ecosystem. The value may be different, but recognition that the collaborative relationship is the best possible way to deliver the solution or drive the innovation is what counts for all.

- Understanding and developing the critical mass of each of the parties within the ecosystem. It is their individual capability to deliver collectively that gives the system its robustness and the ability to thrive.

- Seeking continuous performance and improvement through individual and collective learning. Participants in the ecosystem working together will learn from each other's experiences and create shared meanings and new ways of doing things (Hobcraft, 2011).

Having a sense of responsibility towards the wider ecological systems is not only part of what makes an organization healthy (and is a trait that is increasingly required by consumers of products and services), but is also (to continue the organization/human analogy) part of what makes a healthy human being. The sense of connectedness, the ability and potential to contribute to the greater good, the feeling of something bigger than the individual, and a shared emotional connection to a goal or value set – these have been demonstrated over and over again as essential to emotional and mental balance. For a theoretical underpinning look at the theory of community based on the work of McMillan and Chavis (1986) and referenced in Resources.

Pause for thought

What is the difference between a social network and community/ecosystem collaboration?

Why do organizations need to develop both strong social ties and a commitment to the wider ecological system?

What barriers might there be to organizations' ability to develop collaborative communities and ecosystems?

Exercise

Reflect on the following 12 key beliefs that, according to Bob Sutton, author of *Good Boss Bad Boss*, are held by the best bosses – and rejected, or more often simply never even thought about, by the worst bosses (Sutton, 2010).

As a result of the reflection consider what actions to take to become a better boss, or what actions to advise when coaching someone to become a better boss.

1　I have a flawed and incomplete understanding of what it feels like to work for me.

2　My success – and that of my people – depends largely on being the master of obvious and mundane things, not on magical, obscure or breakthrough ideas or methods.

3　Having ambitious and well-defined goals is important, but it is useless to think about them much. My job is to focus on the small wins that enable my people to make a little progress every day.

4　One of the most important, and most difficult, parts of my job is to strike the delicate balance between being too assertive and not assertive enough.

5　My job is to serve as a human shield, to protect my people from external intrusions, distractions and idiocy of every stripe – and to avoid imposing my own idiocy on them as well.

6　I strive to be confident enough to convince people that I am in charge, but humble enough to realize that I am often going to be wrong.

7　I aim to fight as if I am right, and listen as if I am wrong – and to teach my people to do the same thing.

8　One of the best tests of my leadership – and my organization – is: 'What happens after people make a mistake?'

9　Innovation is crucial to every team and organization. So my job is to encourage my people to generate and test all kinds of new ideas. But it is also my job to help them kill off all the bad ideas we generate, and most of the good ideas, too.

10　Bad is stronger than good. It is more important to eliminate the negative than to accentuate the positive.

11　How I do things is as important as what I do.

12　Because I wield power over others, I am at great risk of acting like an insensitive jerk – and not realizing it.

Key messages

- It is helpful to distinguish between well-being, health and effectiveness in discussions about the organizational health.

- An organization needs to have healthy structures, systems, processes and controls (the body aspects) and also develop mental, emotional and spiritual well-being. These aspects collectively constitute organizational health.

- Organizations, like people, have to be alert to developing and sustaining their mental, spiritual and emotional well-being as much as their 'bodily' or structure/system/process/control well-being.

- Three main aspects of mental, emotional and spiritual well-being to consider are: individual well-being, social interactions, and community or ecosystem building.

References

Adams, T (2011) Douglas Edwards: I was Google employee no 59 [Online] http://www.guardian.co.uk/technology/2011/jul/31/google-douglas-edwards-tim-adams (accessed 2 February 2012)

Apple (2012) Apple supplier responsibility 2012 progress report [Online] http://images.apple.com/supplierresponsibility/pdf/Apple_SR_2012_Progress_Report.pdf: Apple Inc

Bailey, T (2006) *Ties That Bind: The practice of social networks*, Annie E Casey Foundation, Baltimore

Bates, J (2009) Obstacles to worksite wellness programs [Online] http://www.wellnessproposals.com/wellness_articles/obstacles_to_worksite_wellness_programs.htm (accessed 22 January 2012)

Beckhard, R (1969) *Organization Development: Strategies and models*, Addison-Wesley, Reading, Mass

Bilton, M (1992) *Four Hours in My Lai*, Penguin, New York

Bloomberg Business Week (2007) Get healthy – or else [Online] http://www.businessweek.com/magazine/content/07_09/b4023001.htm (accessed 26 February 2012)

Bruhn, J (2001) *Trust and the Health of Organizations*, Kluwer Academic/Plenum Publishers, New York

Burke, M (2010) Walmart, Patagonia team to green business [Online] http://www.forbes.com/forbes/2010/0524/rebuilding-sustainability-eco-friendly-mr-green-jeans.html (accessed 5 February 2012)

EmployeeSurveys.com (nd) Bad bosses [Online] http://www.employeesurveys.com/bosses/badboss.htm (accessed 24 January 2012)

EmployeeSurveys.com (nd) Good bosses [Online] http://www.employeesurveys.com/bosses/goodboss.htm (accessed 24 January 2012)

Fabricant, R (2011) Fighting AIDS armed with design and a savvy partnership strategy [Online] http://www.fastcodesign.com/1665540/fighting-aids-armed-with-design-and-a-savvy-partnership-strategy (accessed 5 February 2012)

Family Services Employee Assistance Programs (nd) A success story [Online] http://thehealthline.ca/pdfs/FamilyServiceEmployeeAssistanceProgram.pdf (accessed 22 January 2012)

Gallup Healthways (2008) Gallup Healthways Wellbeing Index [Online] http://www.well-beingindex.com/ (accessed 22 January 2012)

German Retail Blog (2009) Talk with Reckitt Benckiser [Online] http://www.german-retail-blog.com/2009/04/30/interview-with-bart-becht-ceo-reckitt-benckiser/ (accessed 28 April 2012)

Good Housekeeping (2012) Various articles *Good Housekeeping*, February

Hare, R (2003) Hare Psychopathy checklist – revised [Online] http://www.mhs.com/product.aspx?gr=saf&prod=pcl-r2&id=resources#reports (accessed 28 April 2012)

Harris, R (2002) Why do people – even identical twins – differ from one another in personality [Online] http://www.edge.org/q2002/q_harris.html (accessed 28 April 2012)

Hart, R (2002) Rethinking team building in geographically dispersed teams: one message at a time, *Organizational Dynamics*, 31 (4), pp 352–61

Hobcraft, P (2011) The forming of new structures: the business ecosystem of innovation federations [Online] http://paul4innovating.com/2011/07/05/the-forming-of-new-structures-the-business-ecosystem-of-innovation-federations/ (accessed 28 April 2012)

International Psychological Trauma Symposium (2008) The Istanbul Statement on the use and effects of solitary confinement, *Torture*, 18 (1), pp 63–66

Jobs, S (2005) 'You've got to find what you love,' Jobs says, from *Stanford University News: Stanford Report* [Online] http://news.stanford.edu/news/2005/june15/jobs-061505.html (accessed 17 January 2012)

Lawler, E, Thye, SR and Yoon, J (2009) *Social Commitments in a Depersonalized World*, Russell Sage Foundation, New York

Loeppke, R (2007) Health and productivity as a business strategy, *Journal of Occupational and Environmental Medicine*, 47 (7), pp 712–21

McMillan, D and Chavis, D (1986) Sense of community: a definition and theory, *Journal of Community Psychology*, 14, pp 6–23

Moore, JF (2005) Business ecosystems and the view from the firm, *The Antitrust Bulletin*, autumn, pp 1–58

Moore, M (2012) 'Mass suicide' protest at Apple manufacturer Foxconn factory [Online] http://www.telegraph.co.uk/news/worldnews/asia/china/9006988/Mass-suicide-protest-at-Apple-manufacturer-Foxconn-factory.html (accessed 18 January 2012)

Nerenberg, J (2011) IDEO's next global challenge: using mobile tech to improve maternal care in low-income countries [Online] http://www.fastcompany.com/1720185/ideo-asks-public-for-input-on-mothers-health-and-mobile-phones (accessed 28 April 2012)

Nicolson, A (2010) *Sissinghurst: An unfinished history*, Viking, New York

Nyberg, A (2009) Managerial leadership and ischaemic heart disease among employees: the Swedish WOLF study, *Occupational and Environmental Medicine*, 66 (1), pp 51–55

Organization Development Network (2011) Principles of OD practice [Online] http://www.odnetwork.org/?page=PrinciplesOfODPracti (accessed 21 January 2012)

Rath, T (2010) Your friends and your social well-being [Online] http://gmj.gallup.com/content/127043/friends-social-wellbeing.aspx (accessed 29 January 2012)

Sutton, R (2010) 12 things good bosses believe [Online] http://blogs.hbr.org/sutton/2010/05/12_things_good_bosses_believe.html (accessed 28 April 2012)

Svoboda, E (2010) The Myelin Repair Foundation encourages collaboration for a cure [Online] http://www.fastcompany.com/magazine/150/collaborating-for-a-cure.html (accessed 5 February 2012)

Waber, B, Olguin, D, Kim, T and Pentland, A (2010) Productivity through coffee breaks: changing social networks by changing breaks structure [Online] http://papers.ssrn.com/sol3/papers.cfm?abstract_id=1586375 (accessed 3 February 2012)

Woodward, S (2004) Leading and coping with change, *Journal of Change Management*, 4 (2) (June), pp 155–83

Worley, C (1997) *Organization Development and Change*, 6th edn, South Western Publishing, Mason, Ohio

Zappos.com (2008) *Culture Book 2008*, Zappos Inc, Las Vegas

Healthy technologies

> *Across the globe, people are seeing the benefits of technology in enabling more flexible working, discovering new ways of accomplishing tasks and enhancing productivity. The consumerization of IT – defined as the migration of consumer technology and experiences into enterprise computing environments – is a well-recognized phenomenon around the world.* **(DELL AND INTEL, 2012)**

Objectives

At the end of this chapter you will be able to:

- discuss the need to rapidly adapt organizational IT policies as the technology advances;
- advise on what makes for healthy and unhealthy technology use;
- explain the differing generational attitudes to use and ownership of technology;
- assess the need to change an organization's design in response to new technologies.

New technologies are one of the forces compelling companies to rethink the way work is done. Vodafone UK, a telecoms company, is one that exemplifies this. Since Guy Laurence joined as CEO in 2009 the UK headquarters in Newbury has been transformed. Gone are the offices, private printers and the trappings of status and power. Instead laptops have replaced desktop PCs, mobile and softphones have replaced desk phones, wi-fi has replaced fixed broadband connections and paper is a thing of the past. No one has a dedicated desk, and everyone is so mobile that they can pitch up wherever they are needed. [We] have a range of meeting rooms with the latest AV and video conferencing technologies. (Laurence, 2012)

The technologies are very powerful, enabling dramatic shifts in the way space is occupied and used, and in the way people do their work. Figures 6.1 and 6.2 summarize some of the changes organizations are experiencing.

Deployed thoughtfully, technologies can support significant organizational performance improvements. Vodafone, for example established baseline performance measures in 2006–07, before Laurence joined, and since the start of his leadership has achieved the following:

- an estimated £45 million from reduced travel and energy expenses;
- reduction in office space by 19 per cent;
- a saving of almost 2.5 million sheets of A4 paper;
- a net annual saving of more than 24,000 tonnes of CO_2 emissions and approximately £11.5 million in 2010/11 compared with 2006/07;
- revenue growth of more than 6 per cent, compared with a 0.7 per cent decline seen by its closest competitor (Laurence, 2012).

FIGURE 6.1   Current and future work styles

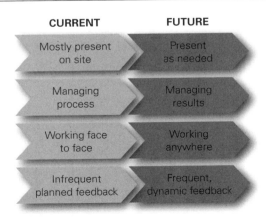

SOURCE: Stanford 2012.

FIGURE 6.2 Current and future workplace

CURRENT	FUTURE
My space Assigned – Sole Occupancy	**Our shared space** Assigned – Shared Occupancy
Roaming/ telework from my space	Roaming/ telework from unassigned space
Private offices	Limited enclosed work space – based on function
Traditional space assignment	Zones with fluid boundaries & common support

SOURCE: Stanford 2012.

But leveraging the technology to improve business performance is not plain sailing. Making the right choices for a particular situation is an art, particularly since technology is advancing at the same time as the choices are being made. A similar situation faces doctors. Technology advances in medicine mean that a wide range of approaches are available to prevent and treat illness, and to maintain health. Helping individuals choose what is right for them requires diagnostic skills, knowledge of the risks and side effects of any treatment plan, and careful monitoring and follow-up of the plan that is then agreed and followed.

And unlike mainstream medical advances, which are subject to well-established regulatory oversight and strict scrutiny before being released for prescription and treatment, technology advances are leapfrogging the regulatory controls, forcing policymakers to scramble to catch up. Take the case of the 2012 US efforts to clamp down on the piracy of copyrighted materials beyond US borders: the Stop Online Piracy Act (SOPA) and the Protect IP Act, both of which failed in the wake of international and multinational company protests. Google, Facebook, Twitter, Zynga, eBay,

Mozilla, Yahoo, AOL and LinkedIn were among others who wrote letters to key members of the US Senate and House of Representatives, saying SOPA poses 'a serious risk to our industry's continued track record of innovation and job creation, as well as to our nation's cybersecurity' (McCullagh, 2012).

This scramble is not only at an international level but also at an organizational level. A government employee working in an IT department makes the point:

> We have well established guidelines and policies on what websites can be accessed on our government-issued laptops and computers. But these are falling apart as we are now issuing smartphones and people can download apps that we are not able to control. We are generating a list of approved apps but this doesn't stop people from doing their own thing and we currently don't have a solution to this.

Beyond the policy and regulatory frameworks, the relationship of the expert to the consumer is changing. Employees push to be able to use their preferred technologies in the workplace, and patients can access information that enables them to feel on a par with the expert doctor. Thus the technology challenges facing organizations are significant, not just in the way technology is and is not regulated but also in the way it is introduced, used and monitored for side effects. Although all registered medical drugs come with a health warning on side effects, this is not the case for technologies.

Without the regulated and tested side-effects warnings, people are prey to technology use misinformation, misuse and rumour. And here technology use and personal health intersect. For example, claims have been made that internet use is addictive and may increase loneliness and depression, or that always-on, multitasking work environments are killing productivity, dampening creativity and making us unhappy, and that mobile phone use causes brain cancer. It is notable that none of these claims have been verified when they are researched and tested. In the case of mobile (cell) phone use and brain cancer the US National Cancer Institute reports:

> Although there have been some concerns that radiofrequency energy from cell phones held closely to the head may affect the brain and other tissues, to date there is no evidence from studies of cells, animals, or humans that radiofrequency energy can cause cancer.
>
> It is generally accepted that damage to DNA is necessary for cancer to develop. However, radiofrequency energy, unlike ionizing radiation, does not cause DNA damage in cells, and it has not been found to cause cancer in animals or to enhance the cancer-causing effects of known chemical carcinogens in animals. (National Cancer Institute, 2011)

TABLE 6.1 Technology and use trends

Technology category (not an exhaustive list)	Organizational examples	Key use trends
User generated media	Wikipedia, blogs, My Space, YouTube, Flickr	**1** Increasing growth of crowdsourcing
Social media	LinkedIn, Yammer, Facebook, Salesforce chatter, instant messaging, Twitter, Sharepoint	**2** Differing intergenerational and cultural use of technology
E-mail	Gmail for enterprise, Microsoft outlook, Lotus Notes	**3** Changing organizational 'ownership' of technology
Tracking and measurement systems	Various surveillance software and hardware	**4** Designing different organizations in response to the possibilities new technologies offer
Mobile devices	Smartphones, notebook computers, laptops, i-pads, MP3 players, e-book readers	**5** Responding to the changing relationship between employees and employer in response to the possibilities new technologies offer.
Internet search	Bing, Google, Yahoo	
Business enterprise software solutions	Business intelligence Customer relationship management Enterprise performance management Governance, risk and compliance Microsoft office products Sustainability management software	

TABLE 6.1 *continued*

Technology category (not an exhaustive list)	Organizational examples	Key use trends
Video, on-line meetings, teleconference technologies (Sometimes bundled as information and communications technology or ICT)	Telepresence, softphones, webex	
Space (real estate) utilization software	Security badge readers, room and resource scheduling software, occupancy detection systems	
Various technical systems to manage specific aspects of the business	For example in 2011 Tesco, a UK supermarket chain installed a "comprehensive 'sat-nav' system inside a store. The new service is able to show you where all your wanted products are on a store map, show you where you are on that map, and guide you round the store to pick up your products using the shortest route." (Techfortesco, 2011, May 23)	
Data visualization	Obizmedia, visual.ly, i-dashboard	
Cloud computing	Amazon web services, Google, Rackspace, IBM, Microsoft	

So what does make for healthy organizational and employee adoption and use of technology, and what does unhealthy use of it look and feel like? Rather than tackling that as a single question, it is more helpful to consider the technology in different categories, look at some associated use trends, and discuss how taken together these might result in healthy and unhealthy deployment in the workplace. Table 6.1 shows in the first column some common categories of organizational technologies, in the second a few examples of the technology type, and in the third some of the emerging trends around technology adoption and use. Note that there is a risk in naming technology companies as examples because many of them have only a short life.

The remainder of this chapter discusses each of the five key use trends and its associated technologies, looking specifically at the impact of these on organizational and individual health.

Pause for thought

What technologies have become mainstream in the last year?

What impact are these having on the way organizations are designed and operated?

What use trends (beyond the five listed in Table 6.1) are evolving as an outcome of new technology introduction?

Increasing growth of crowdsourcing

Crowdsourcing is a term coined by Jeff Howe in a 2006 Wired article 'The rise of crowdsourcing'. Briefly, crowdsourcing is a method of tapping into the general public by asking members to help work on or complete business-related tasks and activities. Often the crowdsourcing initiatives are framed as a public challenge. The US Federal Government has a website **www.challenge.gov** that lists current challenges in various categories. And, similarly, state and city governments offer challenges. For example, in 2011 the US City of Boston and Innocentive, an open innovation and crowdsourcing company, teamed up on a challenge to develop a smartphone app that allows drivers in the city to help track and predict where potholes develop. The Street Bump app keeps track of bumps while driving, as well as their location, and passes all the data on to the city to help it address repairs more quickly and efficiently. Think through the impact of this development on the day-to-day operation of the department that repairs potholes.

Often the challenges are incentivized with monetary or status prizes for the winners. The DARPA (Defense Advanced Research Project Agency) shredder challenge is another example of a US government challenge. This challenge was to work out a method of reconstructing shredded documents.

> Almost 9,000 teams registered to participate in DARPA's Shredder Challenge. Thirty-three days after the challenge was announced, one small San Francisco-based team correctly reconstructed each of the five challenge documents and solved their associated puzzles. The 'All Your Shreds Are Belong to US' team, which won the $50,000 prize, used custom-coded, computer-vision algorithms to suggest fragment pairings to human assemblers for verification. In total, the winning team spent nearly 600 man-hours developing algorithms and piecing together documents that were shredded into more than 10,000 pieces.
> (DARPA, 2011)

Collaboration, open-innovation and crowdsourcing are all similar constructs in that they draw on the collective intelligence of people outside the organization rather than relying only on the brains of employees of the organization. And it is not only governments that are opening up to crowdsourcing to help solve problems, drive innovation or advance knowledge. Increasingly companies are doing this through collaboration with the public: Kraft Foods, Amazon, Fiat and Dupont are among these.

But a leader in the open innovation field is P&G, a household products company, which in 2001 established a programme, 'Connect + Develop', to foster innovation. It did this as a response to declining growth and the felt need to accelerate innovation from both inside and outside the company.

To maximize reach to the public P&G uses a range of technology, including LinkedIn, Twitter and Facebook, and their own website Connect and Develop. Chris Thoen, who runs P&G's open innovation practice, explains the responsibilities that using this technology to reach out to people brings:

> If you put a message out there you have to be willing to engage with the people who connect with you... We want to provide to people and universities, etc, an open door where they can come in and talk about their opportunity. That brings obligations. When someone knocks on your door you have to be responsive to that party and their potential solution. So when you engage you have to be sure you have the resources internally to respond and have the technical people to do the due diligence and to link it to the business units and do this with immediate responsiveness. (Shaughnessy, 2011a)

To get the engagement with the public and partner companies right requires a particular type of employee and again Chris Thoen elaborates:

> If you start in open innovation you need a special profile of people who are seasoned within the organization and know how the business is going and have a strong internal network to create the firm's responsiveness. The best people have three profiles:
>
> 1 What we call a T profile. This means breadth and depth fusing specialization and generalization. They are comfortable to talk today about genomics and tomorrow about nanotechnology and the next day about nuclear. They have the breadth that they need to get these subjects. They have sufficient depth to understand the topic and ask the difficult and dangerous questions and the intuition to know when to dig deeper.
>
> 2 The three legged stool. The technical mastery, the organizational mastery and the business mastery. The technical mastery is straightforward. The organizational mastery, understanding how decisions are made in your company and in other companies, the other company; to understand what drives the company on a business level and on a people level, who are the real decision makers, influencers and executors; how to drive the different audiences with a different message. The business mastery is to put opportunities into the context of a market in words that make sense to an audience through the elevator pitch, the two minutes to explain a technical solution to a commercial colleague.
>
> 3 Balance. A balance between hard skills and soft skills. The soft skills are interpersonal. Ultimately all this is a people business and is all about relationships and building trusts between different cultures and people. You have to represent your company and the partner company within your company. Not everyone can set up these relationships. Talented technologists might be arrogant and could drive people away.
>
> (Shaughnessy, 2011b)

Getting the right level of responsiveness and the right type of engagement with the people whose ideas are being sought is one of the signs of healthy crowdsourcing. Others healthy indicators include:

- development of the connection between the organization and their 'audiences';
- testing of products or services as they are being developed in the informal market, meaning they are more robust from the start;
- reduction in the cost of successful innovation;
- emergence as leaders in the marketplace of people who would not otherwise get the chance to showcase their skills and talents.

On the other hand crowdsourcing is not all great. Some of the unhealthy aspects include:

- lack of acknowledgment of contributions or contributors;
- conflict and competition between employees and the contributors they are working with;
- degradation in the traditional notion of 'professionalism' if amateurs are able to compete in the marketplace in a way that drives out the professionals;
- low quality of a response that does not always match the investment in crowdsourcing;
- unexpected direct and indirect costs in bringing an idea to implementation;
- issues of trust and intellectual property rights if there is insufficient infrastructure in place to support the crowdsourcing venture;
- reliance on people willing to work for free or nearly free.

Differing intergenerational use of technology

The Millennial generation (those born between about 1980 and 2000) are growing up as 'digital natives' with very different learning styles and experiences that are pushing huge changes in the workforce. In a classic piece, *Growing up Digital: How the web changes work, education, and the ways people learn*, published in 2000, John Seely Brown, then Chief Scientist of Xerox, a document services company, defined four key shifts in the way people growing up in a web-based world would learn and interact with each other compared with previous generations:

- Literacy is no longer text based but also image and screen literacy. Seely Brown describes this as having the ability to read multimedia texts and to feel comfortable 'with new multiple-media genres'. The new literacy is 'information navigation' – being able to navigate effectively through confusing and complex information spaces.
- Learning is not now derived from an authority figure standing in front of a class but via discovery learning gained by web browsing. There are formal examples of this; iTunes U is one, and the UK's

Open University OpenLearn courses and various US universities (Yale, MIT) offering similar free programmes are others. And there are hosts of informal learning routes, for example via podcasts, e-books, TED talks, YouTube instructional videos, infographics, blogs and wikis.

- Reasoning is no longer deductive, linear and abstract but construed through judgment and 'bricolage': that is, construction or creation of a point of view or an increase in skills and knowledge from a diverse range of available things, channels and whatever resources are to hand. Seely Brown makes the point that much knowledge comes from social interactions through communities of practice – Meetup is an example of an organization that enables this kind of lateral learning. CEO Scott Heiferman explains:

> When you think, 'this year I'm going to run that half-marathon,' that you don't just watch a video about how to train, you don't just read a webpage about how to train for that half-marathon, but that it just feels natural to say, 'oh I wonder if there's a Meetup in my neighborhood on Saturday of people who are running the half-marathon... because we'll be more likely to succeed'. (Betabeat, 2012)

- People have a bias towards action that is rooted in trying something out rather than being taught first how to do something. Seely Brown sees the digital generation using the web 'not only as an informational and social resource but as a learning medium where understanding is socially constructed and shared... In that medium learning becomes a part of action and knowledge creation' (Seely Brown, 2000).

A 24-year-old data analyst working for a multinational corporation, speaking in 2012, bears out Seely Brown's thinking:

> I've got a work and home laptop, an iPhone, and an iPod. I use twitter, Facebook, e-mail, Google docs, and spend a good amount of time surfing the internet. I probably do about 50 searches a day. Google is my real teacher – anything I need to research I can get there – it's quick and it's learning as I need it. The amount of information people are subject to each day is completely different now than even a few years ago. You have to become much better at filtering out stuff. You choose what to hold on to and what to discard. I probably read 200 tweets on my way into work today.
> It's amazing how quickly things get adopted now. There's increasing speed in the power of technology to evolve, the power of people to adapt to it, and the power of the information available from it. Self-teaching is becoming the norm. And people are learning and teaching themselves in an organic way as needed.

Having grown up via personal computers and mobile phones, it is evident that Millennials do not always draw the line between work and personal, virtual and physical, sanctioned and prohibited. In their use of technology, it is not 'would you approve this, boss?' but 'whatever gets the job done'. Research by Accenture, a consulting company, found that the research underscores the connected-anywhere anytime-multi-tasked-through-any apps-or-gadgets-I-choose-regardless of-official-policy-so-just-deal-with-it nature of Millennials' behaviour (Accenture, 2010).

For the most part, older people in the workforce are much less familiar with the digital territory than their younger colleagues. In healthy organizations this results in upward mentoring, good intergenerational knowledge transfer, and willingness on the part of the less proficient to experiment with new technologies and learn how they work for business benefit. The same 24-year-old explains how he worked with an older colleague:

> I worked with a much older colleague who had a depth of technical expertise that I didn't have but I had the knowledge of the sophistication of Excel that he didn't have. Together we made a good team because we each supported the other. We felt our skills were complementary. Over time he got a lot better at using Excel and I learned a lot about portfolio management.

This example also illustrates the point that devices and software can be adapted and/or used in different ways by different people, depending on their skills, preferences, their role and their job function. With the range of choices available and their inherent flexibility, it is possible for people to stick with systems or approaches that they know and trust but simultaneously be interfacing effectively with people who are much more technologically savvy.

It is worth noting however, that it is not wise to make an assumption that all Millennials are 'digital natives' and all older generation workforce members are stuck in the age of pencil and paper. A quick glance at some 2011 statistics on Facebook use shows that age is not necessarily a factor in technology use.

> In this Pew internet sample, 79 per cent of American adults said they used the internet and nearly half of adults (47 per cent), or 59 per cent of internet users, say they use at least one of the social networking sites (SNS). This is close to double the 26 per cent of adults (34 per cent of internet users) who used a SNS in 2008. Among other things, this means the average age of adult-SNS users has shifted from 33 in 2008 to 38 in 2010. Over half of all adult SNS users are now over the age of 35. Some 56 per cent of SNS users now are female.
> (Hampton, 2011)

The 24-year-old quoted earlier tells the story of his parents and three siblings who all now have smartphones. But they all use them in very different ways.

> We started off by teaching my mum and dad how to use a smartphone but now they have got good at it. It's interesting that everyone in my family uses the same type of device differently. We're using the same technology in different ways. My Dad uses his BlackBerry mainly to message with co-workers or reply to e-mail. My Mum does a lot of photo stuff with her iPhone. And me and my brothers and sister all have different apps that we use regularly. It really shows how technology needs to be (and can be) adaptable to role and function.

Pause for thought

What value is there in organizations assuming that different generations approach technology differently?

How can organizations help avoid employee conflicts and frustration over different abilities to use technology?

What impact does easy access to information have on the way people learn in organizations? Is the learning and development department a thing of the past?

Changing organizational 'ownership' of technology

Access to information on the internet has fundamentally changed the way people maintain their health and interact with their doctors. Research suggests that 70 per cent of the population seeking medical information turn first to online sources (Porter Novelli, 2011). And in the same way that people visiting doctors are now able to go armed with knowledge of their condition, to ask probing questions about medications prescribed, and to work with their doctors to make appropriate health decisions, so employees armed with IT skills and products are changing the relationship they have with their IT departments.

No longer are employees content with using company issued equipment and software. In many cases they are buying, bringing and using their preferred set-up with or without organizational permission – this is the trend known as the consumerization of IT. The capability of personally owned technology now means that employees are increasingly able to blur the boundaries between work and personal life, challenging the role of the IT department as guardians of the type of hardware and software to be used during a traditional 9:00 to 5:00 working day.

This is now forcing IT companies to consider 'bring your own device' (BYOD) or 'bring your own computer' (BYOC) policies and programmes. At Kraft Foods, for example, the IT department's involvement in choosing technology for employees is limited to handing out a sum of money. Employees use the money to buy whatever laptop they want from Amazon.com or the local Apple store.

'We heard from people saying, "How come I have better equipment at home?"' said Mike Cunningham, chief technology officer for Kraft Foods. 'We said, hey, we can address that.' Encouraging employees to buy their own laptops, or bring their mobile phones and iPads from home, is gaining traction in the workplace (Kopytoff, 2011).

Kraft Foods is not alone; the BOYD movement is rapidly gaining pace. Gartner, a technology research company, predicts that 90 per cent of companies will support corporate applications on personal mobile devices by 2014. Their assessment is that this trend is being driven by individual employees who 'prefer to use private consumer smartphones or notebooks for business, rather than using old-style limited enterprise devices' (Plummer, 2011).

Research from Forrester, another IT research company, supports this view, adding that in 2010 formal BYOD programmes were still rare, with only 6 per cent of companies they surveyed having programmes in place. However, 58 per cent of companies surveyed expected a growth in the number of employees bringing smartphones to work, whether BYOD-supported or not (Figure 6.3).

In businesses that allow BYOD today (2012), nearly a third of the mobile devices connecting to the corporate network are employee-owned. Most of these – 66 per cent – are laptops, but a quarter are smartphones and nearly 10 per cent are tablets. This suggests that not only are more people working from their own devices, but they are also accessing their corporate applications and data from more than one personal system (Desktone, 2012). Indeed over 50 per cent of workers reported using three or more personal devices at work (Perez, 2012).

This push from employees to use their own devices has two key ramifications. First employers and their IT departments really have no choice but to go with this flow. For the IT department this means:

FIGURE 6.3   Use of BYOD

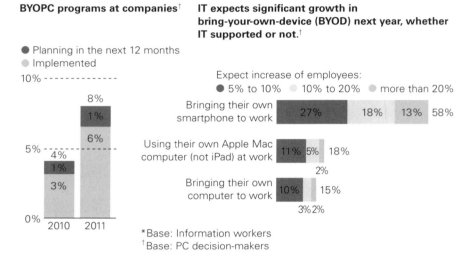

Compared with employees' actions, IT's use of bring-your-own-PC (BYOPC) programs is low.

BYOPC programs at companies[†]

● Planning in the next 12 months
● Implemented

10% - - - - - - - - - - - - -

8%
1%

6%

5% - - - - - - - - - - - - -
4%
1%

3%

0%
2010   2011

IT expects significant growth in bring-your-own-device (BYOD) next year, whether IT supported or not.[†]

Expect increase of employees:
● 5% to 10%   ● 10% to 20%   ● more than 20%

Bringing their own smartphone to work
27%   18%   13%   58%

Using their own Apple Mac computer (not iPad) at work
11%   5%   18%
2%

Bringing their own computer to work
10%   15%
3% 2%

*Base: Information workers
†Base: PC decision-makers

SOURCE: Forrester 2012.

- Thinking differently about the risks, business continuity, security, privacy and confidentiality aspects of technology.

- Reviewing the skills and capabilities of IT employees. A BYOD environment is very different to operate from a traditional organizational IT environment.

- Educating the workforce on the protocols of a BYOD environment.

- Maintaining interfaces and compatibilities between the full range of devices in use.

- Collaborating with other functional areas to enable employees to benefit from bringing their own device. For example, one of the employee benefits is flexibility – an employee can be receiving work e-mails at home on his own device in the evening. But this means examining working hours, possible overtime payments, taxation issues and so on.

- Supporting a variety of mobile platforms.

Second, organizations will have to reinvent the way they measure and reward productivity and being at work. One government organization that is encouraging employees to telework is using the tag line: 'work is what you do not where you are or when you do it,' thus reinforcing the point that a daily presence in a physical space owned by the employer is not the future of work.

Employees are increasingly able, and want, to blur the boundaries between work and personal stuff – for example by doing online shopping while in the workplace, or answering e-mails at the weekend. Failure to recognize this more flexible approach to doing the work will result in loss of motivation and productivity if employees are forced into either an enterprise IT solution box or a cultural norm of a 9:00 to 5:00 day at an employer's facility. Additionally there is the risk to retention and competitive standing if employers hang back from taking the direction of IT consumerization. But going with the flow of BYOD means rethinking the policies and processes of work, specifically:

- managing remote and virtual workers;
- devising valid and appropriate productivity measures;
- developing feedback and performance systems that are more than the annual appraisal;
- instilling values of organizational trust, eg not to surf inappropriate websites;
- recognizing and accommodating the individual differences in technology preferences and use in doing the work;
- developing policies around employee-owned device use and support.

A likely outcome of the move to consumerization of IT and BYOD is the increasing alignment of IT and HR. Indeed one report suggests that workplace IT of the future will not merely be a tool to accomplish tasks, but will be a means of recruiting and retaining staff, of managing well-being, and of facilitating personal and professional development. This raises the intriguing question of whether IT departments will take on significant aspects of the current role of HR departments, with a related shrinking of the size and scope of the latter (Dell and Intel, 2011).

Designing different organizations in response to the possibilities new technologies offer

The huge range of technologies available and in the pipeline is forcing organizations to rethink their business models and designs irrespective of other forces. This is very evident in the medical field; Cisco's Healthpresence, for example, is part of an integrated solution that enables local and remote team collaboration, patient examinations and consultations. The example below illustrates the potential of this approach:

> Deepak Chandrasekar has been wondering why his right eye has been so red recently, which is what brought him to see the doctor today. Dr Seema Sangwan examines his eye and inquires about whether he also has an itchy throat. 'Look up, please,' she asks her patient, peering closely at the eye, finally determining that his symptoms are consistent with allergies. She prescribes some antihistamine eyedrops and recommends scheduling a follow-up appointment. It's a pretty routine medical exam. Except that Sangwan isn't in the same room with her patient – she appears in front of him on a giant home-theater-esque display.
>
> Chandrasekar was diagnosed remotely with the aid of videoconferencing and high-tech medical equipment that transmitted images, blood-pressure readings, and heart-rate data to Sangwan. Xenia Khesin, the on-site nurse, focused a high-resolution video camera on Chandrasekar's eye and instantly a magnified image of his eye appeared on a smaller monitor next to the main video display in their location. Sangwan saw the same image on her computer screen, which was how she was able to diagnose Chandrasekar's problem. (Svoboda, 2011)

Other companies are following suit in overturning conventional models of health care. In 2011 GE Healthcare and Intel joined forces to form a new company, Care Innovations, that went live in January 2011, from a combination of GE Healthcare's Home Health Division and Intel's Digital Health Group. It bills itself as 'aimed at being a catalyst for changing healthcare models. To do so, we create technology-based solutions that give people confidence to live independently' (Care Innovations, 2011).

Similarly HP, a technology company, teamed up with Lifebot, a telemedicine company (see Glossary), to develop an ambulance-to-hospital solution for live streaming video and 'play-by-play' between ambulance personnel, doctors and hospital emergency departments (Moreno, 2011).

What is interesting about these examples is that they are all three indicative of the trend towards new forms of organization that are developing innovative products and services driven by advancing technologies:

- Cisco's Healthpresence is a product and service offered by the company to clients. So in that respect it is doing no more than extending its line. But think now of the organizational processes, systems, control mechanisms, structures and so on that will have changed in the client companies as this type of technology is introduced into conventional medical settings where a patient meets face-to-face with a doctor.

- GE Healthcare and Intel jointly created a new company that is designed around the collaborative model described earlier. As they state 'Our customers are our driving force. We are committed to collaborating with you to deliver human-centered solutions that people will use.'
- HP and Lifebot formed a partnership to leverage each other's capabilities around their respective technologies, products and services.

Although it would be easy to say at this point that there's nothing different about these three organization designs a closer examination shows that:

- The companies involved are directly both responding to and innovating around the capabilities of emerging technology to offer new products and services.
- They are operating much less as independent companies and much more as members of complex business ecosystems.

Current thinking converges around the notion that innovation of the type the three companies exemplify is best developed through business ecosystems, a form of intentional development of communities of economic co-ordination where multiple parties join forces to 'co-ordinate innovation across complementary contributions arising within multiple markets and hierarchies' (Moore, 2005). From this, if things go well, the business ecosystems co-evolve and adapt to continuously changing contexts. Figure 6.4 illustrates the ecosystem in China of Novozymes, a biotechnology company.

The importance of the business ecosystem is underlined by Michael Christensen, president of Novozymes China, who remarked in a media briefing in December 2011 that the company was in talks over a series of collaborative projects with 'six or seven' firms aimed to boost its presence in China (Reuters, 2011). Later, at the 7th EU-China Business Summit held in Beijing in February 2012, he said:

> The technology of turning biomass into biofuels is ready. It is now, more than ever, we need to have a closer tie with the government for policy requirements to secure demand and support production. We believe that, a growing partnership at both business and political level is crucial to further deepen EU–China co-operation on energy and be part of maintaining stable and sustainable economic growth. (Novozymes, 2012)

Although there is a lot of information on the value of the business ecosystem for driving innovation, and there is some information on ecosystem business

FIGURE 6.4 Novozymes' business ecosystem

Building Strong Relationships and Partnerships
Across the Value Chain is Instrumental

SOURCE: Novozymes.

models, there is very little concrete and practical information on the way
to structure them for success. Each member of the ecosystem has its own
perspective, capabilities, goals and incentives. The question remains of how
they can be encouraged and enabled to act in ways that pave the way for this
type of inclusive business model to succeed.

There are some clues and possibilities that could inform healthy business
ecosystem building. These centre around four aspects of the organization:
space, people, process and technology.

- *Space*: Design maximum physical and virtual space for collaboration
  between and within ecosystem members – small meeting spaces,
  coffee areas, casual contact possibilities, and ability to reconfigure
  the space on an as-needed basis, allowing for what the urban theorist
  Jane Jacobs calls 'knowledge spillovers'.

- *People*: Build project teams and networks with diverse members within and between the ecosystem as this enables strong innovation. But simultaneously recognize that much innovation is drawn from individuals thinking in isolation about a problem and solving it themselves. (Think Archimedes and 'Eureka'.)

- *Process*: Structure around work processes. Henry Chesbrough, an academic and writer on innovation, argues that open innovation in products and services is the way forward. By open innovation he means moving outside an organization's boundaries to innovate. For example involving customers in innovation (look back at the crowdsourcing section in this chapter) requires processes that support this kind of initiative, with the surrounding structures acting as support.

- *Technology*: Keep up to date with evolving technology. It is both an innovation enabler and an innovation requirement. Amazon, an e-retailer, is known as a great innovator, and continues to evolve its business model by staying on top of the technology wave and using new technologies to enable its future success.

Responding to the changing relationship between employees and employer in response to the possibilities new technologies offer

The ongoing breakdown of the workplace–personal life divide – enabled by workers using their own technologies and thus bypassing enterprise provision of technology services in order to use what is easiest and most convenient – is a fact of organizational life today. There is no going back to a world of IT department command and control of technology. So given that employees are able to use their own technology devices in the work that they do, and that the technologies allow workers to work flexibly in an anytime/ anywhere way, what does an employee-driven IT demand mean for the relationship between employees and employer?

- It means that human capital management practices and processes themselves have to start using the mobile technologies to enhance employee engagement, increase employee productivity and attract new recruits.

- It means that organizations have to take steps to help employees work healthily and effectively in a potentially always-on environment.

- It means that managers have to learn to manage their workforce in a new way, realizing that traditional command-and-control approaches must give way to 'cultivate and collaborate'.

- It means that employees of all ranks have to be skilled in using the technology to best advantage.

Human capital management (HCM) processes

Gaining ground, starting in around 2009 and partly driven by the expectations of employees and potential employees' organizations, and partly driven by the need to be more efficient and make quicker decisions, organizational HR Departments started to use mobile devices (see Glossary) to make available a full range of HR service applications including:

- filling out travel and expense forms;
- requesting vacation time;
- filling out time and attendance sheets;
- updating benefit information;
- accessing payroll data;
- updating direct-deposit information;
- accessing benefit and retirement data;
- accessing organizational charts;
- accessing sick days and vacation days.

For employees this means that, whether they are in the office or on the move, they have ready access to the full suite of information whenever and wherever they need it. This translates into both higher employee satisfaction and higher productivity. The case of Merck & Co, a $27.4 billion pharmaceutical company, illustrates this form of mobile HR in action. Martin Khun, executive director for strategic marketing operations and commercial support for the Asia/Pacific region of Merck Sharpe & Dohme, a Merck & Co subsidiary, explains:

> I have direct reports scattered from India to Hong Kong, and [before the technology] a local administrator handled all human resources issues. It was painful and tedious. It took 150 e-mails to get anything done. All the employees had to have a local manager, even though they reported to me. Whenever I wanted to make a change for an employee, I had to write to the local HR

person, who by proxy handled every kind of approval – from vacation requests to expense reports. One country had limited electronic access, so every request had to be scanned and sent to me via e-mail, with originals sent by snail-mail for final approval.

[Now] Basic requests can be handled anytime, anywhere in the world, via any computing device, including smartphones and tablets. All my employees can sign on and apply for leave or any other request. When someone gets back from a trip, they submit their expenses, and the request pops up on my screen and I approve it. They get paid in their local currency, but the approval comes from me. (Bloomberg Business Week Research Services, 2011)

Always-on environment

The lowering costs, easy availability and intuitive use of small, portable devices means that 'everyone' in the workforce has access to them. At the same time people are increasingly working with colleagues in other time zones. Martin Khun, quoted above, notes that mobile devices are simply part of working life today.

> Now, whether you're office-bound or not, you have a mobile device. A product manager here in Australia might want to talk to a global brand team in the United States, and there's a 12-hour time difference. That means either going into the office at odd hours or using a mobile device at home. And with that device, if I'm at my kids' hockey game on Saturday morning in Sydney, I can still be in touch with the US where it's Friday afternoon.
>
> (Bloomberg Business Week Research Services, 2011)

Not only that, the range of channels for receiving information – e-mail, telephone, blogs, tweets, and, social networks – make for a tendency to multitask. Who hasn't participated in a meeting while simultaneously answering e-mail and texting a colleague? Multitasking leads to continuous partial attention and 'techno stress'. The result of this is errors, inability to focus, think creatively or make good decisions. Additionally it can have social repercussions. Working on another task while someone is speaking can easily upset the speaker if they feel they are not being paid attention to.

Multitasking and the always-on environment put detrimental stresses on both individual and organizational health. A healthy organization helps individuals learn how to put boundaries around work and personal life, and encourages people to practise:

- *Focusing*: This includes shutting down e-mail, closing web browsers, having phone calls go automatically to voice mail; software like **www.rescuetime.com** that tracks time spent on various tasks can help individuals manage time more effectively.

TABLE 6.2 Changing management approaches

Management aspect to consider	Why it is important	Healthy example	Unhealthy example
Managing with a collaborative, involving style	Easy access to information impacts the traditional notion of hierarchy. A manager may be no more knowledgeable than his team members. Resting on hierarchy gets in the way of getting the work done.	'She's very good at involving us in all forms of decision making – like who we should hire onto the team, what should go into the report to upper management. It's not all brainstorming and stuff but good adults to adults relationship amongst us. She knows we know as much as her about the situation.'	'My manager always thinks he knows best. It's very wearing. Even if I can produce a good business case or evidence for an alternative view he won't take a look at it. Often I think it's like working with my 3-year old.'
Developing a sense of visibility and community membership amongst workers	Remote or virtual workers can feel isolated and out of touch with on-site workers. They worry about career progression if they are not being seen about the place.	'We've set up online chat rooms where we talk daily about work stuff – manager included, we have video conferences weekly and every quarter or so, funding permitting we get together in our regions. The whole global team gets together in one spot about once a year. We had a virtual Christmas Party which was great fun. We all had our webcams, played party games, and ate food we'd made by exchanging recipes online first so we each made another person's recipe that appealed to us. That sort of thing creates a sense of being part of the team and my manager is very conscious of how important that is.	'Weeks could go by and I would just get an occasional e-mail from my manager. I felt she didn't really know or care what I did. I decided I would go back on-site in spite of the long commute. It's better but she still isn't good at small things that would oil the community wheels and I feel sorry for my remote colleagues. I've suggested that my manager hold a teleconference call each week at a minimum to rope everyone in. But she's very reluctant.'

TABLE 6.2 *continued*

Management aspect to consider	Why it is important	Healthy example	Unhealthy example
Managing both outcomes and outputs (See Glossary)	Instituting an outcome based results-only work environment, aims to replace business thinking that equates physical presence with productivity. This form of measurement is more clearly aligned to a mobile, flexible, virtual workforce. Recognizing the importance of mutual trust between employers and employees is the key, but there is still a challenge in finding output measures. For production workers, productivity is readily measured in terms of units of output; for transaction workers, in operations per hour.	Organizations define goals and objectives with their employees that are in line with the job role and function. 'The value of internal consulting is very hard to measure in an outcome way but we are learning how to do it. Each month we work with our manager to set monthly goals. We work out with him what would be successful outcomes of our work. Often it's tied to things like increases in the customer satisfaction score. We also use an online performance management tool that enables us to collect feedback from various people. It's very helpful.'	'There's a lot of anxiety in our department around the performance measures. We're supposed to be working in a results only environment but we don't really know what that means. There's a lot of confusion about what are acceptable outcomes that show we are working and producing benefit for the organization.'

- *Filtering*: This means learning how to let go of things that are distractions, sidetracks, or better delegated.

- *Forgetting about work every once in a while*: In a humorous article about e-mail Lucy Kellaway, a *Financial Times* columnist, references Chris Anderson, 'curator' of the TED conferences, who has a rule to turn off the computer sometimes. He suggests sending an automated reply to e-mails: 'Thank you for your note. As a personal commitment to me and my family's mental health, I now do e-mail only on Wednesdays. I'll reply to as many as I can next Wednesday. Thanks for writing. Don't forget to smell the roses' (Kellaway, 2011).

Changing management approaches

Managers are learning to stop and rethink how to manage differently, given the power and ubiquity of mobile devices in common organizational use. Briefly there are three key aspects to consider when working with technology-enabled employees who may be a mix of remote and on-site, and these are summarized in Table 6.2.

Pause for thought

What other impacts on management role and style is technology making?

How is personal ownership of technology devices affecting the way work is done in functions beyond IT and HR?

What different organizational designs are emerging as a result of the technologies working across business ecosystems?

Is a results-only work environment, where people are measured on outcomes only, a fad that will pass?

Ensuring adequate and appropriate privacy, security and trust in the use of new technologies

The increase in BYOD programmes and the consumerization of IT bring management challenges that many organizations are struggling with. Questions arise like:

- Do we allow employees to use any device they want?
- Should web tools and apps be limited?
- Are there benefits to blurring the traditional technology boundaries?
- What impact does this have on productivity?
- Should we be monitoring what people are using the technology for?

These are being answered in different ways by different companies. In general, organizational responses hinge on addressing issues around data protection, confidentiality and security. As cloud-based solutions are accelerating, the need for international collaboration raises more questions about the capacity for current security protocols to cope. Cloud services are highly exposed to attack and require a relatively high level of security functionality, and with this in mind Gartner, a technology research company, predicts that by 2015, 80 per cent of enterprises using external cloud services will demand independent certification that providers can restore operations and data (Plummer, 2010).

From the individual employees' standpoint they want to feel that when they use their own and the organization's devices that employers trust them to use the technologies appropriately. The fact that monitoring methods are available and can be used does not mean that they should be. A healthy organization works to develop high levels of employer/employee trust, one of the most valuable factors in cultivating productivity and motivation.

Exercise

Technology can aid in micro-management and monitoring. Activities that are often monitored by software include: e-mail, chat/IM, files transferred, application use, websites visited, internet searches, documents printed and data copied to removable storage devices.

Use the six points below on 'Employee monitoring done right' to foster organizational debate and transparency on monitoring. Remember monitoring is not always wrong – monitoring physical health through blood pressure checks, cholesterol screening and so on is considered right and normal. What is different about organizational monitoring of activity?

Employee monitoring done right

Experts recommend these steps to protect your company and yourself if you're asked to monitor employees:

1 Have a formal internet usage policy in writing that spells out what employees are and are not allowed to say or do via e-mail and on the web, including blogs and social networks.

2 Explain the rationale behind the policy (that what employees say electronically can expose the company to legal risk, for example), state specifically what is being monitored and how, and lay out the consequences of violating the policy.

3 In addition to having new hires read the policy, conduct ongoing training and awareness programmes to educate and remind employees.

4 Establish clear procedures to follow when violations are discovered, including who should report the violation and to whom, how it should be documented and who will confront the violator.

5 Ideally, IT, legal and HR should be involved in developing and enforcing the policy. Legal, in particular, should provide guidance on the handling of electronic evidence related to any potential criminal charges or a civil lawsuit. (If there is no in-house legal counsel, hire an outside lawyer with experience in employment law, IT and e-discovery.)

6 Remember that although the IT staff may not realize it, many companies also monitor everyone in the IT department (Harbert, 2010).

Key messages

- Advancing technologies are continuing to drive organizational change.
- Deployed thoughtfully, these technologies bring individual and organizational benefit in terms of productivity improvements and employee motivation and engagement.
- The rise of BYOD possibilities brings challenges to IT, HR and legal departments as they struggle to develop use policies and protect security and confidentiality.
- Monitoring of all aspects of employee activity is easily done via various software. Ensuring monitoring is appropriate and transparent is an organizational responsibility.
- The easy access to information by everyone shifts the role of managers away from one of command and control to one of cultivate and co-ordinate.

References

Accenture (2010) Jumping the Boundaries of Corporate IT: Accenture global research on Millennials' use of technology, Accenture, New York

Betabeat (2012) Interview With Scott Heiferman, CEO of Meetup [Online] http://www.betabeat.com/2012/02/06/interview-with-scott-heiferman-ceo-of-meetup-full-transcript/ (accessed 19 February 2012)

Bloomberg Business Week Research Services (2011) The always-on enterprise: mobilizing the HR–workplace connection [Online] http://whitepapers.businessweek.com/detail/RES/1327504902_76.html (accessed 25 February 2012)

Care Innovations (2011) Shaping the future with new care models [Online] http://www.careinnovations.com/About/Default.aspx (accessed 24 February 2012)

DARPA (2011) DARPA's shredder challenge solved [Online] http://www.darpa.mil/NewsEvents/Releases/2011/12/02_.aspx (accessed 19 February 2012)

Dell and Intel (2011) The Evolving Workforce Report #1 Expert insights, Dell, London

Dell and Intel (2012) The Evolving Workforce Report #2 The workforce perspective, Dell and Intel, London

Desktone (2012) BYOD & the Implications for IT, Desktone, Boston, Mass

Gillett, FE (2012) *Info Workers Using Mobile And Personal Devices For Work Will Transform Personal Tech Markets*, Forrester, Cambridge, Mass

Hampton, KN (2011) *Social Networking Sites and our Lives*, Pew Research Center, Washington DC

Harbert, T (2010) Employee monitoring: when IT is asked to spy, *Computerworld*, June 16 [Online] http://www.computerworld.com/s/article/9177981/Employee_monitoring_When_IT_is_asked_to_spy (accessed 28 April 2012)

Kellaway, L (2011) You've got mail but you need to get your life back [Online] http://www.ft.com/cms/s/0/e851c786-9ea6-11e0-9469-00144feabdc0.html (accessed 26 February 2012)

Kopytoff, VG (2011) More offices let workers choose their own devices [Online] http://www.nytimes.com/2011/09/23/technology/workers-own-cellphones-and-ipads-find-a-role-at-the-office.html?pagewanted=all (accessed 23 February 2012)

Laurence, G (2012) Cutting the cord: Vodafone UK's revolutionary approach to mobility, flexibility & productivity [Online] http://www.managementexchange.com/story/cutting-cord-vodafone-uks-revolutionary-approach-mobility-flexibility-productivity (accessed 13 February 2012)

McCullagh, D (2012) How SOPA would affect you: FAQ [Online] http://news.cnet.com/8301-31921_3-57329001-281/how-sopa-would-affect-you-faq/ (accessed 18 February 2012)

Moore, JF (2005) Business ecosystems and the view from the firm [Online] http://cyber.law.harvard.edu/blogs/gems/jim/MooreBusinessecosystemsandth.pdf (accessed 12 February 2012)

Moreno, AM (2011) Texting 911: the emergency services of tomorrow [Online] http://h30507.www3.hp.com/t5/Explore-Health-IT-with-HP/Texting-911-The-Emergency-Services-of-Tomorrow/ba-p/90011?jumpid=reg_r1002_usen (accessed 24 February 2012)

National Cancer Institute (2011) Cell phones and cancer risk [Online] http://www.cancer.gov/cancertopics/factsheet/Risk/cellphones (accessed 18 February 2012)

Novozymes (2012) EU–China cooperate in bioeconomy [Online] http://www.novozymes.com/en/news/news-archive/Pages/eu-china-cooperate-in-bioeconomy.aspx (accessed 24 February 2012)

Perez, S (2012) Here's what 'post-PC' looks like: over half of info workers use 3 or more devices [Online] http://techcrunch.com/2012/02/23/heres-what-post-pc-looks-like-over-half-of-info-workers-use-3-or-more-devices-at-work/?utm_source=feedburner&utm_medium=email&utm_campaign=Feed%3A+Techcrunch+%28TechCrunch%29 (accessed 23 February 2012)

Plummer, D (2010, November 23) Gartner top predictions for 2011: IT's growing transparency [Online] http://www.gartner.com/DisplayDocument?ref=clientFriendlyUrl&id=1476415 (accessed 28 April 2012)

Plummer, D (2011) Gartner top predictions for 2011: IT's growing transparency and consumerisation [Online] http://www.gartner.com/it/content/1462300/1462334/december_15_top_predictions_for_2011_dplummer.pdf (accessed 23 February 2012)

Porter Novelli (2011) Consumers' health information seeking behaviours [Online] http://wsmconference.com/2011/downloads/12S7SS2%20Melissa%20Kraus%20Taylor.pdf (accessed 23 February 2012)

Reuters (2011) Novozymes to expand [Online] http://www.globaltimes.cn/NEWS/tabid/99/ID/688549/Novozymes-to-expand.aspx (accessed 24 February 2012)

Seely Brown, J (2000) Growing up digital: how the web changes work, education, and the way people learn, *Change*, March/April, pp 11–20

Shaughnessy, H (2011a) Procter and Gamble's Chris Thoen on open innovation [Online] http://www.innovationmanagement.se/2011/04/21/procter-and-gambles-chris-thoen-on-open-innovation/ (accessed 19 February 2012)

Shaughnessy, H (2011b) Chris Thoen on open innovation – Part II [Online] http://www.innovationmanagement.se/author/haydn/ (accessed 19 February 2012)

Svoboda, E (2011) Cisco's virtual doctor will see you now [Online] http://www.fastcompany.com/magazine/155/the-virtual-doctor-will-see-you-now.html (accessed 24 February 2012)

Techfortesco (2011) In-store 'Sat-nav' up and working now in a Tesco branch: come and try it! [Online] http://techfortesco.blogspot.com/2011/05/in-store-sat-nav-up-working-now-in.html (accessed 18 February 2012)

Healthy space

> *I don't believe in offices. They're a thing of the past. Offices produce things like a conventional company.*
>
> **(GUY LAURENCE, CEO, VODAFONE UK)**

> *Work has migrated beyond the conventional boundaries of time and space into a wider environment and those who manage the government estate need to be prepared.*
>
> **(SIR GUS O'DONNELL, CABINET SECRETARY AND HEAD OF THE UK HOME CIVIL SERVICE, JUNE 2008; QUOTED IN HARDY ET AL, 2008)**

Objectives

At the end of this chapter you will be able to:

- explain the relationship between physical space design and employee productivity and motivation;
- discuss the importance of involving stakeholders other than architects in space design, including HR and IT specialists and employees who will work in the space;
- present the case for thinking carefully about noise, light and other ambient environment factors in relation to outcomes desired;
- make the links between the visual and tactile elements of space design and the expression of the organization's 'personality'.

Look around any wi-fi enabled city-centre coffee shop and at almost any time of the day or night people are there with their tablets, smartphones and laptops working individually or having meetings with others. They are part of the always-on, mobile workforce. Several factors are playing into this ability to work in an anytime/anywhere environment and some have been discussed in earlier chapters: Millennials, collaboration, mobile technologies and the push to offer flexible work patterns in response to employee demands are some of these.

But these mobile workers, for the most part, have some 'base camp', a physical corporate office that they work from or go to at times; and as changes occur in the ways people, culture, and information and communications technology interact, so do changes in the way people think about their place of work. For many people now the idea of travelling each day to work in an office between the traditional hours of 9:00 am and 5:00 pm is eroding fast. And if work can be done anytime/anywhere, then there is little value in organizations of any type – government, corporate, non-profit – holding on to expensive office space. Across the board employees are being asked to trade in their offices for a workstation in open-plan offices with little in the way of personal storage space.

Cutting office space yields savings on a number of fronts – real estate costs, energy costs, carbon emissions and storage provision. In most organizations this corporate real estate (CRE)[1] is a high fixed cost that should be reduced as far as possible. But costs, new technologies and employee demand are not the only factors that are influencing the way organizational leaders are thinking about their use of CRE.

Many organizations believe that creative use of space can enhance service delivery to their customers, increase employee health and well-being, encourage knowledge sharing and collaboration between workforce members, involve other stakeholders differently (for example by opening up space for them to use), accelerate innovation, increase organizational flexibility, attract and retain workers, break down hierarchies, express their organization's values and brand, and improve the efficiency and effectiveness of business operations. On this last, a UK Government report, *Working Without Walls*, makes the point:

> Put simply, the workplace can either support or hinder day-to-day operations, as well as help the process of change and improvement. However, many office occupants do not fully recognize the extent to which their physical workspace and its characteristics such as layout, appearance, comfort and functionality, affect their ability and motivation to work and the quality of the work they do.
> (Allen *et al*, 2004)

From an action orientation this translates into working with the interdependencies and interrelationships between the subsystems people, process

FIGURE 7.1   Integrated work planning

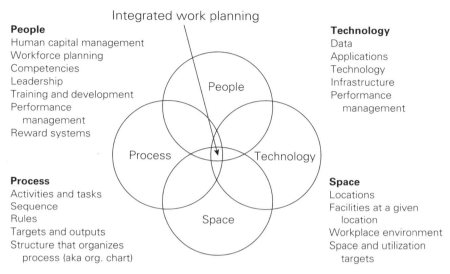

People
Human capital management
Workforce planning
Competencies
Leadership
Training and development
Performance
    management
Reward systems

Technology
Data
Applications
Technology
Infrastructure
Performance
    management

Process
Activities and tasks
Sequence
Rules
Targets and outputs
Structure that organizes
    process (aka org. chart)

Space
Locations
Facilities at a given
    location
Workplace environment
Space and utilization
    targets

SOURCE: Stanford, 2012.

(business operations), technology and space, as Figure 7.1 shows. Note that healthy business functioning and the capacity for organizational adaptability 'demands attention to all four elements, challenging traditional approaches to change which often ignore the role and dynamic of the physical environment. Arguably, space has the strongest psychological impact on people and behaviours allowing it to become a key catalyst for wider change' (Allen *et al*, 2004).

This argument makes sense. People put considerable effort into choosing a home that feels right for them and then making its spaces reflect their personality and style preferences, their lifestyle as it changes, and their values. Specialist home-making journals, websites and countless books help people create a unique home that is functional and expressive, and makes them feel good, as this description of one family's home illustrates:

> Their Victorian house has been clad in flint, in vernacular Sussex style and has been lovingly modernized by the family... After the birth of their two daughters, and in need of extra room they knocked down the back wall to create an airy, sunny dining and family room plus conservatory, with custom-made sliding doors that open onto the garden. This area of the house has a glass roof and is constantly filled with light and the result is a warm, friendly, cohesive family room. The kitchen is the hub of the home with other rooms radiating off of it.

The dining room, a sitting area and a laundry room lead to the playroom, which is one of Simon's favourite spaces. 'I love being in there, playing with the girls,' he says. (allaboutyou, 2012)

What is striking about home redesign like that described above is that it is done with the input and involvement of the occupants. However, it is rare that architects and interior designers work with other than company facility managers to upgrade or redesign the physical working environment. The physical environment is only superficially considered (although things are changing) by these space professionals as relevant to the organization's business model, the delivery of its strategy and as a component of the design of a whole organizational system.

This is a missed opportunity. As stated, the physical environment is a reflector of the culture, values and preoccupations of the organizational members. Even now, the corner office, for instance, is the prime example of a physical space status symbol, usually reflecting positional power. The choices of marble, wood or other surfaces give clues on organizational values – lavish use of hardwood, for example, might be at odds with corporate statements about sustainability.

Additionally, good or poor physical space planning impacts the motivation and morale of workers, their productivity, the way they are able (or not) to communicate both face to face and virtually, and the way they feel about their power and creativity. Kaiser Permanente (KP), a US health care company, is one organization that does recognize the interlinkage between space design and the well-being of the whole organization, making the point that architecture and physical health are interlinked. The organization points to the fact that numbers of studies show that the new hospital designs they have been implemented improve patient outcomes. Having a private room with access to natural light, or controlled intensity of light and sound has a beneficial impact on patient satisfaction, recovery time, soundness of sleep and overall satisfaction. Beyond these factors views of nature 'have been shown to decrease depression, pain, stress and even length of hospital stays'.

From a staff perspective floor plans that are specifically designed to help workers carry out their duties effectively help reduce stress and improve productivity for the benefit of all (Arieff, 2009).

In this instance it is clear that the design is part of a business strategy aimed at changing the way KP delivers its mission and that, beyond space change, it involves changing the business processes, the way people approach and do their work and the technology. KP is not alone in seeing the value of space changes as a catalyst for much more fundamental organizational business change. Many organizations see this in the same way.

For office space architects and designers this presents an opportunity, as one noted:

> Design strategies and solutions must be posed and presented as business cases, a language and format not necessarily in the comfort zone of the design profession... More importantly, for the workplace to serve as a change agent, we must also be in the position to provide change management services... We often speak with clients about the workplace being a transformation opportunity, a place to create innovation and change, yet we have traditionally given clients the physical opportunity for change while leaving them to their own devices to adapt internally to the required operational and mindset changes. (Levin, 2010)

Teaming organizational designers and developers, business strategists, HR practitioners and IT experts with architects and facilities management to ensure organizations are getting the most value from their physical space in terms of operational effectiveness, sustainability and good customer outcomes is a proven way forward for healthy organizations, though achieving this functional integration is easier said than done. The first step is to recognize the value of 'integrated work planning' (see Glossary). Organizations that employ integrated work planners are good at getting involved early in business decision making and informing the business of the full impacts of real estate-related implications of business decisions. They benefit from this in the following ways:

- deeper planning integration with the business;
- more efficient with better outcomes delivered;
- less money spent reacting to business decisions after the fact without having to sacrifice on project timelines;
- able to drive the bigger changes needed to improve productivity and drive savings (ie further shrink footprints) than their peers;
- the business quickly learns about the bigger connection between space and work, and makes the partnerships better than those that focus on precise analytics and formal planning.

The second step is to develop and deploy four competencies within the corporate real estate (CRE) function and across related functions (IT, HR, Business Planning). Table 7.1 lists the four competencies required and illustrates them in use. CRE functions without these competencies struggle with

TABLE 7.1   CRE Competency

CRE Competency	This means
Partnership-facilitation	• Orienting conversations around desired business outcomes, such as driving productivity through the way work is done rather than sticking to space design preoccupations. • Explaining the timelines and decisions required to deliver a successful real estate strategy that supports the business strategy. • Developing tools, for example a criteria development tool for allocating private offices, to trigger business and functional partner real estate questions. • Providing transparency into the impacts that individual partner decisions have on others: eg differing demands for a certain percentage of hotelling (see Glossary) spaces in different parts of the organization will impact employee work patterns and technology requirements. • Clarifying the connections between space and work outcomes. **Example:** Pfizer, a pharmaceutical company, conducts workplace productivity sessions with the business to demonstrate how space drives communication and from this productivity and innovation.
Engagement	• Creating planning models to illustrate how work-related changes impact business objectives. • Focusing conversations on business, not real estate outcomes. • Educating business/functional partners on the potential role for and value of CRE. **Example:** The UK Treasury held a series of charrettes (see Glossary) and focus groups with employees and business leaders, giving several different scenarios to consider that related to different ways the work could be conducted in the different scenarios.

TABLE 7.1 *continued*

CRE Competency	This means
Learning and teaching	• Tracking business unit/functional partner choices to clarify how they think about the connectivity between space and their priorities. • Identifying individual business success drivers and showing the relationship to real estate strategies. • Teaching the business the connection between space, technology, and staff considerations. • Driving the business to consider the implications of future work needs on current decisions. **Example:** Google, a technology company, shows the business how it can improve informal communication flows by spotting influencers and making more informed location and space decisions.
Value-demonstration	• Demonstrating the savings associated with real estate initiatives that make the business more efficient, effective and productive. • Demonstrating that partnering between the functional areas is a good investment and will not overly tax business resources. **Example:** Nationwide, a US insurance company, compels business engagement by reorienting planning discussions around the connection between location, labour decisions and talent supply.

Adapted from: Real Estate Executive Board, 2010.

business scepticism, narrow perspective on real estate impacts, and lack of capacity to engage the rest of the organizational system in meaningful discussions on the design and layout of the space.

The third step is to make a compelling business case for applying systems thinking to the design and use of space. This can focus solely on the subsystem elements of people, process, space and technology shown in Figure 7.1. Or can be extended to draw on the full systems model (See Figure 1.1 shown in Chapter 1). Eversheds, the largest UK legal firm, which in 2009 opened a new corporate office is an example of an organization that considered a fuller systems approach. Their design brief required that the new office reflected and provided for:

- a friendly, non-hierarchical, collegiate and open culture;
- a client-centric focus that gave a first-class experience;
- a vibrant, healthy and sustainable workplace to attract and retain best talent;
- a flexible, adaptable and efficient work platform that allowed teams to grow and contract;
- use of new technologies and new ways of working that improved business efficiency;
- space that improved teamworking and collaboration whilst preserving the requirement for confidentiality and privacy;
- a value-for-money solution;
- unification of the corporate office culture with that of the regional offices.

Mapping some elements of this brief to the systems model shown in Chapter 3 (Figure 3.2) illustrates the relationship of space design decisions to the whole system. With this kind of map to hand it is easy to check whether and how the system is aligned and where to address shortfalls or make adjustments (Table 7.2).

Looking across the systems elements at the design brief elements, it is evident that these are geared towards not just delivering the 'body' design outcomes shown in Column 3 of the table but also towards the 'mind and spirit' aspects of space design. The key 'body aspect' of space design is that it is functional and fit for purpose. And the two key mind and spirit aspects of space design are that it enables the 'feel-good factor' in employees and that it is expressive of the organization's culture, values and brand. In fact, these are exactly the same three aspects that were mentioned in relation to the family home described earlier in the section. The following sections discuss these three aspects and their relationship to office space in more detail.

Pause for thought

What might be the effect of ignoring the drivers towards collaborative, flexible, mobility-supporting office space?

What characterizes space that is 'traditional', 'contemporary', 'modern' and 'period'? What different images of the organization do the different styles create?

What are the arguments in favour of treating space, people, process and technology as interdependent subsystems for healthy organizational functioning?

TABLE 7.2   System alignment

Type of system	Design brief element	Design outcome
Mechanistic (Not purposeful)	Flexible, adaptable and efficient work platform that allowed teams to grow and contract	IT infrastructure designed to ensure that as future technology demands and needs increased and changed, systems could be simply integrated to existing infrastructure.
Animate (Purposeful)	Space that improved team working and collaboration whilst preserving the requirement for confidentiality and privacy	'Studio' principle adopted that combined open plan with some of the autonomy provided by traditional cellular office solutions. One litigation partner commented, 'I have embraced the semi-open plan arrangement ... as I find the increased communication invaluable for my current case.'
Social (Purposeful)	Friendly, non-hierarchical, collegiate, and open culture	The office space adjacent to reception was designed as a café providing staff and visitors with an alternative meeting and work area. The space also acts as a function facility for in-house events as well as a bar in the evening.
Ecological (Not purposeful)	Vibrant, healthy and sustainable workplace to attract and retain best talent	Included 26,000 square feet of green roofing, chilled beam air conditioning, and sustainable and recyclable building materials. The building has a BREEAM (Building Research Establishment Environmental Assessment Method) "excellent" rating. In one response to a post occupancy survey '85% of respondents believe the air quality in the new building is having some degree of positive impact on their motivation to perform their work.' (Woods Bagot, 2009)

Functional and fit for purpose

What makes office space functional and fit for purpose depends on the nature of the work: the range of activities and types of tasks people do on a day-to-day basis both individually and in groups and teams. Some people's work requires them to have specialized tools, for example two large monitors, or sound and video equipment. Others' work requires them to have concentrative space for heads-down tasks like analysing spreadsheets or writing white papers. And some need to be able to interact in groups on a team-based project.

Regardless of the role or type of work, not many people sit at their workstation or desk the entire day. They get up and go to meeting and conference rooms for formal meetings, and to coffee areas or vending machines where they may bump into people and have informal yet still work-related and useful conversations, or indeed have purely social conversations that contribute to building a sense of community and belonging. They leave the building and pass through common space like reception areas, lift lobbies and staircases. And take rest breaks to use the washrooms, stretch or find someone. The space that they are in and move through has to accommodate a range of activity and work style preferences.

Interviewed for a story on Cisco's office space, Woo, a systems engineer, answered the question 'What space will you be using today?' with:

> I booked this small meeting room for our discussion because it's private and my phone conversation won't disturb others. After this I'm planning to move to an individual workstation in the quiet area to finish off writing a report. Then I'll move to the soft-seating area to catch up on e-mails and connect with people who are walking by. I expect I'll go down to the cafeteria around lunchtime and stay there to listen to a webinar through my headphones – I'll take my iPad with me. Then I've got two meetings I have to go to. One with people on-site so we'll be in a mid-sized conference room, and the other with some people on-site and some off-site so we'll be in a room that has video conferencing capability. Adapted from: (Cisco Systems Inc, 2007)

Deciding how to design or redesign for functionality usually involves assessing the type of work that people do, the numbers of people who do that type of work, their utilization rate of each type of space used, and the amount of time they are present or absent from the building. This assessment is conducted by various methods including employee surveys, focus groups, observation, and data collection eg turnstile data. A sample block of questions from a typical space use survey is shown below.

Of the hours you spend in your primary assigned location, please indicate the percentage of that time dedicated to the following activities in your typical workweek (must add up to 100%).

Also, please rate how critical each activity is to your core job role [rating scale not shown in this example]:

Focused individual work (requiring concentration)

0 per cent...100 per cent

Training/learning new skills

0 per cent...100 per cent

Scheduled meetings or phone calls with colleagues
(face-to-face or tele-video)

0 per cent...100 per cent

Unscheduled meetings or phone calls with colleagues
(face-to-face or tele-video)

0 per cent...100 per cent

Scheduled meetings or phone calls with clients and others
(face-to-face or tele-video)

0 per cent...100 per cent

Unscheduled meetings or phone calls with clients and others
(face-to-face or tele-video)

0 per cent...100 per cent

Secondary tasks (faxing, copying, printing, etc.)

0 per cent...100 per cent

Other (please specify):

0 per cent...100 per cent

From this form of data collection, the way people use desk space and the amount of time they are mobile can be classified in various ways. One system, shown in Figure 7.2, uses six categories to describe this combination of activity.

FIGURE 7.2   Six types of work styles

High	**Resident** > 3/4 of total time at their desk	**Roaming** < 3/4 of time at their desk & < 1/4 outside the office	**Remote** > 1/4 of total time outside the office
Level of interaction at their desk	**Interactive** majority of desk time communicating with others	**Interactive** majority of desk time communicating with others	**Interactive** majority of desk time communicating with others
	Resident > 3/4 of total time at their desk	**Roaming** < 3/4 of time at their desk & < 1/4 outside the office	**Remote** > 1/4 of total time outside the office
Low	**Concentrative** majority of desk time on individual work	**Concentrative** majority of desk time on individual work	**Concentrative** majority of desk time on individual work

Low   **Time away from desk (mobility)**   High

SOURCE: GSA.

With this and other data, design plans can be drawn up and decisions made on the number of desk spaces needed, the mix of collaborative spaces and conference rooms, where to site common areas like print rooms and kitchens and so on, and thus the functional aspects become fit for purpose. Remember, however, that all self-report surveys require cautious use for a number of reasons, so do not skimp on the validation of survey data through other activities. Back the findings up with further qualitative and quantitative data, with forecasts, and information from the business strategy group, the HR function (on predictions of workforce ebb, flow, engagement and demographics), and the IT function (on IT plans). Involving anthropologists and social and organizational psychologists gives added insight into the design process.

If surveys ask for input on the 'ideal', like the examples in the box below, remain sceptical of the responses. People cannot realistically envisage an 'ideal' in any useful sense. It is unlikely that the iPhone would have made production if people had been asked to describe their ideal mobile phone. In fact one of Steve Jobs' quotes is, 'It's really hard to design products by focus groups. A lot of times, people don't know what they want until you show it to them' (*Business Week Online*, 1998).

Thinking about your ideal workplace, how much would the addition/enhancement of the following space types improve your job performance (quality and quantity of work)?

Spaces to think and concentrate

0 per cent...100 per cent

Spaces to meet and collaborate

0 per cent...100 per cent

Spaces to socialize informally with colleagues

0 per cent...100 per cent

Spaces for learning, training, discovery

0 per cent...100 per cent

But once you do show it to them, their insights and comments are extremely useful in making adjustments and design changes early enough in the process not to be too costly. Showcasing the 'ideal' space through a prototype is a powerful way of both inviting employee support of changes and getting good insights into the way the space will and should operate in relation to the work they do.

One organization, RadioShack, invested $400,000 in a carefully designed mock-up incorporating the features and elements of their proposed new headquarters office design, including workstations, team spaces, common areas, quiet rooms and more. They called this the Ideas Lab. Ultimately, every HQ RadioShack employee spent time in the Ideas Lab, either working, touring or visiting. Every one of the 70 departments discussed which aspects of the Lab they wanted applied in their own neighbourhoods in the new building. 'Each group was able to get the right things, versus the cookie cutter approach of throwing the same cubes at everyone,' commented Nina Petty, vice president of corporate real estate. The company estimated that the Lab facility and processes saved $1.5 million by preventing application and design mistakes (Steelcase, 2006).

Clearly not every organization can make this significant upfront investment in prototyping but all organizations should make an investment in gathering a range of data from a variety of sources and inputs. From this data a picture of space use in relation to current work can be deduced which forms the basis for discussions on future use in relation to various factors. These factors include:

- The constraints around items like budget for redesigned or new space (including building work, technology investment, furniture, etc), contractual requirements if the space is being leased, regulatory requirements and timescale for delivery of new space.

- The opportunities and desire for making changes on a scale of incremental to radical in the way the business is operated and the way people work. And the amount of resource required in supporting people through the change.

- The building constraints if an existing building is being redesigned. Fixed things like lift shafts, staircases and historical features will have to be incorporated into the design.

- The various ways the design brief can be realized, bearing in mind current and forecasted space use. Note again that paying attention to technology trends, demographics, business strategies, and prototype finding where available, should inform the design options presented.

Designing or redesigning office space that is realistically functional and fit for purpose involves a vital and often omitted process: preparing people for the shock of the new. Even if 'the new' is eagerly anticipated it is nevertheless different from the current state and that can take some adjusting to. Best practice recommends pre-preparing staff for any move or change in four stages as shown in the right-hand column of Figure 7.3: awareness, understanding, engagement and action.

It is all too easy to go inadvertently from awareness to action – the left-hand column of the graphic above – without sufficient understanding and engagement of the people who will work in the building. An extract from an e-mail from an employee in a public sector organization illustrates the response to an unprepared-for announcement:

> We are about to undergo a space renovation to create a new mobile design lab to provide a more collaborative work environment and allow us to start hoteling.
> We announced this initiative at our quarterly all-hands meeting and there was a lot of apprehension from the employees regarding the change.

People who hear an 'announcement' are usually shocked and scared of the unknown. Typically they have a lot of questions that, for the most part, go unasked and unanswered, or if they are asked and answered there is insufficient repetition of the messages to ensure they are heard. In any

FIGURE 7.3 Communicating change: effective and ineffective

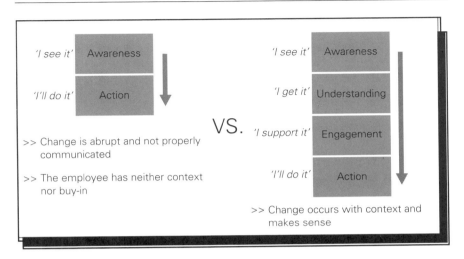

SOURCE: Unknown.

change situation, extensive communication and involvement (using multiple channels) from long before the word 'go' is essential. Additionally, people need to know who the 'owner' is of their new space design. They want to know who is leading it, and who is playing what role in the project. They need this clarity and role definition to know who to go to if there are questions, concerns or requests. Any lack of project organization information gives rise to questions like these two, from the same public sector organization:

- 'Who owns the current project? We don't know. We need to have information shared readily. Transparency is lacking.'

- 'Who is in charge of this? There's a perspective that the people or persons who have decreed this are not interested in how people feel about it. That their view is that this is the way it is and they don't want to hear differently.'

This organization took these kinds of comments to heart and learned from the experience. The project manager lists the key steps they took in a subsequent project:

1 'Running several all-staff meetings to talk about what the new work environment would feel like. We explained that because of new technology and a changing workforce we were no longer tied to our desk.

2 Inviting speakers from organizations who had gone through similar radical space redesign to talk about their experiences. These reassured people that although the new environment would focus on creating less space for the individual it would open the building up allowing people to collaborate and connect from any part of our collaborative space. (We installed wifi everywhere... including the park outside.)

3 Bringing our IT team on-board from the start. They were brilliant in introducing, demonstrating and coaching in the new technologies as they came on stream. They gave ongoing support with short videos, checklists and how-to info.

4 Allowing people who were being assigned a seat (as opposed to being totally mobile) as far as possible to choose the type of workstation they felt would work best for them.

5 Setting up teams of 'mobile change champions'. These people were peers in the organization and each division had a representative. They were there to communicate to the design team what was happening in the space and collecting preferences and requirements on anything we missed along the way (coat hooks, headphones and such).

6 Having our executive team members go out and walk the floor plates assuring employees that the executives were not getting different treatment from the employees, listening to staff and sharing concerns.

7 Investing in development and coaching for middle managers and team leaders who were not confident in managing team members, who in the past had been in an assigned seat, but who were now mobile and could be anywhere at any time.'

Getting the workspace functional and fit for purpose and encouraging staff to see how this is the case, is one aspect of space design. But the encouragement may not be fully effective. People still have to feel good about the space they are in. It is rather like the difference between a house and a home. Both describe a living situation. But 'house' refers to the building, which may be fully functional and fit for purpose, while 'home' is more an emotional concept – and that is much more difficult to design into an office space. Take a housing estate where each of the houses has been built to the same design specification with the same internal layout, hardware and white goods. Go inside a few of them. The occupants will have very different interiors personalized in a way that makes them feel good. In an office space there are multiple occupants and each of them has, as far as possible, got to feel good about their workspace.

Feeling good

What helps workers feel good is having some control over their environments. Backing up this statement, a research article published in *Ergonomics* in 2010 titled 'Can personal control over the physical environment ease distractions in office workplaces?' concludes:

> The results showed that workers' sense of control over physical aspects of their work environment mediated the relationship between perceived distractions and perceived job performance. These results suggest that increasing perceptions of personal control over features of the physical work environment may serve to link work attitudes and work outcomes. (Lee and Brand, 2010)

Three designable features can encourage control and thus aid the feel-good factor: ambient environment, work style preferences, and personalization.

Ambient environment

There are some aspects of ambient office design that are 'must have' feel-good factors: lighting, personal temperature and ventilation controllability, and noise containment are four of these. Of these, the one that causes the most concern to workers is noise. Table 7.3 looks at noise in more detail.

Additionally, research shows that window views influence cognitive functioning, especially distant views or views of nature. 'Benefits include improved concentration, stress reduction, and increased cognitive tranquillity. It appears that the cognitive and psychological benefits of views may result from the ability to weave mini mental breaks into ongoing work, thereby restoring attentional capacity and the ability to concentrate' (Heerwagen *et al*, 2004). This feature is not usually controllable by office workers – although in some organizations position in the hierarchy is rewarded with a window view – but it is worth bearing in mind in space design. If partition heights and cubicle walls can be kept low enough for people to have something of a window aspect, then that is all to the good.

Work style preferences

Beyond having the right ambient environment, having the right mix of accommodation in the right amount so that individual's work style preferences can be met helps with the feel-good factor. Lawyers, for example, are used to having private office space allocated to them on the basis of hierarchy: secretaries in open space, paralegals in cubicles, associates in offices by

TABLE 7.3   Noise problems

Noise problems	Unhealthy result	Behavioural protocols for noise reduction (Note: physical design and layout can also help alleviate noise)
The real noise problems are people having conversations with colleagues on the phone, in their workstations or in adjacent circulation areas. Because it is easier to see colleagues in a more open workplace, this generates more spontaneous conversation and more distractions for others doing quiet work. Research also shows that distractions and interruptions are most detrimental for complex cognitive tasks with high information processing demands.	Shifts in attention that reduce focus may mean: • Increasing efforts to concentrate, which can increase stress levels and fatigue • Abandoning a current task to deal with demands caused by an interruption • Losing flow of thought and the need to re-orient to the task, which can take up to 15 minutes. One worker posting to a blog describes her experience: 'I currently work in a cubicle – my neighbors are a man in the midst of a divorce, a woman with a problem child, another woman with an elderly parent who should be in a care facility. The only cure for my personal hell would be a quiet room with a door. Perhaps my employer would then get his money's worth from my workday... did I mention that I am across from the copier?'	Speak in a low, normal voice. (This is easier when one can see other occupants of the space rather than in the fictional privacy of a 'cubicle' with high partitions.) Keep phone conversations short or move them to an enclosed room. Schedule lengthy calls for enclosed rooms with speaker phones. Do NOT use speaker phones at the desk in the open office. If needed, headphones with voice piece are an acceptable alternative if the voice can be kept at a normal level. Limit conversations in the open workspace; hold meetings behind closed doors or in public spaces away from the open workstations. Be particularly aware of workers who are adjacent to main circulation paths. Be aware that lengthy hall conversations before and after meetings can be heard by desk workers nearby. Where possible, locate conference room entries away from workstations to allow communication that occurs before and after meetings. Look before you interrupt; if someone appears to be concentrating, come back later or use an alternative means to communicate such as e-mail or mail chat features. Avoid noise spill by closing meeting room doors, especially when meeting rooms are located adjacent to the open plan work areas.

Adapted from: GSA Public Buildings Service, 2012.

windows, partners in bigger offices, and senior partners in a large corner office. Eversheds, mentioned earlier, is a leader in the legal profession for moving towards more shared space and a lower real estate footprint; others are finding the concept challenging.

As one lawyer in a public sector organization said:

> Our work is desk-bound and concentrative. Most of us come into our offices daily. We don't do a lot of off-site work. It's not in our psyche. We need individual private offices for privacy, confidentiality and to meet client expectations. The ideas of glass walls to our offices and sharing offices are not ones that we'd go along with. We just wouldn't feel good and wouldn't be able to do a good job.

Accommodating different work styles means having a variety of space types available and then enabling and encouraging people to find the type that works best for them. One employee in a commercial sector organization, commenting on the drive to make the whole enterprise open plan, said:

> I am concerned about all the superlatives that are used to describe the current movement toward the open office. I am working in an 'open environment'. I hate it! It is too loud, too cavernous, allows for absolutely no personal space (the only thing that separates me from the person sitting across from me is my computer screen), and I find it extremely harsh. I think my son described it perfectly, he said, 'wow – you work in a cafeteria!' I don't know any people who really like it. Everyone feels like they are tolerating it. Most people chose to work at home at least two days a week (is that a win?). I know this is the future for office design, but having experienced this environment first-hand, I am not sure all the superlatives are appropriate. I think this definitely needs to be tempered.

This type of response to open offices can be mitigated by responses such as Google's (although it may be less concerned than some other organizations with reducing their real estate footprint). Google has embraced many aspects of open space and collaboration but has simultaneously acceded to 'the engineers demand [for] stationary offices that they could nest in and decorate like digital magpies' (Chang, 2011).

Personalization

In any organization, a quick look at the workstations that are assigned to specific employees (as opposed to touchdown, or hoteling spaces) shows that they reflect their occupants' tastes, experiences and personalities – just as their own homes do. There are pictures, certificates, soft toys, plaques, mottos, plants, books, clothing, electrical appliances and other things.

This 'status armour' (see Glossary) is a method of displaying aspects of employee personality: who they are and how they want to be seen in the organization. People like the ability to personalize their space. Again in the public sector organization, one of the project managers working to move people from old space to new design asked:

> Quick question: how do you all handle awards, certificates, personal pictures and other stuff people like to have at assigned desks? Pictures I figure may not be too big a deal to have people let go – but work awards are supposed to be morale boosters and reminiscent of great work or good team performance. Will we be asking people to take them home, or is there going to be some kind of photo wall or other way of dealing with this?

Allowing for appropriate personalization in an environment where there is shared occupancy, hoteling and unassigned seating is an important aspect to consider in healthy space design. Different organizations have different responses to this desire for the personalization that will help people feel good about the space. Some have community walls where people assigned to that 'neighbourhood' put up their pictures. Others suggest having a very small number of personal items – photos, for example – that can be put away and taken out each morning. Thinking out the issues of personalization and discussing them with the employees in an engaging process may result in creative ideas for getting the right level of personalization without compromising the overall image and experience the office space is partly designed to express.

Expressive

SEI, an international investment services company, has a tag line 'New ways. New Answers'. It also has a conscious philosophy and strategy for expressing what this tag line means, using careful space design and use. In designing a physical environment and technology infrastructure that foster SEI's culture and values of innovation, caring, engagement, egalitarianism, teamwork, flexibility, transparency, and empowerment, it has built a direct link to their people and business processes. Figure 7.4 illustrates this approach.

SEI is an example of an organization that has discovered that culture can be expressed in the workplace design, layout and fittings. 'Everywhere a member of the organization turns, the culture is clearly evident, inescapable. While it may take new employees in some organizations months or years to

FIGURE 7.4   Linking people, process, space

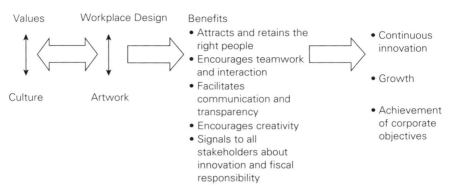

Values   Workplace Design   Benefits
                                  • Attracts and retains the   • Continuous
                                    right people   innovation
                                  • Encourages teamwork
                                    and interaction
                                  • Facilitates   • Growth
Culture   Artwork   communication and
                                   transparency   • Achievement
                                  • Encourages creativity   of corporate
                                  • Signals to all   objectives
                                    stakeholders about
                                    innovation and fiscal
                                    responsibility

SOURCE: SEI.

really know what the company is about, a person who walks into the offices of SEI knows instantly'. For example:

> When a new employee joins SEI, it is an unusual experience. The new hire is given a map and sent down to a storeroom on the lower floor of the main building. There, the employee is issued a chair and desk, both on wheels, with a computer and phone on the desktop. The map shows where in the complex of nine barn-like buildings on the corporate campus in Oaks, Pennsylvania, the new hire will initially be located. The employee then rolls the desk through the buildings, into the oversized elevators designed for this purpose, past hallways filled with a provocative (and sometimes shocking) collection of emerging contemporary art. (Wind and West, 2006)

Facebook is another example of a company that expresses its culture through space design. Its Menlo Park, California, campus was renovated in 2011 at a cost of $250m in what has been described as a 'hacker' style, deliberately intended to express the culture of the organization.

> The office buildings are arranged along a narrow interior courtyard with a jumble of storefronts featuring food, medical, cleaning and other services for employees, all of them free. The complex has internal atriums to increase natural light, rows of white benches topped by 24-inch (61-centimeter) monitors and items brought in by employees, including a tiki bar, Charlie Sheen poster and Sarah Palin bobble-head... Workers roam with laptops, meet on sofas and scribble on [art] walls. (Levy, 2011)

The way a building looks both inside and out is something that has a significant impact on the way people think about and relate to the organization.

(The same is true of the visual layout of websites.) Organizations that do not think carefully about what sort of image they want to create and what values they want to express physically in their buildings and workspaces are disadvantaged compared with those that do.

The image choices matter whether or not the space is being newly or specially designed. Furniture choices and layouts, artwork, the artefacts that are around the space are all expressive of the culture of the organization, in exactly the same way that clothing, accessories and hairstyle choices are all expressions of an individual's personality. As the UK Government report *Working Without Walls* notes:

> The way a building looks inside and out, has a profound effect on what people think about the organization it houses and how they relate to it. Organizations need to think about what sort of image they wish to create and the values they wish to express physically in buildings and workplaces.
>
> In government today those values include: interaction and service to the public, openness and accountability, professionalism and authority, prudence and value for money, and being modern, in-touch, forward looking, accessible and responsible... the government is now learning the lesson that workplaces that look right as well as being functional and cost effective are better value [than those that are functional but are drab and unwelcoming].
>
> (Allen et al, 2004)

It is not just the visual images and experiences that are important. Some interesting research points to the fact that first impressions are also influenced by the tactile environment. Think back to an experience of visiting an unknown organization – how heavy were the entry doors, what materials were the surfaces covered with, how hard or soft were the reception area chairs? These interactions with weight, texture and hardness all matter. In their experiments on tactile experience, researchers' findings showed that heaviness produced impressions of importance and seriousness, roughness led to impressions of decreased social co-ordination (for example, whether the interaction was adversarial or friendly, competitive or co-operative), hardness made others appear strict and stable and not so emotional (Ackerman, Nocera and Bargh, 2010).

Retailers are generally better at expressing their brand, values and culture through their store layouts than those involved with office design. Perhaps this is because office workers are viewed as 'behind the scenes', where it might be thought less important to invest in aligning brand and image. But it is not less important. Employees need to be wooed with the same level of identification with brand, culture, image and values as customers do.

Pause for thought

What trade-offs might need to be made between designing space that is functional/ fit for purpose and that helps employees feel good?

Why is it important to explore and understand the links between physical environment and worker satisfaction and productivity?

What are the productivity concerns and benefits in reducing real estate footprint and encouraging mobile working?

What value is there in consciously aiming to express the organization's culture and values in the office space design, and choices of materials used?

Exercise

Backpack as office space

For many mobile workers, their backpack is their office space. Its look and content reflects their work habits and personality – anyone who could take a look at or in it would get an impression of who they are and how they approach life. Below are one mobile worker's 12 tips for personalizing and feeling in control of backpack office space. Review these and decide which are worth following and/or passing on to other mobile workers in the organization.

1   Get a good backpack (or wheelie bag) that has pockets but not too many. A square backpack with lots of pockets works best for many people. It seems easier to find things in than the traditionally curved ones.

2   Do not to fling things randomly in the bag but put the items back in their 'own' pocket. That way there is less searching through a jumble of stuff when, for example, a pen is needed because someone wants to sketch out something.

3   Have small, neon fabric, ripstop nylon bags for stuff within the pockets. Know which item is in which colour; it helps locate them in the depths of a black backpack.

4   Get a travel mouse – it makes life a whole lot easier than trying to work just with the laptop keyboard. Also get a clear skin to put over a laptop keyboard so that you feel secure against accidentally spilling coffee on it.

5   Carry a basic office kit of supplies. Typical contents include a pencil with eraser, small stapler, scotch tape, paper clips, small pair of scissors, pen, coloured pens, post-it notes and highlighter pen (some are available that also have flags in them for marking pages). Put these in a small clear box or transparent make-up bag; it makes it easier to find the pair of small scissors that are in there somewhere.

6   Pack a bamboo or other reusable cutlery set. It saves using disposable stuff, is easy and light, and some come in a case made from plastic bottles – so sustainability all round.

7   On each of the various tools of the trade that you need at all times – laptop, power cord, BlackBerry, notebook, mouse, ear-piece, etc – put on a sticker with the owner's name, address and phone number. As one mobile worker reported, 'I've had my power cord and my ear-piece returned when I left them places because the finder was able to contact me.'

8   Tag the backpack with a luggage tag or identifier that really speaks you. One person has just a simple red heart one, another got photos made into luggage tags, which is the equivalent of photo on desk. It is very easy when black backpacks are so look-alike to seize the wrong one from an overhead rack on a plane or train.

9   Always have a few documents or stuff in hardcopy to work on. If batteries fail, or there is a long wait for something or a call to switch off 'all portable electronic devices', its a good use of time to be reviewing, researching, catching up on reading or whatever.

10 Develop the mindset of 'anywhere is my office'. Small personal touches – the colour of a luggage tag, a pink crystal stapler, or silver rhinestone computer mouse (yes these are available) and similar will help personalize the office 'space'.

11 Clear out the backpack every single evening. It's amazing how many items are inadvertently collected in a day – business cards, napkins, receipts, pens, documents not needed after the meeting. Don't let the backpack get cluttered up.

12 Carry a couple of empty Ziploc or small plastic bags, and a ripstop folding nylon shopper, and a packet of travel wipes. They all come in handy.

Key messages

- There is a current drive, aided by advancements in mobile technology, to reduce corporate real estate footprint.

- This is achieved through a variety of means, principally by designing space to be flexible, collaborative and non-hierarchical. This is reflected in open-plan designs with a mix of types of accommodation.

- Knowing what type of accommodation to provide usually requires an assessment of current and planned work, workforce numbers, business strategies and other factors.

- Supporting people in shifting mindsets from one form of work space to another requires investment in employee engagement and communication from long before the word 'go'.

- Giving employees some control over their working environment aids well-being and productivity. Three key areas to allow some control are ambient environment, work style preferences and personalization.

- It is not just functionality and fitness for purpose that matter in space design. Expressing the brand, culture and values of the organization through the design matters just as much.

Note

1 For the purposes of this discussion 'real estate' is defined as physical office space – the place where people have traditionally come to work. It excludes manufacturing and commercial space, although some of the principles discussed are equally applicable in those environments.

References

Ackerman, J, Nocera, C and Bargh, J (2010, June 25) Incidental haptic sensations influence social judgments and decisions, *Science*, 328, pp 1712–15

allaboutyou (2012) Real homes: from holiday let to family house [Online] http://www.allaboutyou.com/coast/readers-home-chocolate-makers-Chichester?page=1 (accessed 2 March 2012)

Allen, T, Swaffer, F, Hardy, B, Bell, A and Graham, R (2004) *Working Without Walls*, HMSO, London

Arieff, A (2009) A breath of fresh air for health care [Online] http://opinionator.blogs.nytimes.com/2009/12/13/a-breath-of-fresh-air-for-health-care/ (accessed 2 March 2012)

Business Week Online (1998) Steve Jobs on Apple's resurgence: 'not a one-man show' [Online] http://www.businessweek.com/bwdaily/dnflash/may1998/nf80512d.htm (accessed 6 March 2012)

Chang, J (2011) The Fifth-Annual Smart Environments Awards, Macquarie Bank [Online] http://www.metropolismag.com/story/20110214/the-fifth-annual-smart-enviroments-awards-macquarie-bank (accessed 9 March 2012)

Cisco Systems Inc (2007) How Cisco designed the collaborative, connected workplace environment [Online] http://www.cisco.com/web/about/ciscoitatwork/downloads/ciscoitatwork/pdf/Cisco_IT_Case_Study_Connected_Workplace_POC.pdf (accessed 8 March 2012)

GSA Public Buildings Service (2012, January) Sound matters: how to achieve acoustic comfort in the contemporary office [Online] http://www.gsasoundmatters.com/ (accessed 9 March 2012)

Hardy, B, Graham, R, Stansall, P, White, A, Harrison, A, Bell, A *et al* (2008) *Working Beyond Walls*, DEGW, London

Heerwagen, J, Kampschroer, K, Powell, K and Loftness, V (2004) Collaborative knowledge work environments, *Building Research and Information*, 32 (6), pp 510–28

Lee, SY and Brand, JL (2010) Can personal control over the physical environment ease distractions in office workplaces?*Ergonomics*, 53 (3), pp 324–35

Levin, A (2010) *Opportunities for Changing Perceptions of the Workplace*, unpublished, Seattle

Levy, D (2011) Facebook's 'Cool space' campus points to future of office growth [Online] http://www.bloomberg.com/news/2011-12-20/facebook-s-cool-space-campus-points-to-future-of-office-growth.html (accessed 9 March 2012)

Medici, A (2012) No desk, no nameplate, half the workspace: Feds adjust to 'hoteling', from *Federal Times*, January 21 [Online] http://www.federaltimes.com/article/20120121/FACILITIES02/201210301/ (accessed 3 March 2012)

Real Estate Executive Board (2010) *2010 Research Recap: Aligning CRE with Business Partners*, Corporate Executive Board Company, Washington, DC

Steelcase (2006) Case study: Radio Shack Corporation [Online] http://www.oneworkplace.com/images/dynamic/case_studies/RadioShack.pdf (accessed 6 March 2012)

Wind, Y and West, A (2006) Putting the organization on wheels: how SEI uses workplace design and art to create a corporate culture that drives innovation and growth, from *California Management Review* Special Issue on Workplace Design, June 8 [Online] http://marketing.wharton.upenn.edu/documents/research/0701_Putting_the_Organization_on_Wheels.pdf (accessed 9 March 2012)

Woods Bagot (2009) *Eversheds LLP, One Wood Street Design Intelligence Document*, Woods Bagot, London

Management fads

> *Journalists use the word 'guru' only because 'charlatan' is too long for a headline.*
>
> **(ATTRIBUTED TO PETER DRUCKER, MANAGEMENT THINKER)**

Objectives

At the end of this chapter you will be able to:

- decide whether something is a trend or a fad;
- assess whether or not to invest in something that might prove to be a fad;
- explain the roles of buyers and sellers of fads;
- keep an eye out for upcoming fads.

No one reading management journals, articles and blogs can fail to notice that something suddenly becomes the 'flavour of the month'. It is the same in the individual health and fitness field. There is a sudden torrent of information on the Atkins or South Beach diet, or the benefits of taking large quantities of vitamin C, doing step aerobics, Zumba dancing or hula hooping. Alongside the various high-profile 'flavours' are ideas, theories and concepts that may or may not contribute to individual health and well-being – homeopathy, acupuncture and other approaches generally termed 'alternative' therapies or medicines also fall into this bracket. Some even argue that conventional medical approaches are equally doubtful in their efficacy.

Quackwatch is an international network of people who are concerned about health-related frauds, myths, fads, fallacies and misconduct. Its primary focus is on quackery (see Glossary) and its network of doctors, advisors and academics provide information on what might be dubious medical claims that is difficult or impossible to get elsewhere. Its activities include:

- investigating questionable claims;
- answering inquiries about products and services;
- advising quackery victims;
- distributing reliable publications;
- debunking pseudoscientific claims;
- reporting illegal marketing;
- assisting or generating consumer-protection lawsuits;
- improving the quality of health information on the internet;
- attacking misleading advertising on the internet.

Unfortunately no such quack watch is concerned about the claims of management poobahs, pundits, gurus and panjandrums (aka consultants) touting the benefits to organizations of a fairly constant stream of products and services including: models, frameworks, methodologies, advice, five-point plans, seven steps to success, and statements on what makes a good leader. But there is no doubt that individuals seeking help on personal health matters and managers on organizational performance matters are similarly assailed by confusing advice, conflicting messages and the lure of the latest fad.

A couple of things about fads; first, they may or may not be valuable to invest in. The main point is to know what information is needed in order to make a sound investment decision and to be clear why the decision is being made: ie on what criteria and what the expected outcomes are. There is nothing intrinsically wrong about jumping on a bandwagon, even though the word 'fad' tends to have negative connotations. In the worst case it might provide a useful learning experience, and in the best it might result in success.

Second, a fad is not the same as a trend. Marilynn Larkin, a health and nutrition writer tells a story of writing on 'hot' nutrition topics, in this case the fad for oat bran:

> In 1989, at the height of oat bran's popularity as a panacea to lower cholesterol, the president and chief operating officer of a leading cereal manufacturer estimated that sales of oat-bran cereals would grow to nearly $600 million

annually. I wrote five oat-bran stories that year for various women's magazines. A year later, when a study called oat bran's health-promoting properties into question, sales plummeted 50 per cent within a week; at that point, I couldn't give away an article on oat bran. (Larkin, 2000)

However, the oat bran fad was related to a broader (and continuing) health trend of taking steps to reduce and/or maintain cholesterol levels to within a certain range. So think of a fad as something not expected to last – but which may be a contributor to a trend – and a trend as month-by-month or year-by-year movement. Trends are often shown graphically as 'trend lines' drawn from quantifiable metrics collected over time. Figure 8.1 illustrates a trend line in relation to dropping levels of 'bad' cholesterol in the population. Larkin, writing in 1989 about oat bran as a means of lowering cholesterol, was at the start of a downward trend in cholesterol levels. People jumped on the oat bran bandwagon, which was short-lived, but the downward trend continued, perhaps with another 'flavour of the month' replacing oat bran.

Trends in organizations are collected on performance-based data, obviously the financials, but also including customer satisfaction, company reputation,

FIGURE 8.1   High serum total cholesterol

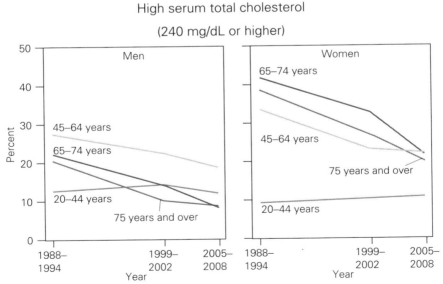

NOTE: High serum total cholesterol is measured serum total cholesterol of 240 mg/dL or higher.

SOURCE: National Institutes of Health http://www.ncbi.nlm.nih.gov/books/NBK54368/#healthrisk.s6

productivity and employee engagement among others. What managers do not know is whether the latest fad is going to contribute positively to the trend direction they are interested in. Who is to know whether the 'latest thing' in whatever decade will move the trend line in the right direction, or whether it will be debunked and/or prove to be fool's gold? Brainstorming, corporate social responsibility, customer relationship management, delayering, double-loop learning, empowerment, lean, learning organization, matrix management, outsourcing, process improvement, project management, quality circles, six sigma, succession planning, sustainability, total quality management, vertical integration and/or zero-based budgeting are some past fads that organizations have invested in. Some have proved valuable and others not.

But it is easy to generalize. For some organizations adoption of a fad will prove successful, while for others adoption of the same fad will not. It is similar for health fads: they deliver results for some people and not others. For example, even with endless diet and fitness fads the trend towards obesity is going upwards in many countries, including the United States and UK. Yet some individuals may well have bucked the general trend by losing weight and becoming fitter following their adoption of the diet/exercise flavour of the month. Remember too that fads are only part of a complex context. A company's success does not necessarily stand or fall by adoption of a fad – although it might.

Over the last 20 years or so, academics have been studying management fads (also called fashions in the theoretical literature) using techniques such as 'bibliometric research' (see Glossary) to track how often certain phrases appear in newspapers, magazines and academic journals in order to follow the rise and fall of keywords that might indicate the inception and life cycle of a fad. Complementing the academic research are various management and popular books on fads and fashions (see Resources).

Even so, although people seem to know when a fad 'hits' it is less obvious how they originate. It is not clear whether fads emanate from the academic research, from consultants coming up with a new idea to sell or from managers themselves seeing what works that somehow get transmitted through memes (see Glossary) and then on to academics and consultants who repackage it into the latest thing.

Neither is it clear whether 'fads' are a kind of necessary evil that bedevil organizations or whether they have a learning value in their own right that makes them worth the investment even though they often fail to deliver on their promises, have relatively short life cycles and swiftly decline into obscurity. However, just a quick look at *The Dilbert Principle: A Cubicle's-Eye View of Bosses, Meetings, Management Fads & Other Workplace Afflictions* (see Resources) illustrates the general response of a line manager to the next new thing. It is one of cynicism and sometimes despair.

Without a reliable 'Quackwatch' for managers, making a decision on whether or not to invest in the latest thing is fraught with difficulty. There is some merit in waiting and seeing – being a 'late adopter' in marketing speak – but that could mean missing the competitive advantage that early adopters might get. One way of taking a healthy approach to fads is to conduct a certain amount of due diligence and, as stated earlier, to be very clear on both reasons for investing in it and the outcomes it is expected to bring. Do not be beguiled by the sweet talk of the seller of the fad.

To help foster a healthy approach to fads this chapter looks more closely at them, offers some insights into the selling and buying of the latest fad, discusses what seem to be newcomers to the fad landscape, and in the spirit of anti-quackery suggests some buyer-beware pointers.

Pause for thought

Why is it useful to distinguish between a fad and a trend?

How true is it to say that managers tend to have a cynical attitude to the next new thing? How healthy is that attitude?

How useful would a 'quackwatch' for managers be?

Fads: definitions and adoption

A fad is something that captures the popular imagination and is adopted with wild enthusiasm for a relatively short period of time. Thus fads progress through a fairly swift life cycle of introduction, growth, maturity, decline and then either 'death' (that is, a drop out of fashion) or 'mainstreaming' (that is, absorption into the way things are done – losing the connotations of 'fad'). The history of Crocs shoes illustrates this.

Crocs, established in 2002, originally manufactured foam resin clogs as a boating shoe for a niche market in Canada. But by 2004 Crocs clogs had become a phenomenal hit and in 2006 the story on Crocs, specifically their clogs, was:

Celebrities adopt them. Young people adore them. The company goes from $1 million in revenue in 2003 to a projected $322 million this year. Crocs Inc's IPO in February was the richest in footwear history, and the company has a market cap of more than $1 billion. (Anderson, 2006)

A year later, one journalist wrote:

As fans will tell you, Crocs aren't just footwear; they're the closest thing to religion that the foot has experienced. The company's stock has skyrocketed in value over the past year, and Crocs is now poised to launch a new product line this fall. Yet Crocs are heinous in appearance. A Croc is not a shoe; it is a Tinkertoy on steroids. How did this peculiar shoe-manqué achieve ubiquity – and can it possibly stick around? (O'Rourke, 2007)

And two years later, in 2009, Deloitte & Touche, the company's auditors, expressed 'substantial doubt' about Crocs' ability to continue as a going concern. Deloitte cited:

[the] maturity of the company's revolving credit facility on April 2 and losses from operations... Crocs said that it is currently evaluating its operating plans for 2009, considering restructuring and right-sizing activities. It said its ability to keep operating is dependent upon achieving a cost structure which supports the levels of revenues we are able to achieve. (Taub, 2009)

By the end of 2011 though, Crocs had done a remarkable turnaround and was back in the black with $1 billion-plus in sales and $160 million in profits, but they were no longer a hot fad. They had become mainstream, offering among other footwear a collection of medical shoes specifically designed to provide therapeutic relief for a number of foot conditions, a collection aimed at recovery after an athletic event or competition, and a collection of work wear shoes for people whose jobs required a lot of standing or walking (Spellman, 2012).

So Crocs clogs is a classic example of a product fad. In Crocs case, it was able to regroup and recover from the dropping of the Crocs clogs fad by taking a number of actions, including extending their product line and thus becoming a more mainstream shoe company.

Management fads are similar to fashion fads and health fads and usually take one of three forms:

- Products, for example standing desks, might be an office furniture fad.

- Services, for example Twitter, discussed below might be a social media fad.

- Concepts, theories, beliefs and ideas that are 'packaged', usually by consultants, as services or interventions such as Six Sigma are also discussed below.

Academics offer many definitions of a management fad: below are five of the more commonly cited ones, variously suggesting that fads are:

- 'Relatively transitory collective beliefs, disseminated by the discourse of management-knowledge entrepreneurs, that a management technique is at the forefront of rational progress' (Williams, 2004).

- 'Widely accepted, innovative interventions into the organization's practices designed to improve some aspect of performance' (Gibson and Tesone, 2001).

- 'A short lived but enthusiastically pursued practice or interest' (Huczynski, 1993).

- 'Patterns of production and consumption of temporarily intensive management discourse, and the organizational changes induced by and associated with this discourse' (Benders and Van Veen, 2001).

- A thing that in the right conditions 'is promoted and disseminated widely by various individuals, agencies and institutions; it is timely, reflecting the problems of the age; and it targets managers who are seeking new ways of doing business' (Fineman, 2001).

Notice that within these five definitions are hints or statements about change and progress, innovation and performance improvement: it appears that organizational fad adoption is part of a concern to take advantage of the next new thing in the hope that it will bring organizational improvements. The case of Twitter, a micro blogging platform, exemplifies this. The company was established in 2006 and though growing in 2009 was dismissed as a fad:

> Twitter – it's fun and useful finding out what friends, co-workers, and industry big-shots are reading and thinking... But Twitter is still a fad, and according to a [recent] study, it looks like its popularity may soon fade. (Helm, 2009)

Yet three years later, in 2012, it was reported that the company was poised to 'be turning into a viable business... although still relatively small with 100 million active users (compared with Facebook's 800 million-plus members), Twitter has become the pulse of a planet wide news organism, hosting the dialogue about everything from the Arab Spring to celebrity deaths' (Stone, 2012).

FIGURE 8.2 Per cent of *Fortune* Global 100 companies with
Twitter accounts

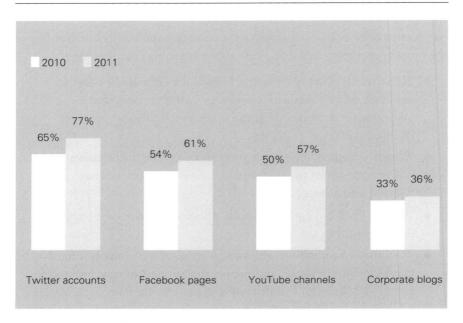

SOURCE: Burson Marsteller, 2012.

Indeed between 2010 and 2011, the adoption of Twitter by Fortune Global
100 companies as one of their platforms for interacting with their customers
grew by 12 per cent – from 65 per cent to 77 per cent – as Figure 8.2 shows.
Companies were using their Twitter accounts to provide company news,
updates, announcements to stakeholders, and information on deals or
contests specifically related to their products and/or services. As well as
this, more than a quarter (28 per cent) of corporate accounts in 2011 were
tweeting to consumers and also using Twitter to engage stakeholders on
customer service issues (Burson Marsteller, 2012).

But adopting a fad can be counterproductive. It can be a huge distraction
from the day-to-day task of running the company. Sam Palmisano, Chairman
of IBM, is of this view. During his tenure as CEO of IBM (January 2002 to
December 2011) he led the company to staggering success. He explained
how he did this:

> We always had the mosaic that we were gonna have a financial guidepost – a
> very straightforward financial guidepost. We were gonna get margin expansion,
> cash generation, and return it to the shareholder. We weren't into PR campaigns:

We're the biggest, we're the smartest, we're the this, we're the that, we're into this trend, right? We're not running fashion; we're not running fashion. It was gonna be that simple: margin expansion, cash generation, and give it back to you. Very, very simple model. (Evans, 2009a)

And we're not crazy kids. So we don't throw numbers out to throw numbers out. Y'know, we're not that short-term oriented... This is IBM, this is not, y'know, we're not running around up here dressed in fads, and sunglasses, and whatever kinda designs. (Evans 2009b)

IBM, does not have a corporate Twitter account. It is not that IBM is 'against' Twitter; rather it stays close to Palmisano's view that IBM is not running round 'dressed in fads'. They stated that they:

don't have a corporate blog or a corporate Twitter ID because we want the 'IBMers' in aggregate to be the corporate blog and the corporate Twitter ID. We represent our brand online the way it always has been, which is employees first. Our brand is largely shaped by the interactions that they have with customers.
(Hibbard, 2010)

So although there are social media guidelines, the basic premise is that individual IBMers are trustworthy users of social media channels.

The view that fads are time-consuming and can result in taking the eye off the operational ball is reflected in reservations from the advertisers who partly finance Twitter. They want to be where their customers are yet, as Joel Ewanick, chief marketing officer of car manufacturing company GM, said: 'maintaining a Twitter presence and supporting a Twitter ad campaign is more resource-intensive than running old-fashioned TV and print ads. All that engagement and authentic-seeming messaging can be exhausting. A company tweet can't look like it came from some corporate thing' (Stone, 2012).

Turning from Twitter as an example of a service fad (that may become mainstream) to the notion of fads as ideas and concepts, a good example is the field of process improvement, specifically six sigma. An academic review, published in 2008, using bibliometrics (see Glossary) concluded that 'the more recent concepts of lean and six sigma have mainly replaced – but not necessarily added to – the concepts of just-in-time and total quality management. Lean and six sigma are essentially repackaged versions of the former, and the methods [of adoption] seem to follow the fad (product) life cycle' (Naslund, 2008).

Just a year earlier, *Business Week* headlined an article 'Six sigma: so yesterday?' outlining the six sigma experiences of various companies, including Home Depot, a home improvements retailer.

> At Home Depot (HD), ousted Chief Executive Robert Nardelli was devoted
> to six sigma. 'Facts are friendly' was a favorite mantra of his, neatly summing
> up his managerial point of view. Six sigma was used to streamline the check-
> out process and strategically place vacuum-cleaner displays, for example...
> The bottom line on Nardelli's tenure: Profitability soared, but worker morale
> drooped, and so did consumer sentiment. (*Business Week*, 2007)

His successor, Frank Blake, 'dialled back' on the approach – allowing local managers choices in how they ran their stores and interacted with their customers, and this response was in line with other companies' including GE, and Sun Microsystems.

Answering the question: 'Has the six sigma moment passed?' Tom Davenport, author and academic (see Resources), responded, 'I think it has. Process management is a good thing. But I think it always has to be leavened a bit with a focus on innovation and [customer relationships]. [Six sigma] was developed as a systematic way to improve quality, but the reason it caught fire was its effectiveness in cutting costs and improving profitability.'

These examples of IBM, Twitter and six sigma show some of the complexity surrounding fads. For a fad to 'take', a whole host of factors need to simultaneously be in play. Broadly these can be grouped into socio-psychological factors and techno-economic factors.

Socio-psychological factors

In the book *The Tipping Point* (see Resources), author Malcolm Gladwell uses a medical analogy to explain the emergence of a fad. He suggests thinking of it as an epidemic. 'Ideas and products and messages and behaviors spread just like viruses do.' In this respect they are contagious. His popular book discusses three socio-psychological 'rules' that come into play to make a fad tip from the few interested in it to the many that turn it into an 'epidemic': the law of the few, the stickiness factor and the power of context. Much of the book is oversimplification; indeed some reviewers put it into the 'quack' category, and suggest that it needs to be taken with a pinch of salt. Nevertheless, the book serves to illustrate that social and psychological factors are instrumental in fad take-up and acceptance.

Eric Abrahamson's classic academic article on management fashion written in 1996 (the same year that Gladwell wrote his original *New Yorker* article 'The tipping point', which was expanded into the book with the same title) developed the socio-psychological element of fad adoption, suggesting that managers are vulnerable to this if they are:

- Frustrated that the way things are going is not resulting in progress or improvement and they are looking for some kind of magic bullet that will provide the cure.

- Seeking novelty – so that rather than sticking with the perhaps boring status quo they are looking for a new way of doing things that will re-energize and re-motivate people, with an outcome of performance improvement.

- Striving for organizational status differentiation. In this case senior managers aim to differentiate their organizations by adopting something intended to give them a higher reputational edge than their competitors (Abrahamson, 1996).

Techno-economic factors

This category of factors relates to the external and internal technical and economic forces that shape the supply and demand of fads. Abrahamson suggests, for example, that during periods of economic expansion there will be a demand for management techniques that focus on technologies to increase productivity, while during periods of contraction there will be a focus on techniques that stress employee engagement as a means of increasing productivity.

Adoption of the techno-economic fad itself can rebound, causing a swing to an opposite fad; for example in aiming to make productivity (economic) gains a drive to centralize is likely to follow a period of decentralization if that has not yielded the expected gains or if it compromises the socio-psychological element. Like Home Depot, Cisco, a technology company, is another case in point, as indicated in Table 8.1.

Thinking about the factors that need to be in play for a fad to 'take' as socio-psychological factors and techno-economic factors is not either/or. Both have to be present. Additionally there has to be a 'buyer' of the fad and a 'seller' of it, and this aspect is discussed in the next section.

Fad buyers and sellers

A look back at the definitions of fads shows that innovation is commonly one of the characteristics of a fad, but it doesn't have to be. Sometimes a fad is a recycle of something previous that suddenly re-sparks interest. Malcolm Gladwell cites Hush Puppy shoes as an example of this. Other examples

TABLE 8.1   Cisco, centralizing and decentralizing

2008	2012
John Chambers, CEO, reorganized starting 2001 so that 'The leaders of business units formerly competing for power and resources now share responsibility for one another's success. What used to be 'me' is now 'we.' The goal is to get more products to market faster, and Chambers crows at the results. 'The boards and councils have been able to innovate with tremendous speed. Fifteen minutes and one week to get a [business] plan that used to take six months!' Cisco, Chambers argues, is the best possible model for how a large, global business can operate: as a distributed idea engine where leadership emerges organically, unfettered by a central command.	John Chamber, CEO, e-mailing employees: 'Today we face a simple truth: we have disappointed our investors and we have confused our employees. Bottom line, we have lost some of the credibility that is foundational to Cisco's success – and we must earn it back. Our market is in transition, and our company is in transition. And the time is right to define this transition for ourselves and our industry. I understand this. It's time for focus. We will make it easier for you to work at Cisco, as we make it easier for our customers and partners to work with Cisco. We will simplify the way we work and how we focus our attention and resources. We will significantly rework our systems, tools and funding models to do this. **http://blogs.cisco.com/news/message-from-john-chambers-where-cisco-is-taking-the-network/**

include 'retro' cars, or furniture. At other times it can be an iteration or 'improvement' of the previous fad. Some commentators have suggested that out of 'disintegrating fads come remnants which, often under new names, become new fads or blend into standard operating practice' (Naslund, 2008) – the evolution of process improvement methods: Japanese Total Quality Control (JTQC), total quality management (TQM), Deming's system of profound knowledge, business process reengineering (BPR), lean thinking and six sigma is illustrative of this line of thinking.

This characteristic of the 'next new thing' seems to be one of the motivators of a purchase decision by both managers as the consumers of the fad and consultants as the sellers of the fad. And in pushing the next new thing consultants are popularly seen as snake oil salesmen, rather than true consultants. One manager made this point eloquently:

> He is a good salesman, though he would be appalled to know that. I don't think he can park his ego enough to be a great consultant. Several of my mates who know him from his work fall about laughing at the self-puffery that goes on around some of his stuff. It's amazingly unselfconscious for one who ought to realize how he comes across and be more humble, given he has never run much in the way of a business himself. I think consultants are way off base. Delivering today is not a trivial and banal activity for the little people; it's what earns you the right to think big thoughts about what needs to be done tomorrow and the day after.

But managers are not helpless beings unable to resist the lure of the salesperson. Several researchers argue (in the words of one of them) 'that the phenomenon of management fad succession is the result of the conscious and unconscious collusion between managers as consumers of management ideas and consultants as suppliers of such ideas' (Huczynski, 1993). This collusion is a complex interaction which operates at a number of levels: organization, competition, individual and suppliers.

Organization

Organizations are continuously searching for improvements in their business performance and tend to look at fads for one or more of four reasons – all related to improving performance: they have an immediate problem that needs to be solved, they want to generate internal motivation around a cause – for example, 'putting the customer first' – they want to try out a new approach to an intractable problem, or they want the fad to accelerate a planned change.

Where these reasons are known, or advice is solicited around them, pressure can be brought to bear on organizations by consulting firms, management gurus and popular authors or speakers to at least entertain the idea of the next new thing. Brochures and marketing collateral are often threaded with data and claims that aim to convince readers of the value of investing in the new approach. And if the fads have the following eight characteristics it becomes an easier sell.

Organizations are likely to be attracted to a fad if it is:

- Simple to understand, easy to communicate and associated with buzzwords and catchphrases.

- Prescriptive in its approach – it tells managers what to do in things like seven steps, or five phases.

- Encouraging of successful outcomes by raising hopes, even if there is little in the way of evaluative process attached to the sales pitch.

- Universally relevant or one-size-fits all, as shown by exemplars who have already adopted the fad.

- Easy to apply in practice, or even partially apply, by taking some elements of the method – this makes it easier to graft on to existing operations without whole scale change.

- Able to speak directly to business issues of the day, eg to downsizing in a recession.

- Interesting because of its novelty but not so radical as to disturb the underlying status quo.

- Given legitimacy by consultants and/or their successful devotees – an endorsement by a management celebrity and/or their followers goes a long way even without any evidence of true results (Miller and Hartwick, 2002).

Competition

Ignoring what the competition is doing in the way of fad adoption could well be a high-risk strategy. Given that fads are often linked to innovation and innovation diffusion, not participating could mean being overtaken by a competitor. Additionally companies want to be seen by their customers to be ahead of their competitors – 'a market leader' – and some kinds of fads promote that type of image. Greening the supply chain is an example of this as Andrew Winston (2010), a *Harvard Business Review* blogger, implies:

> While the 'greening of the supply chain' has been in the works for decades, the movement has really taken off in 2010. In the last few months, a number of corporate giants have announced new initiatives that pressure suppliers to do much more to measure and manage their environmental impacts. The big guns asking the questions include Pepsi, P&G, and IBM... IBM execs know that the green path is a profitable one.

With the 'big guns' firing, it is only a matter of time before the next tier leaps into greening their supply chains. (See the 'Pause for thought' question at the end of this section.)

Some fads act as incentives to attract and retain staff – thus keeping talent from straying to a competitor. Flexible or cafeteria benefits schemes are an example of this; they allow staff to select the benefits that suit them.

Individual

In the section above on fads and fad adoption, three reasons are given for why individual managers adopt fads. They are frustrated by the way things are going. They are seeking novelty. They are striving for organizational status differentiation. But there are additional reasons: individual managers are often attracted to a fad, first, not because it may offer a solution to an organizational problem but because it might offer a path to that person's greater power and influence in the organization. Latching onto a new idea may be a good career move because it helps distinguish one person from another in a crowd. For example, becoming a six sigma black belt may bring individual benefit in the form of enhanced pay or prestige.

Second, adopting a fad is sometimes a kind of managerial defence tactic in that it demonstrates a willingness to seek remedies to a problem. Being interested in a new topic provides some evidence that a manager is not a 'stick in the mud' but is willing to take a look at what is new out there in order to get things working. The scenario below illustrates this:

> Place yourself in the position of a mid-level manager of an organization. Things aren't going too well for you. Productivity is lagging. What could be the problem? Something you haven't done? Certainly not! No, it's those employees out there. They're just not motivated. So the answer is to start up a new idea motivation programme. That ought to do the trick. And look what you accomplish with this. First, the problem is acknowledged and officially identified as a problem of individuals, not of the management system. Next, you can pat yourself on the back for having taken corrective action. Crisp, hard-hitting decision-making. You've gotten yourself a big name 'motivation consultant' (talk funny, make money) and you'll put a programme in place. There, that should take care of it. (Ritti and Levy, 2003)

Third, managers want a panacea or quick fix, even though rationally they know this is not likely to work. There are no magic bullets or simple recipes for business success. But in the fast-paced always-on world that managers live in, the attraction of the quick win that does not involve much in the way of thought is almost irresistible. As Peter Drucker, a management thinker said, 'Thinking is very hard work. And management fashions are a substitute for thinking.'

Suppliers

Suppliers of management fads can, from the get-go, be reasonably assured that the fad will have a life cycle that is on the lines of:

1 An academic article is written on a new discovery or theory.
2 The study is discussed, summarized and repeated.
3 The concept is popularized in a best-selling book.
4 Throngs of management consultants carry the new technique to their client base.
5 Managers embrace the fad and champion the concept.
6 Time passes, enthusiasm dims, and doubts and cynicism arise.
7 New discoveries occur and consultant interest turns elsewhere (Naslund, 2008).

Note: An alternative, and well-known in academic circles, fad life cycle is five stages: discovery, wild acceptance, digestion, disillusionment and hard core (Ettore, 1997). This follows a bell curve, with digestion at the top, and hard core (only the total believers in the fad) at the end.

Thus, suppliers have first to work with a built-in obsolescence in mind, and second with the knowledge that are they vying not only for 'their' fad to have a higher appeal than suppliers of the same fad offered by other consultants but also a higher appeal than a different fad. At any one time managers and organizations are assailed by fad sellers and are often making decisions on them relative to other decisions on other fads. (For example, is investing in outdoor management team-building events a better bet than investing in lean techniques?) Knowing that what they sell is probably going to go out of fashion relatively rapidly, consultants have to have the next big thing ready in the pipeline to offer to clients. A look at Table 8.2 in the following section that lists 2012 contenders for the next new fad award shows what might be a consultant's line up. Readers of this book beyond 2012 will be able to see which were fads, which became mainstream, and which never got off the ground. Bear in mind Scott Adam's (originator of Dilbert cartoons) point on prediction:

> There are many methods for predicting the future. For example, you can read horoscopes, tea leaves, tarot cards, or crystal balls. Collectively, these methods are known as 'nutty methods.' Or you can put well-researched facts into sophisticated computer models, more commonly referred to as 'a complete waste of time.'

Second, suppliers have to balance a degree of authenticity with recognition that they have a vested interest in their fad being adopted. This is not an easy thing to do and only a few succeed, which contributes to the stereotype of consultants being people who steal a client's watch in order to tell him the time. In a review of the book *The Management Myth: Debunking modern business philosophy* by Matthew Stewart (see Resources) the reviewer points out Stewart's whistleblowing on the profession. Following in the tradition of Frederick Winslow Taylor (see Resources), who was accused by both his enemies and colleagues of fudging his data, lying to his clients and inflating his successes:

> Stewart did the same things during his seven years as a management consultant; fudging, lying, and inflating, he says, are the profession's stock-in-trade. Stewart had just finished a DPhil at Oxford in philosophy when he took a job rigging spreadsheets to tell companies whose business he barely understood how to trim costs, and he feels sullied by it. (Lepore, 2009)

Third, suppliers are information sorters and guides: in essence managers are delegating the work of sifting through the multitude of white papers, tweets, journals, Ted talks (see Resources), management websites, case studies, MBA lectures (see Resources), conference presentations and so on to the consultant whose role is to make certain the uncertain, to simplify the complex, and to present 'solutions' in an easy to work with approach. Often this involves presenting materials through anecdote, story, sound bites and simple visuals rather than sound data, either quantitative or qualitative. Managers, maybe unconsciously, collude in this on at least two counts: a) they appreciate the talent consultants have for making the connections between what's going on in the outside world and what's going on in that specific organization's world – albeit at a high level; b) they like the idea of a 'hand holder' who will give them confidence to keep changing the organization on the premise that 'everything will be okay in the end and if it's not okay it's not the end' (attributed to John Lennon among others).

In summary, the way fads are bought and sold bears examination. Returning to the health analogy currently the relationship of buyers to sellers is:

> like the practice of medicine in the Middle Ages. A leech under the armpit, and one to the groin, with no understanding of bacteria, viruses or how the body worked, there were lots of prescriptions... But cures were largely the product of random chance. A parallel holds today. Lots of remedies but few examples of authentic transformation. Organizations churn through one technique after another and at best get incremental improvement on top of business as usual. At worst, these efforts waste resources and evoke cynicism and resignation.
>
> (Crainer, 1996)

Pause for thought

What stands in the way of taking the long view rather than getting overly caught up in the latest trends and infatuated with the latest fashions?

How much is the buying and selling of management fads a conscious or unconscious collusion between manager and consultant/seller?

What is the difference between a fad and a movement?

How true is it to say that 'fundamental and enduring truths will always trump fads and fanfare?' (Evans, 2010).

Fad watch

Through various media channels, conversations and often vague intuition, managers are aware of what they might be expected to adopt with alacrity. Table 8.2 gives a list of some of these items. Note that they have not been selected using bibliometrics or on any valid or reliable basis. Bear in mind the two types of forecasters that the economist John Kenneth Galbraith identified – 'Those who don't know, and those who don't know they don't know' – and take the list as something to think about rather than a forecast. Look down the list and reflect on whether the item is a fad and if so where it is in the life cycle of fads.

Pause for thought

What management/organizational fads have come and gone in the last five years?

What aspects of organizational life and operation have started off as a fad and have now been integrated into the way business is conducted?

What is it about fads that sidelines or mainstreams them?

How easy is it to predict the next new thing? Why/why not should it be attempted?

TABLE 8.2   Are these fads?

Fad?	Description
B corps.	A certification system for companies aiming to build a more inclusive, resilient, and sustainable economy. Success in the 21st century not only making money but doing so carefully and in a way that creates public benefit.
Behavioral analytics	Many companies are using behavioral analytics, also known as personalization, to better serve consumers. Netflix and Amazon popularized the concept of using previous buying history and profile information to recommend products to their customers. This kind of intelligence enables targeting advertising.
Big data analytics Data reduction Data visualization	Tapping into enormous reservoirs of information – for example 1 billion tweets every three days, or voice patterns in customer service calls – to yield useful analytical insights for organization performance improvement. Hand in hand with capturing 'big data' goes 'data reduction' that transforms and orders it into usable forms – often these are visualizations, or info graphics. See Figure 8.4.
Biomimicry	Biomimicry (from bios, meaning life, and mimesis, meaning to imitate) is a new discipline that studies nature's best ideas and then imitates these designs and processes to solve human problems. Studying a leaf to invent a better solar cell is an example. Think of it as 'innovation inspired by nature.' (Benyus, 2007)
Clean tech	An umbrella term to describe the 'green and clean' technologies, especially including solar, biofuels, fuel cells, water remediation, and renewable power generation that venture capital investors were turning to in increasing numbers as the next trend in technology investing after the collapse of the tech boom in 2001. (Dikeman, 2008)
Collaborative work spaces	Office space designed to enable people to interact informally as well as formally, including a variety of adaptive space, and excluding private offices for named individuals.

TABLE 8.2   *continued*

Fad?	Description
Cradle to cradle	Gained ground following publication of the book *Cradle to Cradle* (see Resources). Briefly suggests that aiming to reduce the negative impacts of commerce should be replaced by a new paradigm of increasing its positive impacts ('eco-effectiveness'), around the three elements of people, planet, profit. Advocates for all product components to be designed for continuous recovery and reutilization. Includes a certification programme. InterfaceFLOR is an example of an organization using this approach.
Crowdsourcing	Developing ideas, products, and services through the power of the many often without payment to them but relying on their interest and goodwill. (Wikipedia is an example of this).
Design thinking	The application of product and architecture design approaches to the design of business strategies and operations.
Gamification	Gamification, which differs from the traditional use of video in the workplace, is based on using game mechanics and game theory to drive behaviour by injecting some fun and a sense of community into the workplace. 'In terms of health and wellness, companies like zamzee, basis, and Massive Health have gamified diet, exercise, and monitoring routines, while companies such as BreakAway have launched successful medical education, training and simulation modules. (Spitz, 2011)
Green jobs	A green job, also called a green-collar job is, 'work in agricultural, manufacturing, research and development (R&D), administrative, and service activities that contribute(s) substantially to preserving or restoring environmental quality. Specifically, but not exclusively, this includes jobs that help to protect ecosystems and biodiversity; reduce energy, materials, and water consumption through high efficiency strategies; de-carbonize the economy; and minimize or altogether avoid generation of all forms of waste and pollution.' (United Nations Environment Program, 2008)

TABLE 8.2 *continued*

Fad?	Description
Positive psychology, wellness, happiness	Positive Psychology is the scientific study of the strengths and virtues that enable individuals and communities to thrive. The field is founded on the belief that people want to lead meaningful and fulfilling lives, to cultivate what is best within themselves, and to enhance their experiences of love, work, and play. Positive Psychology has three central concerns: positive emotions, positive individual traits, and positive institutions. Understanding positive emotions entails the study of contentment with the past, happiness in the present, and hope for the future. (Positive Psychology Center, 2007)
Neuro (marketing, economics, etc)	Neuromarket researchers essentially connect sensors to a person and monitor brain activity. It can help marketers deduce why a person found an ad to be interesting by mapping what areas of the brain were stimulated by the ad. Neuroeconomists
No offices/ hoteling Co-working	Some organizations do not house their workers at all. They work from home or otherwise remotely, perhaps in a co-working environment. (see Glossary). If workers want to come into their corporate office they can 'touch down' and/or book a space via a hoteling system.
Outsourcing	Contracting with another company or person to do work or a job that was previously done in-house. City councils in the UK have outsourced a number of functions that they previously did themselves – architecture and waste collection, for example.

TABLE 8.2   *continued*

Fad?	Description
Organizational energy	Organizational energy is described as the force which an organization uses to purposefully put things in motion. There is a notion that this energy is decisive for a company's capabilities, particularly for growth, change and innovation as the degree of organizational energy shows to what extent an organization utilizes its emotional, mental and behavioural potential in order to pursue its goals. Organizational energy is expressed through intensity, vigour and pace of work, change and innovation processes. Lack of organizational energy appears as organizational inertia, burnout, and resignation
Post PC era	The post PC era describes a point where people's computing needs and habits will be satisfied on a smartphone or tablet. They will not need to sit at a laptop or desktop PC to access information and computing functionality will be incorporated into other devices for example, cars and household appliances. This mobility is enabled by cloud technology and the increasing availability and use of mobile devices. Alongside mobile functionality is the development of software that can provide additional context. For example alerting a user to the immediate availability of a local parking spot. It may be that The Post-PC world is more than a shift in device use. It may be a shift in computing as we know it.
Prediction markets	A method of taking the informed guesswork of many and consolidating it into hard probability. As the name suggests prediction markets are all about predicting how the business and money markets will behave in the future and making the most out of the accurate predictions. (Intrade.com is a well established prediction market).
Results only work environment (ROWE)	A management strategy where employee performance is evaluated on outcome – results achieved – and not on presence or output.

TABLE 8.2   *continued*

Fad?	Description
Self-managed teams, erosion of hierarchy, end of leadership	A view that with technologies, politics, and ideas changing the notions of 'leading' are based in obsolete paradigms. The leadership industry has failed to live up to promises and expectations and followers are disillusioned. Other forms of leadership need to be brought into play.
Social advertising	Advertisements tailored to particular individuals by following their preferences in data retrieved from their web activity. For example, people will see on their screen messages from a marketer such as 'John and three of your other friends like Smarties'.
Social data	Social data can reveal consumer preferences, feedback on products, and ratings, and, of course, social media response to a new product launch or campaign can boost performance.
Social media	Social media is user generated content that is shared over the internet via technologies that promote engagement, sharing and collaboration. (Tomassi, 2012)
Sustainability	The integration of economics, operational business practices and relationships as well as environmental considerations, to build something lasting. (Walsh, 2012)
Virtual and remote working	Working from home, or in a remote environment not immediately accessible to company headquarters.

Buyer beware

Dismissing a fad out of hand is not a sensible learning mechanism, but neither is leaping in to adopt it. There is danger in believing that a fad peddler is an expert who knows more about the topic than the potential buyer. In answer to the questions 'Can we do without experts?' Richard

Tetlock, an organizational behaviour researcher on experts, said 'No way. We need to believe we live in a predictable, controllable world, so we turn to authoritative-sounding people who promise to satisfy that need. That's why part of the responsibility for experts' poor record falls on us. We seek out experts who promise impossible levels of accuracy, then we do a poor job keeping score' (Schurenberg, 2009).

As in the field of medical care, it is good practice to do research and seek second opinions before making a decision to act. Be aware of the possibility of 'mimetic isomorphism'; this occurs if the organization is aspiring to mimic the performance, structures and practices of other organizations as a response to situations of uncertainty in which management is under pressure to improve performance, but does not know how to reach this objective. At this point some good advice is to:

> Trust yourself. Trust your own experience and apply it to the current market place. You won't do any worse than the consultants to whom you'd otherwise pay good money. To truly understand what any given business is doing right or doing wrong, you have to fully understand what it is doing. Most businesses don't have the machinery and/or can't afford the time to do that, so we stagger on as best we can with the best-available data. (Mason, 2010)

One way of deciding about whether or not to adopt a fad is to consider it as a field experiment. So in the case of determining whether, for example, to adopt Twitter (either organizationally or individually), follow the scientific method:

1 Make observations (about Twitter use in the general population and other organizations).
2 Formulate a hypothesis (about how it will benefit or work in the organization).
3 Design and conduct an experiment to test the hypothesis – this is the part that is often missed out in organizations. There is no pilot test, just a blanket 'let's adopt this'.
4 Keep a close eye on what is happening.
5 Evaluate the results of the experiment – this is another step that is often left out in organizations.
6 Accept or reject the hypothesis.
7 If necessary, make and test a new hypothesis.

Using this approach means taking the view that fads are successive experiments to secure the future, and as such are worth looking at, remembering as the experiment unfurls to 'Be prepared to turn back if circumstances turn against you' (advice from English Mountain Rescue) and that the experience garnered in one place is generally not much use elsewhere. Some other sound advice comes from a book review on intervention in a foreign country's affairs – *Can Intervention Work?* by Rory Stewart and Gerald Knaus – where, in answer to the question 'So, does intervention work?' (Take the word 'intervention' as a substitute for fad), the response is: 'As any Bosnian peasant may tell you, "maybe yes, maybe no." It depends on the circumstances and requires modest ambitions. Muddle through with a sense of purpose, says Mr Knaus. Do what you can, where you can and no more, agrees Mr Stewart' (*Economist*, 2011).

Exercise

Checklist to reflect on before adopting a fad

Use the checklist plus comments in the table below to take stock before plunging into fad adoption. If there are more 'yes' answers to the 11 questions than 'no' answers, it may be in order to go ahead. If there are more 'no' answers than 'yes' answers think very carefully and assess the risks before committing to adoption.

Question	Comments
1. Has the fad been around long enough to have a proven track record for performance and measurable outcomes in other similar companies facing similar challenges to ours?	Do some due diligence before investing. Without impartial and evidence-based metrics of success it is taking a risk to be the testing ground for untried and unproven fads.
2. Does the goal of the fad complement the needs of the organization?	Understand what problem, issue or opportunity is expected to be addressed by adopting the fad. Assess the likelihood of success against the resources invested.
3. Does the fad address problems or opportunities that are a high priority for our company?	Know what is a high priority for your company. Do not invest in something that is not a high priority just because it seems like a good idea to follow the masses.

Question	Comments
4. Does implementation of the fad mesh with the organizational culture?	Check that the new fad meshes with the current organizational culture. Consider whether the culture can adapt quickly enough if the fad/organization fit is not good. (For example, a fad for self-managing teams will not mesh well in a command-and-control hierarchy where people expect to be told what to do.)
5. Will adopting the fad help the organization remain competitive?	Fix on the competitive advantage that fad adoption is expected to bring. If there is no competitive advantage think carefully about adopting it.
6. Does the organization have the capabilities and resources needed to implement the fad?	Determine what the total direct and indirect resource investment is likely to be in terms of introducing, implementing and embedding the fad.
7. Do the expected benefits of the fad outweigh the direct and indirect costs?	Develop a soundly argued, fact and evidence-based business case for fad adoption. Lay out the assumptions, limitations and risks of adoption.
8. Can the fad be implemented in small sections of the organization to test the new concepts with minimum risk?	Conduct a pilot or test the prototype before launching into enterprise-wide fad adoption. Review progress. What works in some parts of the organization may not work in others. Learn from the test experiences.
9. Has the organization's track record with previous fad adoptions been positive?	Review past fad adoption experiences. What happened? What worked well? What needs to be done differently in introducing this new fad to raise its chances of success?

Question	Comments
10. Can you wait for the long-term benefits from fad adoption?	Limit expectations of instant results. Fads take time to implement and embed. They are not a quick fix.
11. Can organizational inertia and resistance to change be managed to successfully implement the fad?	Ensure that organizational policies, infrastructures, technologies and readiness are supportive of the new fad. People and organizational systems must be aligned to support successful fad adoption.
12. Are you conscious of the different context between your organization's and others' who have adopted it?	Take care that the notion of fad adoption is not just a 'copycat' response to what other organizations are doing.
13. If you were to adopt the fad, are advocates for it in possession of a mental model of how this change could benefit the organization or not and have a programme to measure it in some way?	Make sure that the reasons for adoption of the fad are clear, agreed and transparent, and that the intended benefits are measurable along points in time.
14. Do you have a choice?	Examine the level of political or other pressure that is being brought to bear to adopt this fad. Some managers want to jump on a bandwagon to look good, up to date, or progressive. Be realistic about motivations in adopting the fad.

SOURCE: adapted from Gibson and Tesone, 2001.

Key messages

- There is no oversight or control of the claims made by consultants and others involved in selling management fads.

- Fad adoption may or may not contribute to a trend direction that an organization is interested in, eg improving customer satisfaction.

- There are many definitions of a management fad but most imply change, innovation and improved business performance. Fads tend to have a short life cycle before they die or become mainstream.

- A number of factors – socio-psychological and techno-economic – have to be in play for a fad to take.

- Fad adoption involves the different motivations of a seller and a buyer.

- Knowing whether or not to adopt a fad requires due diligence, caution and a certain amount of intuition.

References

Abrahamson, E (1996) Management fashion, *Academy of Management Review*, 21 (1), pp 254–85

Anderson, D (2006) When Crocs attack: an ugly shoe tale [Online] http://money.cnn.com/2006/11/02/magazines/business2/crocs_whatworks.biz2/index.htm (accessed 23 March 2012)

Benders, J and Van Veen, K (2001) What's in a fashion? Interpretative viability and management fashions, *Organization*, 8 (1), pp 33–53

Benyus, J (2007) What is biomimicry? [Online] http://biomimicryinstitute.org/about-us/what-is-biomimicry.html (accessed 25 March 2012)

Burson Marsteller (2012) The global social media check-up 2011 (Burson-Marsteller) – FEB2011 [Online] http://www.slideshare.net/sociatriacom/49056658-theglobalsocialmediacheckup2011bursonmarstellerfeb2011 (accessed 24 March 2012)

Business Week (2007) Six sigma: so yesterday? [Online] http://www.businessweek.com/magazine/content/07_24/b4038409.htm (accessed 24 March 2012)

Canalys (2012) Smart phones overtake client PCs in 2011 [Online] http://www.canalys.com/newsroom/smart-phones-overtake-client-pcs-2011 (accessed 15 March 2012)

Crainer, S (1996) UK: the rise of guru scepticism [Online] http://www.managementtoday.co.uk/news/410860/UK-RISE-GURU-SCEPTICISM/?DCMP=ILC-SEARCH (accessed 24 March 2012)

Dikeman, N (2008) What is clean tech? [Online] http://news.cnet.com/8301-11128_3-10012950-54.html (accessed 25 March 2012)

Economist(2011) When to hold and when to fold [Online] http://www.economist.com/node/21533357 (accessed 25 March 2012)

Ettore, B (1997) What's the next business buzzword?*Management Review*, 86 (8), pp 33–35

Evans, B (2009a) Global CIO: Sam Palmisano's grand strategy for IBM revealed in $5b global financing plan [Online] http://www.informationweek.com/news/ global-cio/interviews/217700880?pgno=1 (accessed 17 March 2012)

Evans, B (2009b) IBM CEO Sam Palmisano tells investors, 'we got it all' [Online] http://www.informationweek.com/blog/main/archives/2009/05/ ibm_ceo_sam_pal.html (accessed 17 March 2012)

Evans, B (2010) Global CIO: IBM top product exec discusses strategy, systems, & oracle [Online] http://www.informationweek.com/news/global-cio/ interviews/227001077 (accessed 17 March 2012)

Fineman, S (2001) Fashioning the environment, *Organization*, 8 (1), pp 17–31

Gibson, J and Tesone, D (2001) Management fads: emergence, evolution, and implications for managers, *Academy of Management Executive*, 15 (4), pp 122–33

Helm, B (2009) Twitter is a fad [Online] http://www.businessweek.com/the_thread/ brandnewday/archives/2009/04/twitter_is_a_fa_1.html (accessed 17 March 2012)

Hibbard, C (2010) How IBM uses social media to spur employee innovation [Online] http://www.socialmediaexaminer.com/how-ibm-uses-social-media-to- spur-employee-innovation/ (accessed 22 March 2012)

Huczynski, A (1993) Explaining the succession of management fads, *International Journal of Human Resource Management*, 4 (2), pp 443–63

Kass, D (2011) IDC: PC sales worldwide rose 13.6 percent in 2010 [Online] http://www.itchannelplanet.com/trends/article.php/3920931/ IDC-PC-Sales-Worldwide-Rose-136-Percent-in-2010-Despite-Lackluster- Q4-and-Strong-Tablet-Sales.htm (accessed 15 March 2012)

Larkin, M (2000) Confessions of a former women's magazine writer [Online] http://www.nutriwatch.org/12Media/confessions.html (accessed 11 March 2012)

Lepore, J (2009) Not so fast [Online] http://www.newyorker.com/arts/critics/ atlarge/2009/10/12/091012crat_atlarge_lepore?currentPage=all (accessed 25 March 2012)

Mason, L (2010) The management myth: debunking modern business philosophy by Matthew Stewart [Online] http://www.thebookbag.co.uk/reviews/ index.php?title=The_Management_Myth:_Debunking_Modern_Business _Philosophy_by_Matthew_Stewart (accessed 25 March 2012)

Miller, D and Hartwick, J (2002) Spotting management fads, *Harvard Business Review*, October, pp 26–27

Naslund, D (2008) Lean, six sigma and lean sigma: fads or real process improvement methods?*Business Process Management Journal*, 14 (3), pp 269–87

O'Rourke, M (2007) The Croc epidemic [Online] http://www.slate.com/articles/ news_and_politics/the_highbrow/2007/07/the_croc_epidemic.html (accessed 23 March 2012)

Positive Psychology Center (2007) Positive Psychology Center [Online] http://www.ppc.sas.upenn.edu/ (accessed 25 March 2012)

Ritti, R and Levy, S (2003) *The Ropes to Skip and the Ropes to Know: Studies in organizational behavior* (6th edn), John Wiley, New York

Schurenberg, E (2009) Why the experts missed the crash [Online] http://money.cnn.com/2009/02/17/pf/experts_Tetlock.moneymag/index.htm (accessed 25 March 2012)

Siegler, M (2011) Vinod Khosla on the Post-PC Era and Stealth Hamburger Companies [Online] http://techcrunch.com/2011/09/13/meat-two-point-o/ (accessed 12 July 2012)

Spellman, J (2012) How a trendy shoe nearly lost its footing [Online] http://www.cnn.com/2012/03/16/living/american-comeback-crocs/index.html (accessed 23 March 2012)

Spitz, M (2011) The gamification of healthcare and what it means for mobile [Online] http://www.pharmaphorum.com/2011/12/09/mhealth-monthly-mashup-release-6-0-the-gamification-of-healthcare-and-what-it-means-for-mobile/ (accessed 25 March 2012)

Stone, B (2012) Twitter, the startup that wouldn't die [Online] http://www.businessweek.com/articles/2012-03-01/twitter-the-startup-that-wouldnt-die#p2 (accessed 17 March 2012)

Taub, S (2009) Crocs steps onto going-concern turf [Online] http://www.cfo.com/article.cfm/13315331 (accessed 23 March 2012)

Thompson, W (2011) Worldwide survey of fitness trends for 2012, *ACSM's Health and Fitness Journal*, 15 (6), pp 9–18

Tomassi, M (2012) 50 definitions of social media [Online] http://thesocialmediaguide.com/social_media/50-definitions-of-social-media (accessed 25 March 2012)

United Nations Environment Program (2008) Green jobs: towards decent work in a sustainable, low-carbon world [Online] http://www.unep.org/labour_environment/PDFs/Greenjobs/UNEP-Green-Jobs-Report.pdf (accessed 25 March 2012)

Walsh, M (2012) MBA diary: switching from the accelerator to the sustain pedal [Online] http://www.economist.com/whichmba/mba-diary-switching-accelerator-sustain-pedal?fsrc=nlw%7Cmgt%7C3-7-2012%7Cmanagement_thinking (accessed 25 March 2012)

Williams, R (2004) Management fashions and fads: understanding the role of consultants and managers in the evolution of ideas, *Management Decision*, 42 (5/6), pp 769–89

Winston, A (2010) IBM's green supply chain, HBR Blog Network [Online] http://blogs.hbr.org/winston/2010/07/ibms-green-supply-chain.html (accessed 26 March 2012)

GLOSSARY

Bibliometric research is the application of mathematical and statistical methods to books and other media of communication. It is used to track and measure the number of citations of an author's work, and/or occurrences of specific keywords in various media.

Charrette A charrette, in its simplest form, is a period of intense design and planning for solving a design challenge and a powerful and effective tool for creative and collaborative problem solving in communities. Whether designing a community master plan, designing a park or solving housing challenges in urban neighbourhoods, the charrette provides a physical framework for a community to implement its visions and engage its citizens.

Closed system A closed system maintains itself on a limited amount of resources that are entrenched in that particular system. Energy can be exchanged with other systems, but not any actual matter.

Conway's Law concerns the structure of organizations and the corresponding structure of systems (particularly computer software) designed by those organizations. In various versions, Conway's Law states that: a) organizations that design systems are constrained to produce designs that are copies of the communication structures of these organizations; b) any piece of software reflects the organizational structure that produced it (Wikipedia).

Co-working is a style of work that involves a shared working environment, sometimes an office, and sometimes space designed for independent workers to work in with others in a way that avoids isolation and encourages community and sharing whilst conducting independent activity.

Hoteling is similar to 'hot desking', but differs in that desks/facilities are specifically reserved, ideally by using software that tracks all an organization's resources. Employees can access the hotelling reservation software and log in with a password to reserve work spaces/facilities.

Human capital is the set of skills that employees have or acquire on the job, through training and experience, and that increase individual and collective value to the organization.

Human systems dynamics (HSD) is a collection of concepts and tools that help make sense of the patterns that emerge from chaos when people work and play together in groups, families, organizations and communities.

Integrated work planning is a method of ensuring that office furnishings, space layout, technology and work processes, and people skills support the seamless flow of work and people to deliver the business strategy.

Memes A cultural unit (an idea or value or pattern of behaviour) that is passed from one person to another by non-genetic means (as by imitation); 'memes are the cultural counterpart of genes'.

Mobile devices   smartphones, web and SMS-enabled phones, netbooks, tablets, hand-held e-mail devices, e-book readers.

Open system   In an open system, necessary resources are renewed and exchanged on a regular basis. Many ecosystems, for example, rely on the sun to constantly import energy into their basic cycles.

Output v outcome   Delivering a policy that is never used may be an *output* measure of productivity. Delivering a policy that is implemented and can be shown to have added value to the organization is an *outcome* measure.

Quackery   derives from the word quacksalver (someone who boasts about his salves). Dictionaries define quack as 'a pretender to medical skill; a charlatan' and 'one who talks pretentiously without sound knowledge of the subject discussed'. Quackery's paramount characteristic is promotion ('Quacks quack!') rather than fraud, greed or misinformation. Quackery can be broadly defined as 'anything involving over promotion in the field of health'. This definition would include questionable ideas as well as questionable products and services, regardless of the sincerity of their promoters. In line with this definition, the word 'fraud' would be reserved only for situations in which deliberate deception is involved.

Social capital   is a way to describe the value (solidarity, information, support, etc) that can accrue through the network. The concept of social capital is logically distinct from the concept of a social network. In general terms social capital is about the value of the connections in a social network.

Social network   consisting of lines (relations) and nodes (actors, groups, things, organizations, etc) that can be described in mathematical terms.

'Status armour'   is a phrase used to describe the artefacts of grade, rank or skill displayed by employees in their office space. These include items like certificates, merit plaques and awards, newspaper items mentioning their achievements, and photos of them taken with an important person.

Techno stress   is a term referring to stress stemming from the excessive use of multi-tasking technological devices. Techno stress and ADT may be related although current research into these subjects is extremely limited.

Telemedicine   (also referred to as 'telehealth' or 'e-health') allows health care professionals to evaluate, diagnose and treat patients in remote locations using telecommunications technology. Telemedicine allows patients in remote locations to access medical expertise quickly, efficiently and without travel.

RESOURCES

Any intelligent fool can make things bigger, more complex, more structured, more competitive, more violent. It takes a touch of genius and a lot of courage to move in the opposite direction (ALBERT EINSTEIN).

Below is a list of further articles, blogs, books, websites and films that relate to the ideas discussed in each of the chapters but that are not referenced directly in the chapters. Where commercial websites are mentioned this is not an endorsement of their products or services.

Chapter 1: Organizational health

Jacques, E (1998) *Requisite Organization: A total system for effective managerial organization and managerial leadership for the 21st century*, Cason Hall & Co, Arlington

Morgan, G (1996) *Images of Organization*, Sage, Thousand Oaks

Proventive Solutions, an organization specializing in organizational health [Online] http://proventivesolutions.com.au/

The Dilbert Principle: A cubicle's-eye view of bosses, meetings, management fads & other workplace afflictions

Von Bertalanffy, L (1968) *General Systems Theory: Foundations, development, applications*, Braziller, New York

Chapter 2: Organizational structures

Face it: organizational charts don't work, John McKee [Online] http://www.techrepublic.com/blog/tech-manager/face-it-organizational-charts-dont-work/5861?tag=untagged

Gallup Q12 [Online] http://gmj.gallup.com/content/511/item-10-0-0-0-best-friend-work.aspx

Organizational hierarchy, adapting old structures to new challenges, by Valdis Krebs [Online] http://www.orgnet.com/orgchart.html

Seizing the white space: business model innovation for growth and renewal, by Mark W Johnson, published by Harvard Business Press [Online] http://www.innovationmanagement.se/2010/09/23/seizing-the-white-space-business-model-innovation-for-growth-and-renewal

The org chart is not the org, Aaron Silvers [Online] http://www.aaronsilvers.com/2010/10/the-org-chart-is-not-the-org/

The rise and fall of Marks & Spencer: and how it rose again, Judi Bevan [Online] http://www.amazon.com/gp/search?index=books&linkCode=qs&keywords=1861978987

Tribal knowledge, John Moore (story of Starbucks) [Online] http://www.amazon.com/Tribal-Knowledge-Business-Starbucks-Corporate/dp/1419520016

Watts, DJ and Strogatz, SH (1998) Collective dynamics of 'small-world' networks

Chapter 3: Systems and processes

Idealized design: how to dissolve tomorrow's crisis... today, Russell L Ackof, Jason Magidson, Herbert J Addison

JISC infoNet aims to be the UK's leading advisory service for managers in the post-compulsory education sector promoting the effective strategic planning, implementation and management of information and learning technology. Its primary resources are online infoKits, [toolkits] which promote the effective strategic planning and management of information and learning technology within institutions. One of the infokits is on Process review [Online] **http://www.jiscinfonet.ac.uk/about-the-service**.

Systems thinking for curious managers: with 40 new management f-laws, by Russell L Ackoff

The LSE Complexity Group. The Group has been working for over 16 years, to address practical complex problems. In the process it has developed a theory of complex social systems and an integrated methodology using both qualitative and quantitative tools and methods. The work of the LSE Complexity Group is at **www.lse.ac.uk/complexity**.

Chapter 4: Control

Great business leaders database [Online] http://www.hbs.edu/leadership/database/
Here Comes Everybody, Clay Shirky
Leadership in an age of uncertainty [Online] http://mitleadership.mit.edu/pdf/LeadershipinanAgeofUncertainty-researchbrief.pdf

Levers of Control: How Managers Use Innovative Control Systems to Drive Strategic Renewal, Robert Simons

Love Crime (2011) A French film directed by Alain Courneau that depicts a contest of will between two women executives in the French headquarters of an American multinational

Occupy together [Online] http://www.occupytogether.org

Occupy Wall Street [Online] http://occupywallst.org/

Occupy Wall Street's media team (newspaper report) [Online] http://www.cjr.org/the_news_frontier/occupy_wall_streets_media_team.php?page=all

Padovani, E (2012) *Managing Local Governments: Designing Management Control Systems that Deliver Value*, Routledge

Peoples' assemblies [Online] http://takethesquare.net/2011/07/31/quick-guide-on-group-dynamics-in-peoples-assemblies/

Pfister, Jan (2009) *Managing Organizational Culture for Effective Internal Control: From Practice to Theory*, Physica-Verlag (This is a research study)

The Management Control Association (MCA) is a network of researchers who are interested in the broad area of control in organizations. The ethos of the MCA is to develop critical insights into control processes and encourage research that recognizes the organizational, personal and social contexts of control [Online] **http://www.managementcontrolassociation.ac.uk/**

Chapter 5: Developing well-being

Flourish: A Visionary New Understanding of Happiness and Well-being, Free Press, Reprint edition (2011)

Gallup-Healthways wellbeing index [Online] http://www.well-beingindex.com/

http://www.hare.org/links/saturday.htmlInfed: the encyclopedia of informal education explores the development of theory around community, and the significance of boundaries, social networks and social norms – and why attention to social capital and communion may be important [Online] http://www.infed.org/community/community.htm

Nudge: Improving Decisions About Health, Wealth, and Happiness, by Richard H Thaler and Cass R Sunstein, Penguin Books, 2009

Nudge, Nudge, Think, Think: Using experiments to change civic behavior, Peter John, Sarah Cotterill, Hanhua Liu and Liz Richardson, 2011, Bloomsbury

People and Organizational Development: A New Agenda for Organizational Effectiveness, Francis, H, Holbeche, L, Reddington, M, CIPD

Sense of community: a definition and theory, *Journal of Community Psychology*, 14, January 1986, DW McMillan and DM Chavis

Seven neurotic styles of management, Kurt Motamedi, PhD, *Graziado Business Review*, 2006, 9 (4) [Online] http://gbr.pepperdine.edu/2010/08/seven-neurotic-styles-of-management/

Organization Development Network. The Organization Development Network is an international, professional association whose members are committed to practising organization development intentionally and rigorously as an applied behavioural science [Online] **http://www.odnetwork.org**

Rodgers, C (2007) *Informal Coalitions: Mastering the hidden dynamics of organizational change*, Palgrave MacMillan
Snakes in Suits: When psychopaths go to work, by Paul Babiak and Robert D Hare, Harper, New York, 2007
The Shift: The future of work is already here, Lynda Gratton, Harper Collins UK, 2011
Up In the Air (2009) Follows Ryan Bingham (George Clooney), a 'career transition' counsellor, as he criss-crosses the country firing employees whose bosses won't pull the plug themselves, directed by Jason Reitman
What Happy People Know: How the new science of happiness can change your life for the better, Dan Baker PhD, 2003 Rodale

Chapter 6: Healthy technologies

Morgenstern, J (2005) *Never Check E-mail in the Morning: And other unexpected strategies for making your work life work*, Fireside

Techcrunch is a technology site profiling start-ups, reviewing new internet products, and breaking tech news [Online] **http://techcrunch.com**.

Turkle, Sherry (2011) *Alone Together: Why we expect more from technology and less from each oth*er. In *Alone Together*, MIT technology and society professor Sherry Turkle explores the power of our new tools and toys to dramatically alter our social lives.

Mashable [Online] **http://mashable.com/** Mashable is an independent online news site dedicated to covering digital culture, social media and technology.

Technology Review [Online] **http://www.technologyreview.com/** Technology Review identifies emerging technologies and analyses their impact for technology and business leaders, published by Massachusetts Institute of Technology (MIT).

Wired [Online] **http://www.wired.com/** In-depth coverage of current and future trends in technology, and how they are shaping business, entertainment, communications, science, etc.

Bits [Online] **http://bits.blogs.nytimes.com/** Online newspaper's technology content is not often outdone due to its timely and well-written tech news; considered by some as the premiere source of informed tech news.

Organizational Systems Research Organization. OSRA promotes research and application of information technology in the end-user environment to support work processes, improve employee performance, and enhance overall organizational effectiveness in direct support of goals and strategies. OSRA is a special interest group (SIG) of the Association for Information Systems (AIS) [Online] **http://www.osra.org/index.html**.

UCISA represents the whole of higher education, and increasingly further education, in the provision and development of academic, management and administrative information systems, providing a network of contacts and a powerful lobbying voice [Online] **http://www.ucisa.ac.uk/representation/ activities/ITIL/Continual per cent20service per cent20improvement.aspx**.

Digital Trends [Online] **http://www.digitaltrends.com/** This site has become an indispensable resource for discovering the best of what technology can offer. It provides sneak peeks, one-of-a-kind reviews, editorials and news about trend-setting consumer technology products.

Lifehacker [Online] **http://lifehacker.com/** This may be everybody's favourite go-to site for tech-related productivity tips, news and how-to articles. Lifehacker continues to help all of us work smarter and save time via recommended app and software downloads that we would miss if not for this site's coverage.

Jane Jacobs, a short biography [Online] http://en.wikipedia.org/wiki/Jane_Jacobs
IBMs social computing and blogging guidelines [Online] http://www.ibm.com/ blogs/zz/en/guidelines.html

Chapter 7: Healthy space

Cornell University Ergonomics Web, CUErgo, CUErgo presents information from research studies and class work by students and faculty in the Cornell Human Factors and Ergonomics Research Group (CHFERG) focuses on ways to enhance usability by improving the ergonomic design of hardware, software, and workplaces, to enhance people's comfort, performance and health in an approach we call Ergotecture [Online] **http://ergo.human.cornell.edu/** Design Matters with Debbie Millman, iTunes podcast.

GSA's Workspace Requirements Development Process (RDP) provides tools, guidance and consultant help that goes beyond delivering traditional office design. Current workplaces are often a poor fit for changes made to organizations, initiatives, technologies and staff. Traditional workplace planning that focuses on data does not solve problems that ultimately benefit the organization. RDP is a process aimed at understanding the customer's business, employee work patterns, constraints, and mission before the space design process begins. **www.gsa.gov/workspacedelivery**.

Hardy, Bridget, Graham, Richard, Stansall, Paul, White, Alison, Harrison, Andrew, Bell, Adryan and Hutton, Les (2008) *Working Beyond Walls: The government workplace as an agent of change*, DEGW, London

CoreNet Global's mission is to advance the effectiveness of corporate real estate professionals and the entire industry engaged in delivering value to corporations through the strategic management of corporate real estate and workplace resources [Online] **http://www2.corenetglobal.org/**

The Real Estate Executive Board provides the data-driven insight, analytic tools, and advisory support that enable corporate real estate executives to improve individual, functional, and corporate performance [Online] **https://www.reeb.executiveboard.com**.

The Telework Research Network is an independent research and advisory firm. We specialize in making the management case for telework, workplace flexibility and alternative workplace strategies. We can investigate and model the economic, societal and environmental benefits of telework and workplace flexibility for your organization or community, and help you implement programmes [Online] **http://www.teleworkresearchnetwork.com/**

Work Wise UK is a not-for-profit initiative that aims to make the UK one of the most progressive economies in the world by encouraging the widespread adoption of smarter working practices [Online] **http://www.workwiseuk.org/**

The Workplace Network is a global community of senior executives in public sector real estate. Members are leaders and decision makers from public sector real estate organizations worldwide, from corporations, institutions and government agencies spanning 15 different countries [Online] **http://www.theworkplacenetwork.org**.

The WorldWide Workplace Web (W4) is an international forum of public sector real property professionals. It provides a unique learning environment for the next generation of executives in public sector organizations by facilitating collaboration, sharing best practices and discussing issues of common concern [Online] **http://www.w4web.org**.

Ross, P *The Creative Office*, *The 21st Century Office* and *Space to Work* (all co-authored with Jeremy Myerson)

Chapter 8: Management fads

Quantified self. A place for people interested in self-tracking to gather, share knowledge and experiences, and discover resources [Online] **http://quantifiedself.com/**

McDonough, W and Braungart, M (2002) *Cradle to Cradle*, North Point Press

Two recent popular articles, Groupthink the brainstorming myth, by Jonah Lehrer [Online] **http://www.newyorker.com/reporting/2012/01/30/120130 fa_fact_lehrer**, and The rise of the new groupthink by Susan Cain [Online] **http://www.nytimes.com/2012/01/15/opinion/sunday/the-rise-of-the-new-groupthink.html?pagewanted=all,**

Francis, R, Moss, S *The Science of Management: Fighting fads and fallacies with evidence-based practices*
Furnham, A *Management and Myths: Challenging the fads, fallacies and fashions*
Open services innovation: rethinking your business to grow and compete in a new era [Online] http://www.amazon.com/Open-Services-Innovation-Rethinking-Business/dp/0470905743/ref=sr_1_1?s=books&ie=UTF8&qid=1328501128&sr=1-1-1
Stewart, M *The Management Myth: Debunking modern business philosophy*
Wooldridge, Al *Masters of Management: How the business gurus and their ideas have changed the world – for better and for worse*

The Business Model Canvas

Key Partners

Who are our Key Partners?
Who are our key suppliers?
Which Key Resources are we acquiring from partners?
Which Key Activities do partners perform?

MOTIVATIONS FOR PARTNERSHIPS:
Optimization and economy
Reduction of risk and uncertainty
Acquisition of particular resources and activities

Key Activities

What Key Activities do our Value
Propositions require?
Our Distribution Channels?
Customer Relationships?
Revenue Streams?

CATEGORIES
Production
Problem Solving
Platform/Network

Key Resources

What Key Resources do our Value
Propositions require?
Our Distribution Channels? Customer
Relationships?
Revenue Streams?

TYPES OF RESOURCES
Physical
Intellectual (brand patents, copyrights, data)
Human
Financial

Value Propositions

What value do we deliver to the customer?
Which one of our customer's problems are
we helping to solve?
What bundles of products and services are we offering
to each Customer Segment?
Which customer needs are we satisfying?

CHARACTERISTICS
Newness
Performance
Customization
"Getting the Job Done"
Design
Brand/Status
Price
Cost Reduction
Risk Reduction
Accessibility
Convenience/Usability

Customer Relationships

What type of relationship does each of our Customer
Segments expect us to establish and maintain with them?
Which ones have we established?
How are they integrated with the rest of our business
model?
How costly are they?

EXAMPLES
Personal assistance
Dedicated Personal Assistance
Self-Service
Automated Services
Communities
Co-creation

Channels

Through which Channels do our Customer
Segments want to be reached?
How are we reaching them now?
How are our Channels integrated?
Which ones work best?
Which ones are most cost-efficient?
How are we integrating them with customer routines?

CHANNEL PHASES:
1. *Awareness*
   How do we raise awareness about our company's products and services?
2. *Evaluation*
   How do we help customers evaluate our organization's Value Proposition?
3. *Purchase*
   How do we allow customers to purchase specific products and services?
4. *Delivery*
   How do we deliver a Value Proposition to customers?
5. *After sales*
   How do we provide post-purchase customer support?

Customer Segments

For whom are we creating value?
Who are our most important customers?

Mass Market
Niche Market
Segmented
Diversified
Multi-sided Platform

Cost Structure

What are the most important costs inherent in our business model?
Which Key Resources are most expensive?
Which Key Activities are most expensive?

IS YOUR BUSINESS MODEL:
Cost Driven (leanest cost structure, low price value proposition, maximum automation, extensive outsourcing)
Value Driven (focused on value creation, premium value proposition)

SAMPLE CHARACTERISTICS:
Fixed Costs (salaries, rents, utilities)
Variable costs
Economies of scale
Economies of scope

Revenue Streams

For what value are our customers really willing to pay?
For what do they currently pay?
How are they currently paying?
How would they prefer to pay?
How much does each Revenue Stream contribute to overall revenues?

TYPES:
Asset sale
Usage fee
Subscription Fees
Lending/Renting/Leasing
Licensing
Brokerage fees
Advertising

FIXED PRICING
List Price
Product feature dependent
Customer segment dependent
Volume dependent

DYNAMIC PRICING
Negotiations (bargaining)
Yield Management
Real-time-Market

INDEX

NB: page numbers in *italic* indicate figures or tables